Murder & Mayhem

52 Crimes that Shocked Early California

1849 - 1949

Michael Thomas Barry

Schiffer Publishing Ltd®

4880 Lower Valley Road, Atglen, Pennsylvania 19310

Dedication

This book is lovingly dedicated to my wife, Christyn.

All text and images by author unless otherwise noted

Other Schiffer Books By The Author:

Final Resting Places: Orange County's Dead and Famous ISBN: 978-0-7643-3421-4 $16.99

Fade to Black: Graveside Memories of Hollywood Greats 1927 – 1950 ISBN: 978-0-7643-3709-3 $24.99

Library of Congress Control Number: 2011941354

Designed by Mark David Bowyer
Type set in Rosemary Roman / Zurich BT

ISBN: 978-0-7643-3968-4
Printed in the United States of America

Schiffer Books are available at special discounts for bulk purchases for sales promotions or premiums. Special editions, including personalized covers, corporate imprints, and excerpts can be created in large quantities for special needs. For more information contact the publisher:

Published by Schiffer Publishing Ltd.
4880 Lower Valley Road
Atglen, PA 19310
Phone: (610) 593-1777; Fax: (610) 593-2002
E-mail: Info@schifferbooks.com

For the largest selection of fine reference books on this and related subjects, please visit our website at **www.schifferbooks.com**
We are always looking for people to write books on new and related subjects. If you have an idea for a book, please contact us at proposals@schifferbooks.com

This book may be purchased
from the publisher.
Include $5.00 for shipping.
Please try your bookstore first.
You may write for a free catalog.

In Europe, Schiffer books are distributed by
Bushwood Books
6 Marksbury Ave.
Kew Gardens
Surrey TW9 4JF England
Phone: 44 (0) 20 8392 8585; Fax: 44 (0) 20 8392 9876
E-mail: info@bushwoodbooks.co.uk
Website: www.bushwoodbooks.co.uk

Contents

Acknowledgments

A book of this magnitude and scope cannot be written without the help and support of a vast array of people and sources. I am especially indebted to the following people and organizations for their assistance in writing this book, without whose help and support, could never have been completed: First and foremost to my wife, Christyn, our three daughters, and the rest of my extended family, my eternal gratitude and love for your support during this exhaustive writing process; secondly, to all of the staff at Schiffer Publishing, especially Dinah Roseberry, an exceptionally talented editor, who gave me my big break, taking a chance with an unproven author, and continues to be an advocate for my numerous literary ideas, I am forever grateful; thirdly, a big thank you to the employees at the Los Angeles and San Francisco Public Libraries, the University of Southern California Digital Archives, the University of California, Los Angeles Digital Archives, the California State University, Fullerton Library, the Santa Ana History reading room at the Santa Ana Public Library, who all helped me with the arduous task of finding just the right photographs.

To those I have inadvertently forgotten to acknowledge, my sincere apology and thanks. Lastly, this book is written in recognition of all the men and woman of law enforcement, whose tireless, self-sacrificing, and noble dedication to providing us with safety often goes unheralded. This book is also written and dedicated to the memory of all the victims of crime; those who have, at the hands of criminals, suffered numerous indignities and immeasurable pain. Their lives and stories are worthy of commemoration and have not been forgotten.

Introduction

"And where the offense is, let the great axe fall."

~William Shakespeare (1564-1616)
English Playwright
Hamlet, Act IV: Scene 5

For European man, California began in the imagination. His eyes, when dreams began, had not yet seen its long, bold coast, its vast deserts, its great mountain ranges, its pastoral valleys. The land was to be given its very name out of a romance, Las Sergas de Esplandin, one of those epics of fictional knights on unreal quests. In 1510, a decade before Cortez conquered Mexico, decades before Cabrillo, there was described in this widely read Spanish work of fiction by Garcia Rodriguez Ordonez de Montalvo, an island, said to be home of the powerful Queen Calafia:

> Know ye that on the right hand of the Indies there is an island called California, very near the terrestrial paradise and inhabited by women...living in a manner of Amazons...Their island is one of the most rugged in the world, with bold rocks and crags. Their arms are all of gold, as is the harness of the wild beasts, which, after taming, they ride...Over this island of California rules a queen, Calafia, statuesque in proportions, more beautiful than all the rest, in flower of her womanhood, eager to perform great deeds, valiant and spirited, ambitious to excel all those who have ruled her.

That it was no island, that the Indies were across a vast and perilous sea, that gold was still held in the beds of mountain creeks and in the grips of quartz, made little difference. The dreams of wealth, of adventure, of courageous deeds, of beautiful women were fashioned by the aggressive and ambitious long miles away. Thus was the fanciful beginning of California for which many have dreamed. Millions have come to these golden shores in search of fame and fortune but scores have found misery and pain. From the Gold Rush of 1849 to the rise of Hollywood, this book details much of that hurt and wretchedness. It is not my intention for this manuscript to be an all inclusive anthology of crime in the state of California. My objective is to bring to light, what I perceive to be some of the most notorious and long-forgotten crime stories of the first 100 years of this state's history, as told through newspaper headlines of the time. In choosing which crimes to include, I kept an eye on history and variety, while looking for stories that would surprise and that were relatively obscure. When researching and writing these stories, I was struck by how much I thought I knew, but didn't. Stories discussed include the exploits and dastardly deeds of notorious bandits Juan Flores, Joaquin Murrieta, and Tiburcio Vasquez, infamous stage coach robber Black Bart, the murderous rampages of fiends such as John Anschlag, Mose Gibson, Leon Soeder, Theodore Durrant, and the infamous Black Widow, Louise Peete. Also within these pages will be discussed the treasure trove of unsolved murders such as the notorious Black Dahlia case and the killing of mobster Bugsy Siegel, just to name two. It must be noted that history is replete with tales of valor, glory, and good, but with that there is a flipside, a much more sinister and darker side to the past. The history of man's inhumanity towards his fellow man; so hauntingly and poetically stated in 1784 by the Scottish poet, Robert Burns in his celebrated poem, Man was made to mourn: A Dirge

> Many and sharp the num'rous ills
> In woven with our frame!
> More pointed still we make ourselves
> Regret, remorse, and shame!
> And man, whose heav'n-erected face
> The smiles of love adorn,
> Man's inhumanity to man
> Makes countless thousands mourn!

Why then is the human mind so fascinated by true crime stories? It defies logic, or maybe it defines it. It goes back to the very beginning with the first recorded crime story, that of the killing of Abel by his brother Cain in the Bible. Genesis 4:1-16 of the Holy Bible reads in part;:

> [1]Adam knew his wife; and she conceived, and bare Cain, and
> said, I have had gotten a man from the Lord. [2]And she again bare
> his brother Abel. And Abel was a keeper of sheep, but Cain was a
> tiller of the ground. [3]And in process of time it came to pass, that
> Cain brought of the fruit of the ground an offering unto the Lord.
> [4]And Abel, he also brought of the firstlings of his flock and of the
> fat thereof. And the Lord had respect unto Abel and to his offering:
> [5]But unto Cain and to his offering he had no respect. And Cain was
> very wroth, and his countenance fell. [6]And the Lord said unto Cain,
> "Why art thou wroth? And why is thy countenance fallen? [7]If thou
> doest well, shalt thou not be accepted? And if thou doest not well,
> sin lieth at the door. And unto thee shall be his desire, and thou shalt

> rule over him." [8]And Cain talked with Abel his brother: and it came
> to pass, when they were in the field, that Cain rose against Abel his
> brother, and slew him. [9]And the Lord said unto Cain, "Where is Abel
> thy brother?" And he said, "I know not: Am I my brother's keeper?"
> [10]And he said, "What hast thou done? The voice of thy brother's blood
> crieth unto me from the ground. [11]And now art thou cursed from the
> earth, which hath opened her mouth to receive thy brother's blood
> from thy hand; [12]When thou tillest the ground, it shall not henceforth
> yield unto thee her strength; a fugitive and a vagabond shalt thou
> be in the earth." [13]And Cain said unto the Lord, "My punishment is
> greater than I can bear. [14]Behold, thou hast driven me out this day
> from the face of the earth; and from thy face shall I be hid; and I
> shall be a fugitive and a vagabond in the earth; and it shall come to
> pass, that every one that findeth me shall slay me." [15]And the Lord
> said unto him, therefore whoever slayeth Cain, vengeance shall be
> taken on him sevenfold. And the Lord set a mark upon Cain, lest any
> finding him should kill him. [16]And Cain went out from the presence
> of the Lord, and dwelt in the land of Nod, on the east of Eden.

Thus began mankind's fascination with crime. The question needs to be asked, are we a society fascinated by crime? Now, you may wonder why I associate "fascination" with the pressing social problem of crime, given its harmful and destructive consequences. After all, we often associate being fascinated with something as being charmed by someone or something. How might such feelings then be associated with those fearful things we call crimes? How many examples can you think of from TV or literature that illustrate our fascination with crimes and criminals? Look at the TV schedules and you will see a high-crime diet of murder tales and detective thrillers as well as "true-life" documentaries, especially about law enforcement. Browse your local bookstore and you will find vast arrays of fictional crime thrillers. In some book shops you will also find a whole section dedicated to "true crime" and books which claim to explore the "mind of the criminal" or recount the gruesome biographies of serial killers. Pick up today's newspaper and count how many crime-related stories made the headlines. Some even end up in the entertainment sections.

Our society, then, is characterized by a culture of fear about crime but also a culture of fascination. We are seemingly both seduced and repulsed by crimes and criminals. Nor is this fascination with crimes and criminals simply the stuff of fiction. Acts defined as criminal may both seduce and repulse us because they involve on occasions both risk-taking and challenges to "normal" ways of doing things. Generally, there are two types of story in circulation. One set of stories is prominent in public discussions and the media. It describes crime as something to be feared and diminished: a society frightened by crime. The other set of stories we tell and consume, more privately perhaps, is of crime as fearful but fascinating. It seems that we cannot get enough of this kind of crime and these stories: a society fascinated by crime. Everyone remembers the infamous O.J. Simpson murder case; it broke records on many fronts, one being that it was watched by millions of people nonstop for months. It didn't matter what race they came from, religious affiliation, or social background, we were all spell-bound. Why? What makes the human mind seek and cling to facts about a gruesome murder, rape, or ritual killing with such resolve that they just cannot seem to let it go?

It is interesting that such stories are talked about for so long; they end up becoming legend, it shows you that however old a true crime story is, it does not lose its allure. For years, psychologists and criminologists have tried to explore it, asking why something so gruesome remains so fascinating. Thus far, no one has been able to come up with a solid explanation. They end up with best guesses and conjecture, and some are discussed here: First, most people live a relatively mundane existence. Once something outside of this reality occurs, especially when a gruesome or violent crime happens, we tend to obsess on the details as a way of escaping our dull everyday life. You may, or may not agree with this, but it rings true to some extent.

It is normal human psychology to want to know the facts behind a criminal act, and then immediately after that, question why it was committed. Some criminals will speak out and say why they did it, but this is very rare. Most of the time a crime story grows more and more fascinating as people continue to speculate as to why a crime was perpetrated. Some experts say that humanity as a whole is seeking justice; in seeking justice, they seek to know all the details of a crime which in itself leads to great fascination with the crime itself. There have been some arguments that people are fascinated to see just how far others will go, because it makes them feel good about themselves, knowing that they could never commit such an act themselves. Some experts argue that there is a genuine fear in people that the same crime could happen to them, and so they want to arm their minds with the details in subconscious preparation were something similar to happen. The counter argument to this, however, is that in most violent crimes, the victims can do little or nothing to protect themselves, therefore this fascination cannot prepare you for defense should you be under attack. And lastly of course, the media is a factor. Like everything else, media attention tends to hype crime and criminals. It chases down every bit and morsel and shows you bloody crime scenes, car chases, and even bodies. Listen to or watch news broadcasts for a day, and you will most likely hear of three or four crimes. If the media were to highlight crime less, perhaps society would be less aware of it, and its fascination would somehow lessen. Whatever the justifications given for fascination with crime, we must admit that being human, we want to know what happened, we want the gory details, and we will go after them until we get the last bit of information that we possibly can.

The eighteenth century Italian playwright Vittorio Alfieri wrote in his play Orestes, "providence sees to it that no man gets happiness out of crime." In his version of Antigone, Alfieri added another thought: "Disgrace does not consist in punishment, but in the crime." Both Dick Tracy and the Shadow echoed this sentiment in their 1930's radio shows, with the famous slogan "Crime doesn't pay!" And yet, throughout history, thousands have risked disgrace and whatever chance might exact, to pursue what they saw, rightly or wrongly, as the profit of crime.

Crime is a nasty business, to be certain, but it is also a fascinating one (something Alfieri knew well when he filled his pages with crimes large and small). We disapprove of crime, and find ourselves shocked and appalled by a story, and then find a moment later that we simply can't get enough of it. Not all misdeeds are created equal. Some are more sensational than others, some more baffling, some more audacious. The fifty-two notorious crimes revisited in this book are all of these things and more. In the end crime is awful, but it can be, in retelling, awfully exciting.

~ Michael Thomas Barry
Orange, California

Part One

The Sensational Crimes of the Nineteenth Century

1849 – 1899

Poena potest demi, culpa perennis erit. Latin to English translation: The punishment can be remitted, the crimes are everlasting.

~ Ovid (43BC-18AD)

Roman Poet From the Epistulae ex Ponto Written in 13 A.D.

A Brief History of the State of California

1849 - 1900

When the founding fathers of the United States were writing in letters of gold the name "American Republic" upon the binding of our nation's history, the fertile valleys of California slept in the sunshine undisturbed by the tramp of busy feet, and almost as virgin to the plough as they were when the rugged Sierras first rose above the waters of the Pacific. California was separated from what are now her sister states by an ocean of untraveled prairie. Like an angel of destiny, she stood grandly alone with her feet planted firmly in the surf of the Pacific and her face turned toward the setting sun. A time would come when she would call to her eastern sisters and display to them the golden sands washed down from the rugged hills by centuries of rain; the quiet valleys whose sun-warmed bosom lay the fertile soil of which depleted granaries of the over-crowed east could be replenished.

The padre contentedly traveled in the shadow of the old adobe missions and watched the Indians work among the clusters of grapes, which afterwards served the purpose of a graveyard. The herder, whose sole occupation was to ride after cattle and strip them of their hides, dreamed away a listless existence in their native Mexican sky. And with that, the territory, which became the State of California, lay sleeping in the sunshine of nearly a century. Under the repressing influences, the native Californian was happy in his own self-satisfaction. Not knowing that there were other spheres of action and development, he did not complain about his low estate, but contentedly idled away his existence. While the padres displayed a most admirable zeal in establishing missions and for looking after the interests of the Indians, they also lent a helping hand to who came afterwards. With the progress of the years and the advancement of thought, there came a change which was to mold the destinies of this state. The change was a radical one, but it took place quietly and without serious opposition.

When Mexico cast off her Spanish shackles in 1822, she laid claim to that comparatively unexplored and undefined territory known as California; and when the newly freed province of Spain wheeled into the ranks of the republics, this whole country was solemnly taken possession of as Mexican territory. The first accessions to the population of California were composed of seafaring men and trappers, who settled about the ports and bays along the coast. A sudden surprise befell the Mexicans in 1846 when Commodore John Sloat and his fleet entered Monterey Bay; the *Portsmouth*, a sloop of war entered the harbor, and the American flag was hoisted in the plaza. Following the Treaty of Guadalupe Hidalgo in 1848 (which ended the Mexican War), the western territory of Alta California (California Republic) was annexed as a territory of the United States.

California suddenly emerged from comparative obscurity to be the center of world-wide attention on January 24, 1848, when gold was discovered at Sutter's Mill. This could not have come at a more opportune time. The news reached the east coast on the heels of the announcement of American acquisition of the province. It caught the United States on the rebound from its Mexican War activities and when the American frontier was piling up against the baffling sub-humid and treeless Great Plains. Soon after, people from all parts of the world began to descend upon the territory, and under the circumstances, it is entirely understandable why. On September 9, 1850, California was granted statehood. Like other frontier regions of the United States, California struggled with its share of crime and criminal behavior. Becoming a civilized society with rules and regulations had its growing pains. Because of the obsession with seeking fortune, fame, and cheap land, California became the destination for thousands of righteous people, along with countless numbers of unsavory characters for the next five decades on ward.

Before delving into the most sensational crime stories of California during this period. One must also explore demographics in order to fully understand the circumstances, in which these horrific crimes were committed. In 1848, the non-native population of California was estimated to be no more than 15,000. After gold was discovered, the population increased dramatically with the influx of thousands of fortune-seeking U.S. citizens, Europeans, and other immigrants. The population of San Francisco in 1850 was 21,000, and by 1900, it had rose to 342,782, which ranked ninth most populous in the union. Los Angeles' population on the other hand was 1,610 in 1850, and by 1900, had risen 102,479. San Diego's population was 650 (non-native) in 1850 and 17,700 by the year 1900. The total population of the state of California in 1850 was 92,597 (non-native), and by 1900, had risen to 1,485,053. Fortune, fame, and cheap land were the main catalyst for the population boom.

There has always been a small segment of the population that has chosen to live outside of the laws of civilized society. Whatever the reason for committing the crime, be it socio-economic or mental defect, crime does not pay and must be punished. For better or worse some of these stories have become legends. The stories and exploits have been handed down for generations and sometimes the facts have been mixed with fiction. It is my intention to bring to light the true facts of these crimes. This is the backdrop to one of the first recorded crimes in California state history.

Slaughter at Mission San Miguel

(San Luis Obispo County, 1849)

The awful story of the massacre at Mission San Miguel has been rarely discussed and basically forgotten in the annals of this state's history. With this crime and the discovery of gold, the easy-going lifestyle and culture of pastoral Mexican California was changed forever. The shocking story begins at Sutter's Mill in the fall of 1848 with a man named Peter Raymond. Very little is known about this man other than the fact that he was a veteran of the Mexican War, and served in General John C. Fremont's California Battalion. Raymond had come to Sutter's Mill with the hopes of striking it rich. But Sutter's Mill was not in operation that fall, and instead, was used to house local residents and miners. For unknown reasons, during the early morning hours of October 1, 1848, a drunken scuffle erupted between Raymond and a fellow miner named John R. Von Pfister. The fight turned lethal when Raymond pulled a knife and stabbed Von Pfister in the heart, killing him instantly.

Raymond was seized immediately, taken into custody, and transported to Sutter's Fort, where he was to be confined until trial. Unfortunately, Raymond, who was heralded as the "first murderer of the gold fields," was not to be confined for long. A few weeks later, Raymond was able to escape. A reward notice was printed in the San Francisco *Californian*, October 28, 1848, offering $5000 (this was a misprint with the actual reward being $500) for the capture of the fugitive.

During Raymond's desperate escape from the law, he befriended a fellow veteran of the Mexican War named Joseph Lynch. The two kindred souls quickly bonded, finding that they both had a penchant for murder and mayhem. Eventually, this criminal duo was joined by three others, Peter Quin, Peter Remer, and Bernard Barnberry. Having no money and no other plan, Quin, Remer, and Barnberry were eager to join Raymond and Lynch on their criminal escapades.

For over a year, this criminal gang was able elude authorities, robbing and stealing their way south. On the fateful morning of December 4, 1849, the criminal quintet of Raymond, Lynch, Quin, Remer, and Barnberry happened upon the dilapidated ruins of the Mission San Miguel in rural San Luis Obispo County. The mission and the surrounding land were owned by William Reed and Petronilo Rios. Being hospitable, Reed invited the four men to spend the night. A talkative man and not knowing he was in the company of thieves and murderers, Reed foolishly mentioned over dinner that he had just returned from selling a herd of sheep, for which he had been paid a substantially sum. The next morning, the tiny band of desperadoes resumed their journey, but not long after leaving stopped for a discussion. They discussed Reed's gold and the possibility of there being more booty on the premises. After coming to a unanimous decision, the five started back to Mission San Miguel with evil intent. Returning to the mission, they were cheerfully greeted by Mr. Reed, who agreed to house and feed the men for another night, if only they would agree to help with a few chores around the ranch. Raymond and his henchmen heartily accepted the offer, and set about their assigned tasks.

The early evening hours were spent in jovial conversation by the fire. Reed's wife, Maria (who was pregnant) had excused herself and retired to her bedroom with their three-year-old son. Others at the mission that night were Jose Vallejo (Maria's younger brother), Josefa Olivera (a midwife), Mrs. Olivera's fifteen-year-old daughter and four-year-old grandson, along with other servants and guests. All told there were thirteen people at the mission, excluding Raymond's band of thugs.

Around 8 p.m., as the men lounged around the fire, Mr. Reed came into the room and joined the conversation. Chopping wood and lurking behind Reed was Barnberry. After throwing some kindling onto the fire, he raised his pick axe, then struck Reed on the back of the head, killing him instantly. Reed tumbled to the floor dead in a heap of blood his head cleaved in two. Standing there with blood dripping from the axe, Barnberry yelled out: "I have struck the first blow and there is no backing out." The murderous frenzy had begun. Stalking through the darkened mission buildings, the homicidal band burst into Mrs. Reed's room; there Raymond greeted her, "Buenos noches, Senorita," then stabbed her in the stomach with a sword. The children tried to hide under the bed, but were pulled out and butchered heartlessly. For hours the marauding band of murderers roamed from room to room searching out and killing all the inhabitants of the mission.

Just as the carnage had concluded and while admiring their handiwork, a horse was heard galloping across the courtyard. They all hid as the lone rider approached, calling out to the darkened and barren mission. Jim Beckwourth, a government dispatch rider had come to the mission in the hopes of receiving a hot meal and to get out of the cold. As he entered the living quarters of the mission, he was surprised to find that no one was stirring. Finding a body on the floor of the kitchen, and sensing something was amiss, he immediately retrieved his pistols, and then commenced a room by room search. Much to his horror, he stumbled upon body after body. Quickly returning to his horse, he proceeded to ride to a nearby ranch for help. A group of vaqueros and Indians quickly returned to the mission, where they found that all of the victims bodies had been piled into one room and set on fire. The killers had looted the entire mission, and disappeared into the night. But before leaving, they made a half-hearted and failed attempt at hiding their foul deeds by burning down the mission.

Word of the massacre was dispatched to military authorities in Monterey. A fifteen-member posse under the leadership of Cesario Lataillade was sent from Santa Barbara to track down the murderous desperadoes. Raymond and his gang headed south passing through San Luis Obispo on their way to Santa Barbara. On December 10, 1849, a few miles south of Santa Barbara, Lataillade and his posse spotted Reed and his gang along a stretch of beach (today known as Summerland). Quickly realizing that judgment day was upon them, Reed and his gang attempted to flee. A short gun battle ensued in which Quin was wounded and Barnberry was killed. Raymond leaped from his horse and attempted to evade capture by swimming out to sea. The entire posse opened fire on Raymond from the shore and after taking several hits, attempted to swim back to shore but soon disappeared under the waves, never to be seen alive again. Several days later, his body washed ashore on a nearby beach. The bodies of Raymond and Barnberry were left to rot and decay, where they lay.

The gun battle was over as quickly as it had begun, the three remaining outlaws, Quin, Remer and Lynch raised their hands in surrender. They were led back to Santa Barbara to stand trial for their crimes. On December 24, 1849, their trial commenced, during which Raymond and Barnberry were described as being the ring leaders and aggressors the night of the murders. It must be noted that proof of whether or not Raymond and Barnberry were indeed the aggressors in this crime must be taken within the context of eyewitness testimony. The only living eyewitnesses to this crime were trying to save they own necks by pinning the murders squarely on the shoulders of Raymond and Barnberry, who were conveniently both deceased and could not dispute their actual involvement. Thus by down playing their roles in this crime as patsies, Quin, Remer, and Lynch hoped to avoid the executioner. In the end, this testimony did not save them, the jury found the trio guilty of murder and sentenced them all to death by firing squad.

On December 28, 1849, the three convicted murders were led from jail to a nearby ravine where a firing squad of nineteen men carried out the order of the court. Quinn, Remer, and Lynch paid the ultimate punishment for their crimes and all three are buried at the Mission Santa Barbara Cemetery.

All told, thirteen innocent people were deliberately and senselessly murdered at the Mission San Miguel; they include Reed, his family, numerous other servants, and guests. Their bodies were all buried together in a communal grave located on the mission grounds. Today, as tourists walk the grounds of Sutter's Mill, the historic Mission San Miguel, and wander the beautiful stretch of beach today known as Summerland south of Santa Barbara, very few have any idea of the senseless slaughter and terrible events that took place at these locations, so many years ago. The image and innocence of the age of pastoral Spanish California would be forever broken and changed by this senseless crime.

Mission San Miguel (Circa, 1898). *Courtesy of the Library of Congress, Prints and Photographs, (Lot 13923, No. 172).*

The Murder of Fred Cannon

(Gold Country, 1851)

Fourth of July in Downieville, California, in 1851 was a very celebratory affair that included political speeches, a picnic, and a grand parade down Main Street. Nearly 5,000 people, mostly gold miners, crammed into the tiny town and most were in a very jovial mood, ready to celebrate. This year's event was special because it marked the seventy-fifth anniversary of America's independence and the miners were ready to drink, gamble, and fight.

The Downieville of 1851 was little more than a muck-filled road lined with gambling halls and whorehouses. The town was situated at the convergence of the Downie and Yuba Rivers and the hills surrounding the town were populated with hundreds of gold mines. Settled in late 1849, Downieville was first known as "The Forks" for its geographical location. It was renamed after Major William Downie (1820-1893), a Scotsman who led an expedition up the North Fork of the Yuba River and who was the town's first mayor. The town reached its peak population of over 5,000 people in 1851 but declined sharply by 1865.

The 1851 celebration of our nation's birth would never be forgotten and Downieville would forever have the dubious distinction of being the first town to hang a woman in the state of California. The frivolities and celebrations of July 4, 1851, lasted into the wee hours of the morning and several miners, including Fred Cannon and Charley Getzler, were in no mood to end the party. In a very feisty mood, both men were drunk and ready to cause trouble. They began to bang on doors in an attempt to reignite the celebration. One such home was the residence of a beautiful Mexican woman named Juanita (whose last name is lost to history). She was the common-law wife of a local gambler named Jose (whose last name is also lost to history). The beautiful Juanita was originally from Sonora, Mexico and was often the target of unwanted amorous advances from miners. Ironically, one of these would-be suitors was Fred Cannon.

Juanita was preparing for bed when Cannon and Getzler began pounding on her front door. So ferocious was their pounding that the door came off its hinges. Juanita yelled at the two unwanted intruders to leave her home, but before departing, unpleasant words were exchanged. The following morning their argument continued when Juanita angrily confronted Cannon outside of the town barbershop. She demanded that he apologize for his rude behavior and pay for the broken door. Cannon refused both and insisted that the door was already broken. Enraged by Cannon's lack of respect and failure to comply with her simple request, Juanita flew into a rage and the pair exchanged additional unpleasant words. When Cannon called her a whore, Juanita had heard enough, and in a moment of compete insanity, pulled a large Bowie knife from the fold of her dress, and plunged the weapon deep into the center of Cannon's chest. Clutching his torso in agony, he fell to the ground, dying moments later.

Juanita retreated to a local saloon in attempt to hide from the angry mob which had begun to assemble. Seeing that her situation was hopeless, she surrendered to authorities. She was placed under arrest and housed in log cabin (being there was no jail in town). A miner's court was hastily convened and the accused murderess was provided with two defense lawyers. Outside the makeshift courtroom, a large group of angry men (estimated at 3,000) gathered. An eyewitness to the event described the mob as being "the craziest and wildest mob" he had ever witnessed. Juanita's lawyers and the appointed judge begged the mob to let the judicial system takes its course. After a brief and biased trial, Juanita was found guilty and sentenced to death.

At 3:45 p.m., on the afternoon of July 5, 1851, Juanita, proud and holding her head high, was led out to the suspension bridge that spanned the Yuba River. A crowd estimated at over 5,000 stood nearby to witnesses the historic and tragic event. Juanita, emotionless as she approached her pending demise, refused a blindfold, and when asked if she had any final words about the crime, she simply nodded and said "I'd do it again, if provoked." She bid "adios" to the men standing near and placed the noose around her own neck. At the sound of a pistol shot, her body was flung over the edge of the bridge.

She was the first woman to be executed in the state of California, but not the last. Her lifeless body was left hanging on the bridge for over twenty-two minutes before finally being cut down. Her remains were given to friends for burial at the town cemetery. Ironically, both she and Cannon rest forever side by side in the same grave at the Downieville Cemetery.

A Terrible Case of Mistaken Identity The Story of English Jim

(San Francisco & Sacramento River Valley, 1850-1851)

The history of the Barbary Coast begins with the California Gold Rush of 1849. If gold had not been discovered in the sands of the Sacramento River Valley, San Francisco's criminal underworld would have in all likelihood developed according to traditional patterns like other large American metropolises. Owning almost entirely to the influx of gold seekers and hordes of gamblers, thieves, harlots, and other felonious parasites, there arose a unique criminal district that for almost seventy years was the scene of more viciousness and depravity, but which at the same time possessed more glamour, than any other area of vice and depravity in all of the North American continent.

The nucleus of which the Barbary Coast developed was the colony of harlots and thieves that clustered around the waterfront at Broadway and Pacific Streets and on the slopes of Telegraph Hill. Here gathered all types of ruffians, escaped convicts, and ticket-of-leave men from British penal colonies in Sydney, Australia. This wave of undesirable immigration, which to all intents and purposes was 100 percent criminal, began to wash ashore in California about the middle of 1849. So numerous, these men thoroughly dominated the underworld of San Francisco, and the area became known as Sydney Town. The villains that inhabited Sydney Town were commonly known as the "Sydney Ducks."

Perhaps one of the most infamous of these so-called "Sydney Ducks" was a chap by the name of James Stewart, better known as "English Jim." Stewart had been deported from England at the age of sixteen, following his conviction of forgery and served almost twelve years at the British penal colony at Sydney. He received his "ticket-of-leave" sometime during the late 1840s and made his way to New York. There he met and associated with numerous shady characters and embarked on a life of crime. Eventually, like so many of his kind, he found himself in San Francisco. There he embarked on an extraordinary career of crime, not only in the city, but in the gold fields. It is during this time that he is said to have committed or assisted in more murders and burglaries than any other man in California at the time. In December of 1850, Jim was arrested in Sacramento for killing Sheriff Moore of Marysville and stealing $4,000 from the Sheriff's home, but was able to escape after a few days of incarceration. It is at this point English Jim's story grows to become one of the most celebrated cases of mistaken identity in the annals of American crime.

On the late evening of February 19, 1851, two men entered the Jansen & Bond Company, on Montgomery Street in San Francisco, knocked manager J.C. Jansen unconscious, and fled with over $2,000 in gold coin. The next day, San Francisco police arrested Thomas Berdue, believing him to be James Stewart and transported him back to Marysville to stand trial for the murder of Sheriff Moore. Berdue had mistakenly been identified by nearly half a dozen men as being English Jim, men who supposedly knew Stewart well. He was also identified by J.C. Jansen as one of the two men who had assaulted him the night before. Berdue vehemently protested his innocence, and attempted to no avail, to prove that he was not Stewart. These protestations were in vain and against overwhelming circumstantial evidence, which included a striking physical similarity between him and the infamous Sydney Duck. English Jim was known to have a small scar above his left eye and ear, and his left forefinger had been amputated at the first joint; ironically, and most unfortunate for Berdue, he also suffered the exact same injuries. Berdue was quickly tried and convicted of assaulting and robbing Jansen and was sentenced to fourteen years imprisonment. Soon after, he was transferred to Marysville to stand trial for the murder of Sheriff Moore, and was misidentified for a second time as being the infamous "English Jim." This time the jury brought back a much more grim verdict of guilty and sentenced him to death. Fortunately for him the execution was postponed for several months.

Early in July 1851, the real James Stewart, for whose crimes Thomas Berdue awaited execution in Maryville, returned to San Francisco from the interior, and made a bold and unsuccessful attempt to rob a ship anchored in the harbor. The ship's crew was able to capture and subdue Stewart, and on the morning of July 11, 1851, the trial of the real "English Jim" began. It was necessary to present very little evidence, for Stewart at once confessed to a long list of crimes, including murdering Sheriff Moore and assaulting storekeeper Jensen, thus by giving this confession, he exonerated Berdue. After his confession was read in court, it was unanimously agreed upon that Stewart was to be executed immediately. Less than two hours after being sentenced to death, the real "English Jim," heavily manacled, was led under heavy guard from the courthouse jail. He appeared to be nonchalant to his fate, and when asked if he wished to make a final statement, replied, "This is a damned tiresome business. Get it over with." A scaffold had been hastily erected at the Market Street wharf and at the sight of the gallows, "English Jim" finally lost his nerve, collapsing into the arms of his guards. He was dragged the hundred or so feet to the scaffold, a rope was looped around his neck, and a score of men jerked him to the top. His lifeless body swung on the gallows for several minutes before being cut down. Thus the career of the most infamous Sydney Duck was at an end.

The real "English Jim" was scarcely dead, when members of the Vigilance Committee had taken steps, as far as possible, to right the injustice which had been done to Thomas Burdue. They briskly rode to Marysville, to inform the authorities that the real James Stewart had been hanged, and procured Burdue's release. Thomas Berdue was at last a free man; the committee gave him a sum of $2,000 to ease the pain he had suffered. Several days later, Berdue was seen boarding a small boat in the harbor and was never seen again. This ended one of the strangest and most celebrated cases of mistaken identity in the annals of American crime.

The Curious Case of Yankee Jim

(San Diego, 1852)

Very little is known about the early adventures of James "Yankee Jim" Robinson. It has been speculated that he came to California sometime between 1849 and 1851, but little else is known. Like thousands of other fortune seekers, "Yankee Jim" came to the gold fields of the Sacramento River Valley in search of treasure and fortune. What he found instead was a life of crime that would end in tragedy. His time in the gold fields was quite unproductive, and whether the loss of a possible fortune soured Yankee Jim on the human race is unknown.

What *is* known is that he turned to a rather revengeful occupation of stealing other people's horses. It was certainly lucrative, and far less strenuous than digging for gold. In this profession, Yankee Jim thrived. That is, until the level of lawlessness reached such proportions that the miners demanded retribution. After a rogues' gallery of cutthroats descended on the gold country, miners' committees were formed to issue summary justice. The penchant of these committees was to hand out harsh punishments that most often included death. Sensing that it was the right time for a change of venue, Jim saddled up his best horse and high tailed it for Southern California. He made short stops in Stockton and Los Angeles, but his main objective was San Diego, which, while known as a law-and-order town, offered desperados the advantage of close proximity to the Mexican border.

On the evening of Friday, August 13, 1852, Captain James Keating happened to be standing on a pier at La Playa on Point Loma. He noticed three men, one wearing a red shirt, take a rowboat from the beach and row toward Keating's untended schooner, the *Plutus*. Concerned, Keating yelled out: "Whose boat is that?" One of the men shouted back that it was their own. Knowing this to be false, the captain demanded the man return the dingy to shore, or else be fired upon. The man in the row boat muttered something unintelligible to Keating, and continued to row out into the channel. Raising his shotgun to his shoulder, Keating aimed at the red-shirted man and pulled the trigger. The buckshot fell short, the men changed course and rowed to shore, abandoned the rowboat, and ran away.

The next morning, Keating reported the incident to the authorities; Mayor Tebbett, Judge Hays, Deputy Sheriff Reiner, and Sheriff Crosthwaite set out to find these men apprehending two of the fugitives but failing to locate the man wearing the red shirt. Later, Deputy Sheriff Reiner rode out to continue the search, stopping to tell the Mexican caretaker at Rose's Ranch north of old town (San Diego) to be on the lookout for a man in a red shirt. That evening, by chance, a man in a red shirt did appear at the door of the caretaker, asking for food. After eating, the man lay down to rest, but became suspicious of the movements of the caretaker and began to run. The caretaker's wife quickly handed her husband a lasso and an old artillery sword. He gave chase and began to gain ground on the man, whirled his rope and threw it over the escapee's head, pinning his arms to his sides. The man struggled to get free, but a terrific wallop on the head with the sword brought him to the ground. The caretaker then lashed him to a mule and led him to the Old town jail.

The next morning, a committee of citizens interrogated the three captives. The man in the red shirt was James Robinson, commonly known as Yankee Jim. His fellow detainees were William Harris and James Gray. As the *San Diego Herald* put it, "before night (they) persuaded them that they had better own up." The trio confessed to having come down from Stockton, stealing and selling horses. In Old town, they had sold their horses and bought provision, then attempted to steal the *Plutus* to make their way to Baja, Mexico.

These arrests and confessions created a whirlwind of excitement in Old Town. The town had suffered from a crime wave for the last year and a half. It started with volunteers from San Francisco (many of whom were criminal in nature and known as Sydney Ducks), who came to town to help suppress the Garra Uprising. Even though the Indian revolt never fully materialized, they satisfied their yearning for trouble by boisterously tearing through town causing all forms of mischief. The sheriff and the courts were unable to curb the lawlessness, and the mood of the town can be accessed from a brief item in the *Herald* on July 10, 1851:

> HORSE THIEVES: Mayor Tebbetts had his horse stolen on Wednesday night about 12:00 from his very door. If thieves are caught they will be hung up to the flagstaff in the Plaza without trial.

Yankee Jim and his cohorts could not have picked a worse time or place to run afoul of the law. Harris and Gray were arraigned separately, found guilty, and sentenced to one year in state prison. The trial of Yankee Jim opened on August 17, 1852, at the Plaza Court House, just three days after he received the severe head wound at Rose's Ranch. Yankee Jim, not being in his right mind (after suffering the head wound) and ill advised, served as his own attorney. During the proceedings, he foolishly exercised his right to challenge four of the prospective jurors; this unfortunately prejudiced the remaining jurors and sealed his fate. After a short trial that lasted but one afternoon, the jury retired to deliberate, returning thirty minute later with a verdict of guilty. The judge then sentenced Yankee Jim to death and set the execution date as the next afternoon August 18, 1852. Being delirious from his head injury, Jim was unable to comprehend what had just happened, and before he could come to his senses, he was hauled away to the town jail to await his fate. For unknown reasons his execution was delayed until September 18, 1852.

When the fateful day finally arrived, Yankee Jim was put on a wagon and driven a short distance to the newly erected gallows. Yankee Jim chatted calmly with Sheriff Crosthwaite, still disbelieving he would be hung, and perhaps thinking this was a hoax to scare him half to death as punishment. Asked if he had any last words to say,

A recreation of the first San Diego Courthouse on Old Town Plaza.

Yankee Jim spoke to the crowd at length rambling on and on about nothing in particular. Finally, the sheriff gave the order to whip the mules, which pulled the wagon from underneath Jim. He was a rather tall man, (which was not taken into consideration when estimating the length of the rope) and his toes nearly touched the ground. Thus instead of dying rapidly, Jim slowly and quite painfully strangled for nearly forty-five minutes, until finally succumbing. Thus ended the comical and tragic escapades of Yankee Jim and also answered the question of whether the citizens of San Diego were serious. James "Yankee Jim" Robison is buried at El Campo Santos Cemetery, which is just a short distance from where he breathed his last breath.

Today, the spot where Yankee Jim allegedly met his fate, is where the Whaley House now stands, known nationally as one of the most haunted locations in all of the United States by the Travel Channel's *America's Most Haunted*. Numerous visitors to the house claim to have heard the sounds of heavy boot steps in the upstairs rooms. They also claim that these sounds end at the edge of the stairs, which is directly above the archway between the parlor and the music room. This is the exact spot where the gallows stood from which Yankee Jim was hung. Numerous visitors have also claimed to encounter a feeling of strangulation near this spot. Does the restless spirit of Yankee Jim's still roam the halls of the site of his final demise? No one really knows for sure.

Yankee Jim's gravesite at El Campo Santo Cemetery in Old Town San Diego.

Whaley House, Old Town San Diego (present day), California State Historical landmark #65.

The Robin Hood of El Dorado Joaquin Murrieta

(Gold Rush Country, Central Valley, & Southern California, 1849-1853)

The first significant wide spread outbreak of criminal violence in California and one of the darkest pages in California history did not originate in the vice-ridden streets of the Barbary Coast, as one might think. On the contrary, it began in the gold fields with the systematic and heartless persecution of the Spanish-American. The miners, particularly those from other parts of the United States, harassed those of non-white descent in every conceivable manner: stealing and destroying their goods and mining equipment, driving them from their claims and farms, raping their women, beating their children, or killing them on little or no provocation, then hanging them with elaborate pretensions to justice, if there was so much as an attempt to defend themselves or failure to vacate property, which an American desired. The immediate cause of this ill treatment of Spanish-Americans was probably anger and jealousy over the fact that they, being first on the ground, had naturally occupied the richest gold claims. Thus it has been generally theorized that the rise of the California Bandito (1850-1875) was a direct result of this widespread persecution.

Many historians have tended to oversimplify the main issue as a political conflict between the Californians and the Americans and that the raids by these so-called banditos and the subsequent retaliations on numerous citizenry of Mexican heritage were partisan in nature. It is foolish to label these incidents as just "good guys" versus "bad guys." The evidence does not lend itself to the same conclusion. A quick glance at the history of this place and time reveals that it is often very difficult to separate the differences between a "revolutionary" and the "bandito."

The California Bandito was indeed a very real way of life before the American entered the picture, going back as far as the first years of the Spanish possession of Alta California in the 1700s. During the first twenty-five years of Mexican rule (1821–1848) of Alta California, a new class of dissident arose that developed a tradition for mischief and crime. They included disillusioned Spaniards, Indians, angry soldiers, misfits, and degenerates, and they came from a different strata of society, preferring to live on the fringes, and all favored the vagabond way of life. Civil authorizes had very little power and were liberal in dealing with the criminal exploits of these banditos. Many of these outlaws were viewed at being heroic and justified in their exploits.

During the often troubled and turbulent years of Mexican control, the California bandito was allowed to flourish. When the United States annexed Alta California as a territory in 1848, and the subsequent discovery of gold at Sutter's Mill, these banditos had a new-found foe and source of riches. It is unclear as to whether these bandits were legitimate revolutionaries or just criminal opportunists. A clear answer is not apparent but a perfect storm of convergence between opportunity and circumstance allowed banditry, and all forms of criminal activity to flourish for almost twenty five years, from the central coast and valley to Southern California. This region was a natural retreat for men of Mexican origin who were wanted by the law. The beginning of the golden age of the California bandito was at hand.

Time as it lengthens weaves strange illusions. A murderer of today is a villain, who is ostracized from society and sent off to prison. A wholesale killer of one hundred and sixty plus years ago is a hero of romance. Joaquin Murrieta was one of the most ruthless bandits that lived. His career was crimson with blood and his trails were littered with corpses. But time has dropped a sentimental veil of poetry about him. Myth and fable have enveloped him. The murderous robber has become a picturesque figure of fantasy; high idealed, as chivalrous as he is brave, riding merrily with a sparkle in his eye through hundreds of adventures. He is the protector of women. He robs the rich and gives to the poor. He is the Robin Hood of El Dorado.

Murrieta was both loved and despised, being described as both a blood-thirsty desperado and Mexican patriot. His story has become so legendary that the truths of his exploits have often become blurred between reality and myth. Had it not been for author John Ridge's fictionalized version of his exploits *The Life and Adventures of Joaquin Murrieta* (1853), the bandit would have been remembered as just another cold-blooded western outlaw.

Murrieta's outlaw career is believed to have begun toward the close of 1850, though the exact date is unknown. It is alleged that it ended with a bullet on July 25, 1853. He was twenty years old when he became an outlaw. He was twenty-three when he was killed. But in those three years, one of the most lurid chapters in criminal history was written. Daring robbers and murders followed upon each other's heels in rapid succession and an unknown Mexican youth became one of the most famous figures of his day.

Very little is known about his youth; most historians agree that Murrieta was born around 1832 in the state of Sonora, Mexico. He came to Alta California at the age of seventeen accompanied by his young bride, Rosita Feliz (alias Antonia Molinera), who remained loyal and by his side throughout his entire criminal career. She often rode alongside her husband, and took an active part in many of the robberies and murders.

When the gold rush began, Murrieta was in San Francisco. He followed the crowd and in the spring of 1849, staked a claim at Saw Mill Flat in Stanislaus County. It is alleged that soon after arriving, he was attacked by white American miners, who were jealous of his claim and attracted to his beautiful wife. One evening, a band of five miners confronted Murrieta at his cabin. They beat him unconscious and raped Rosita. Murrieta vowed to make them all pay for their actions, to kill them all and if necessary, follow them to hell to accomplish it. Bitter about being driven from land that he believed to be rightfully his and seething with hatred and vengeance, he was forced into a life of crime. Thereafter, he was an outlaw, and for almost three years, left a bloody trail from the gold country to southern coast of California. Sometimes, he was attended by as many as eighty horsemen, all of whom had a significant reason to hate the American miners. They robbed stagecoaches, lone travelers, held up mining camps, robbed small towns and generously shared their stolen booty with their mistreated friends – while plundering and murdering their way throughout the gold fields, central valley, and coastal areas of California. Murrieta is believed to have killed every one of the men, who had driven him from his mining claim and raped his wife.

In 1852, tiring of Murrieta's activities, the California Legislature offered a $5,000 reward for the bandits capture, dead or alive. One legend states that Murrieta rode into Stockton, just as one of these reward posters were being affixed to a tree. Pushing through the crowd, he wrote on the bottom of the poster: "I will pay $1,000 myself, J. Murieta (sic)."

His deprivations finally became so numerous and so violent that in May of 1853, the Legislature authorized Harry Love, Deputy Sheriff of Los Angeles, to raise a company of twenty-five men to hunt down and kill the bandit. Love and his men took to the trail, accompanied by William Burns, a gambler who had been friendly with Murrieta. Burns agreed to betray the bandit leader for a few hundred dollars. On the evening of Saturday, July 25, 1853, Love, Burns, and other members of the posse came upon Murrieta, Manual Garcia, known as "Three Fingered Jack," and several others who were sitting before a camp fire near Pacheco Pass in San Benito County, fifty miles from Monterey. A brief skirmish ensued and members of the gang scattered. Murrieta attempted to reach his horse but was hit by a volley of bullets. Being mortally wounded and seeing that further escape was futile, Murrieta threw down his rifle, raised his hands, called out to Deputy Love: "Shoot no more. The work is done." The bandit slowly slumped to the ground and died.

Today, the location of Murrieta's capture and death is memorialized by California State Historical marker #344, which is found near the intersection of Routes 33 and 198, nine miles north of Coalinga. After his death, Murrieta's gang was led by Luis Bulvia, who for a brief time continued the reign of criminal behavior until he too was killed.

The life and times of Joaquin Murrieta was a violent affair filled with numerous robbery and killings. Although his exploits were filled with innumerable tales of appalling cruelty, what prevails today is the legend of great kindness to his fellow countrymen. It is easy to see that he regarded himself as the champion of his country rather than as an outlaw. He was only a few months older then twenty-three when he died, and whether considered a revolutionary patriot or coldhearted thief and murderer, there is no doubt that during his short life, he left an indelible mark on the history of crime in the state of California.

Anticipating public skepticism to whether the notorious bandito was indeed dead, Love ordered that Murrieta's head be cut off and preserved in a jar of alcohol. Many people still refused to believe that Murrieta was in fact dead, and numerous reliable witnesses came forward to state that the head in the jar was not that of the outlaw. Even his wife, Rosita, believed that the famous outlaw had escaped back to Mexico. Don Eugenio Plummer, a well-respected citizen of Los Angeles and owner of extensive ranch land on what eventually became West Hollywood, claimed a different fate befell Murrieta:

> That was not the head of Don Joaquin the gringos paid to see in the museum. It was an Indian who was killed for the reward. He (Murrieta) established a fine hacienda below the city of Hermosillo in Mexico and lived there until he died a very old man.

For three plus decades, thousands flocked to see the head of the desperado, who was alleged to have killed more than 300 hundred men. Long after the bandit was allegedly killed by Harry Love's California Rangers, many Californians believed Murrieta had escaped and would return to harass the state.

As for the alleged pickled head of Joaquin Murrieta, it was put on display in numerous county jails and saloons across California. The mere possession of it seemed to bring bad luck to its possessor. Joaquin's head found a permanent home when it was put on display at Doctor Jordan's Museum of Horrors in San Francisco, but bad luck again followed, when the exhibition was destroyed in the Great Earthquake and Fire of 1906 and the alleged head of Joaquin Murrieta was lost forever. As for Murrieta's captors, William Burns was killed shortly after by friends of the bandit leader, and Harry Love also found an early grave, when he was gunned down by a disgruntled former employee on June 29, 1868.

Joaquin Murietta, artist's rendering (circa, 1848), published in the *Sacramento Union Steamer* April 22, 1853.

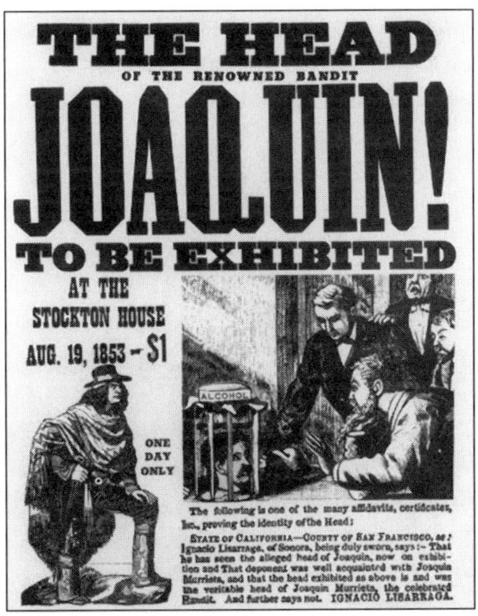

Poster proclaiming the exhibition of Joaquin Murrieta's head at the Stockton House, August 19, 1853.

The Assassination of James King of William

(San Francisco, 1855-1856)

On the evening of Thursday, November 15, 1855, Charles Cora, an Italian gambler, attended the performance of *Nicodemus*, or *The Unfortunate Fisherman* at the American Theater in San Francisco. He was accompanied by his mistress, known both as Belle Cora and Arabella Ryan, the daughter of a Baltimore clergyman. She had long ago abandoned the habits of the church, and was notoriously known throughout San Francisco as the proprietor of a house of prostitution on Pike Street, which was well known to offer the prettiest and most skillful girls, at the highest prices, of any bordello in the city. Also in attendance that night was William H. Richardson, United States Marshal for the Northern District of California. He and his party were offended that a woman of Belle Cora's character was allowed to show herself in public; Richardson demanded that she be ejected from the theater. The manager refused, and Richardson and his party left after a heated exchange of words with Charles Cora.

The next day Cora and Richardson met in the Cosmopolitan Saloon. They appeared to have agreed to forget the previous evening's incident but a quarrel erupted in the streets in which Richardson was quoted as saying to Cora "If I ever see you again on this street, I will slap your face."

Two days later, on November 17, 1855, Cora was drinking in the Blue Wing Saloon when Marshal Richardson entered. The latter approached the bar with evident intent of carrying out his previous threat; Cora drew a derringer and shot Richardson through the heart. He was immediately arrested for Richardson's murder. Belle Cora hired a formidable array of lawyers for his defense that included John McDougal, former California Governor (1851-1852), and Edward Dickinson Baker, who would later become a United States Senator from Oregon and Civil War martyr. Miss Cora agreed to pay Baker $30,000 for defending her lover.

Although the killing of Marshal Richardson aroused a storm of public indignation and resentment, it is quite likely that Cora would

James King of William. *Courtesy of the Bancroft Library/ University of California, Berkeley.*

have gone unpunished, had it not been for James King and his persistent editorials in the *San Francisco Daily Evening Bulletin*. James King of Williams as he liked to be called elected to play gadfly in San Francisco, as Socrates had done in Athens. California editors of the 1850s had an extraordinary command of pungent and insulting language, and King was magnificently equipped in this respect. With impartial acrimony, he attacked the powerful banking houses, David C. Broderick, and James P. Casey, a notorious politician and racketeer.

No sooner had Cora been lodged in jail, then King began calling for the death penalty, and at the same time predicting that the gamblers political friends would never let him be convicted. On a daily basis King would call attention to the many wild rumors which swept throughout the city. One such rumor was that Cora was to be permitted escape with the help of Billy Mulligan, then the County jailer, or that the jury was to be bribed by Cora's friends. In the *Bulletin,* King wrote:

> Look well to the jury, if the jury is packed, either hang the Sheriff or drive him out of town and make him resign. If Billy Mulligan lets his friend escape, hang Billy Mulligan or drive him into banishment.

Such extraordinary journalism so stirred up the town that Cora was brought to trial within two months after the murder. During the first trial of Cora, the jury promptly justified King's fears, reporting a disagreement after forty-one hours of deliberation. A mistrial was declared and a second trial was ordered. Cora was remanded to jail to await a second trial, which no one ever thought would be held.

One of James King's most unrelenting journalistic enemies, was James P. Casey, editor of a weekly political paper and a member of the San Francisco City Board of Supervisors. Casey and King took frequent political pot-shots at each other, Casey in particular berating King for his attitude toward Cora. One of King's most vicious attacks on Casey came on May 14, 1856, when King referred to Casey's prior prison record and asserted that he was deserved "having his neck stretched" for the fraudulent manner in which he had procured his post as Supervisor. Ordinarily, Casey would have replied in kind even to an attack of this manner, but friends of Cora, anxious to create a diversion that would take the public's mind off of the gambler, convinced Casey that only King's death, could wipe out the affront to his honor. Incensed by the *Bulletin's* onslaughts, Casey challenged King to a duel; King calmly ignored both challenge and the open threats which Casey made against his life. But Casey was not bluffing; as King left his office to go home on the afternoon of May 14, 1856, Casey met him at the entrance to the *Daily Evening Bulletin* building (corner of Montgomery and Washington Streets), shoved a pistol against his chest, and fired a shot. King fell to the sidewalk mortally wounded, and Casey immediately surrendered to police.

King was not the most popular man in San Francisco but he was easily the most forthright and best known. He was shot at five o'clock in the afternoon, when the streets were filled with people, and within an hour, the news was all over the city, arousing a sensation such as San Francisco had never experienced. For several days after the shooting of King, business in the city basically came to a standstill as the people awaited the outcome of the editor's wounds. Great throngs continued to threaten the jail where Casey was being held.

Cora was the first to come to trial before the Vigilance Committee. The proceeding began on Tuesday, May 20, 1856. When Cora came to court he pleaded that all prejudices and rancor be laid aside and that he be given a fair and impartial hearing. Many witnesses were called, and the trial last until evening. He was found guilty of murder. The committee rested for two hours and then began the trial of Casey. While Casey was being tried, word came that James King had succumbed to his wounds; it had been six days since the historic shot had been fired. By a unanimous vote, a summary verdict was rendered that called the murder premeditated and unjustifiable. Casey was found guilty of killing King. Both men were sentenced to death by hanging.

On May 22, 1856, a vest number of people estimated at near 15,000 attended the funeral of James King. Before many of them could return from the burial at Lone Mountain Cemetery, both Casey and Cora had been hung from the roof top of the Vigilance Committee headquarters, on a make shift gallows. An hour before his execution and with the consent of the Vigilance Committee, Cora was allowed to marry his mistress Arabella Ryan with whom the whole incident had begun. Arabella "Belle" Ryan Cora sold her house of prostitution shortly after the incident, and became widely known for her generosity to charity. She lived alone until her death on February 18, 1862. She is buried alongside her husband Charles at the Mission Dolores Cemetery.

The hanging of James P. Casey and Charles Cora in front of the Vigilance Committee rooms, San Francisco, May 22, 1856. *Courtesy of the Library of Congress, Prints and Photographs, (LC-USZ62-103212).*

Juan Flores and the Los Manilas Gang

(Central Coast and Southern California, 1852-1857)

The rendezvous tree (located on Junipero Serra Road). Legend states that this is the tree where the Flores Gang met prior to their raid on San Juan Capistrano.

A group of four worn-out and used-up mules pulled a column of buckboard wagons loaded with coffins over the parched, sandy landscape twelve miles north of the sleepy village of San Juan Capistrano. Further on in the remoteness were a group of dead bodies scattered across the valley floor. Distorted dead horses, bloating in the heat, lay beside their dead owners. All of the corpses were wearing badges; three of the men were deputies and one was Los Angeles Sheriff James R. Barton. Each of the lawmen had been riddled with bullets; they had been stripped of all their personal belongings and their right eyes had been shot out.

The purpose of the ill-fated posse, sent out on January 22, 1957, was to capture and arrest Juan Flores and members of his bandit gang. Flores' criminal activity had begun several years earlier and his criminal gang had run rough shod over a stretch of California that extended from San Luis Obispo to San Diego. Along the way, Flores had recruited more than fifty outlaws to assist him in his unlawful behavior. The ensuing search for Juan Flores and his gang was one of the largest (yet virtually forgotten) manhunts in the annals of Western United States history.

Southern California in the 1850s was a lawless and ruthless place. Roving bands of criminal groups roamed the countryside of the region. With powerful leaders such as Poncho Daniel, Manuel Marquez, and Joaquin Murrieta, these gangs of bandits terrorized the "white" settlers of the area. One of the most powerful and deadly bandit gangs to develop was led by Juan Flores and Poncho Daniel. Juan Flores was born in 1835 in Santa Barbara, where his parents were well-respected members of the community. Why Flores embarked on a life of crime is unknown but it is clear that he harbored a deep hatred for whites. He saw his native land being overrun and was not opposed to taking it back by illegal means. He left home at age seventeen and was first arrested in 1855 for horse stealing and imprisoned in San Quentin. He escaped in October 1856 and joined forces with Daniel and a dozen or so other bandits, ex-convicts, and fugitives forming a ruthless gang called the "Los Manilas." This gang of bandits would terrorize Southern California for several months, looting small towns, ransacking prospector camps, and kidnapping lone travelers. Flores was seen by many Spanish-Americans as a vigilante folk hero, akin to the likes of Joaquin Murrieta and Jesse James. Many dead bodies were left in the wake of their mayhem. Due in part to attention by newspapers, opposition to what became known as the "Flores Revolution" began to take form by public officials and law enforcement as well as upper-class Californians such as Pio and Andres Pico, Juan Sepulveda and Tomas Avila Sanchez, some of whom later participated in the capture of Flores.

The Garcia Adobe (present day), the first floor was used by merchant Michael Krazewski.

Six times, James R. Barton was elected Sheriff of Los Angeles County, serving five consecutive years (1851-55) with a one-year hiatus. Barton refused to run again after a vigilante group lynched his prisoner. Two other men tried unsuccessfully to fill his shoes before Barton took the reins once more. Crime was rampant in Los Angeles, averaging one violent death per day, but Barton was successful in quelling the criminal activity. He arrested several bandits; among these was Andres Fontes, who had been convicted of horse stealing and sentenced to two years in prison. It is said that, as Fontes was being placed on the stage to be transported north, he threatened Barton, saying, "When I return, I'm going to kill you." A few historians have speculated that Fontes' resentment toward Barton was a personal matter, stemming from an attraction each had for the same woman. Fontes served his term and was released. He came back and joined the gang led by Juan Flores.

The beginning of the demise of the Flores-Daniel gang occurred in January of 1857, when Flores and his band of outlaws raided the tiny village of San Juan Capistrano. This incident would leave a wide path of death and destruction in its wake. On Sunday, January 18, 1857, a local teamster named Garnet Hardy of San Juan Capistrano was advised that Flores and his bandit gang were hiding out in the local hills, waiting to rob wagon trains and unsuspecting travelers. Hardy sent word of the pending trouble to his brother Alfred, a prominent citizen in Los Angeles. The message was passed on to Los Angeles County Sheriff James Barton, who organized a posse of six men that included constables William Little, Charles Baker, Charles Daly, Frank Alexander, and an unknown scout.

The six-man posse left Los Angeles in the early evening of Thursday, January 22, 1857, in pursuit of the bandits. Andres Fontes had remained in Los Angeles as a lookout for the gang, and learning of the sheriff's plan, immediately rode to San Juan Capistrano to inform Flores and Daniel of the posse's destination.

Earlier that same day Flores and his gang, impatient and needing supplies, raided the town of San Juan Capistrano – where members of the gang attacked and robbed the store of merchant Michael Krazewski. What the gang could not carry out, they destroyed. That evening the gang return to the town, and looted the stores of Henry Charles, Manuel Garcia, and George Pflugardt. Charles and Garcia were lucky and fled unharmed, Pflugardt was not as fortunate. He attempted to stop the looting, and was shot and killed. The gang members then ordered his wife to make them dinner, while the body of Pflugardt lay on the floor nearby. Securing all the supplies they would need, the Flores gang then fled to the local foothills.

Photograph of Michael Krazewski. *Courtesy of University of Southern California, on behalf of the USC Libraries Special Collections.*

Early the next morning, Friday, January 29, 1857, Sherriff Barton and his group arrived at El Refugio, the main house of the Rancho San Joaquin, which was southwest of present day Santa Ana. It was owned by one of California's finest old Dons, Jose Sepulveda, described as "a princely character and genial host." The 1,000 acres upon which El Refugio sat were located west of Bristol and south of First Street; however, historians disagree as to the actual location of the adobe compound. Some accounts place the house at First and Sullivan Streets, while others claim the adobe and its compound were at Artesia and Myrtle Streets. Artesia is now South Raitt. In 1876, the last remnants of the great El Refugio adobe were torn down.

Martina "Cholla" Burruel (circa, 1907). *Courtesy of University of Southern California, on behalf of the USC Libraries Special Collections.*

Gathered about the Don's adobe buildings were dozens of vaqueros and servants, Indians and Mexicans. Among these was Martina "Chola" Burruel, an Indian girl who happened to be the sweetheart of Flores. Leaving their guns on a table in an outbuilding, the posse members sat down to breakfast. Don Jose warned Barton that Flores had a large force of fifty or sixty men, who were well armed and mounted. He advised the Sheriff against going further, since the posse was so pitifully outnumbered. Barton, however, insisted on continuing the pursuit, and immediately after breakfast resumed his search of Flores.

About twelve miles north of the Sepulveda Ranch (near present day Irvine at the junction of the 133 and 405 freeways); they observed a lone rider galloping about a mile off in the distance. Deputy's Little and Baker rode forward to see what the man wanted. When they advanced about 400 yards, the men were suddenly attacked by a band of about twenty men, who rushed out from between the hills. When the scout saw the advancing band, he called out to Barton, "These are the robbers; shoot them, shoot them." Barton and the remaining members of the posse immediately rushed to the assistance of Little and Baker, but before they could reach them, the latter were killed. The four remaining lawmen advanced on the charging bandits, they grabbed their guns to return fire, only to discover that someone had removed the ammunition from the weapons. One of the bandits (presumed to be Fontes, or possibly Daniels) was heard to shout at Barton, "God damn you, I have got you, now," to which Barton replied, "I reckon I have got you, too." Their guns were being leveled at each other during the exchange, when the bandit's gun discharged, and Barton fell from his horse, shot through the heart. Deputies Daly, and Alexander, cut off from the party, broke and ran for their lives. Daly was run down and killed, while Alexander affected his escape, owing to the fleetness of his horse. Members of the bandit gang pursued him for twelve miles, until they came within sight of the Sepulveda Ranch; they then broke off the pursuit, and vanished into the local mountains. It has been suspected, but never proven, that Flores' girlfriend, Martina Burruel, had removed the rounds from the guns of the posse, while Barton and his men were having breakfast with Don Jose.

Details of the murders of Sheriff Barton and his men quickly spread across southern California. Law-abiding citizens were outraged. Within two hours, a posse of approximately sixty men was organized by Don Andres Pico. He had commanded the pro-Mexican forces in Alta California during the Mexican War, defeated U.S. General Stephen Kearny at the Battle of San Pasqual, December 7 and 8, 1846. Pico was, for a brief period in 1847, Governor of Mexican Alta California. He signed the Treaty of Cahuenga on January 13, 1847, which ended military action in Alta California during the Mexican War.

Don Andres Pico (1810-1876), Governor of Alta California, 1847.

Another posse was formed and started immediately for San Juan Capistrano, under the leadership of James Thompson, who later became sheriff. A third posse was led by another future Sheriff, J. Frank Burns, who at this time was Barton's deputy in the San Gabriel district. Another group of fourteen citizens was dispatched to recover the remains of the slain lawmen. Arriving the next morning, Saturday January 23, 1857, they came upon the scene of the bloody massacre. The bodies of Barton, Baker, and Little were found within about ten feet of the road, near the side a small hill (today, known as Barton Mound; State Historical marker #218). Daly's body was found three miles north. Sheriff Barton had been shot through the heart, his left arm was broken, and his right eye had been shot out. His pockets had been rifled through, and all of his personal belongings were missing. Little, Baker, and Daly all had multiple gunshot wounds to their heads and bodies and their right eyes had also been shot out. There was evidence that all of the slain lawmen had been fired upon after they were deceased.

Flores hearing that a large company of men were in hot pursuit, ordered his gang to disperse into small groups. For almost a week, Flores was able to evade capture. On Thursday, January 29, 1857, a scout located Flores, and several other bandits, hidden in Santiago Canyon. The initial plan was to storm the camp by moonlight, but when it was seen that a slow, silent approach would not put the posse in position before the moon set, the time of attack was changed to dawn. Detachments led by Andres Pico and others, moved in as the sun edged above the horizon, but Flores had risen before first light, and had climbed to a rocky lookout above the canyon. After alerting his men to the danger, he leaped onto his horse and raced away. Three other bandits were also able to mount and ride off before the posse closed in on the camp. With Pico's party in pursuit, Flores climbed the ridge near a rocky summit, known today as Flores Peak (designated State historical marker #225), abandoned his horse, and plunged down a cliff face. He gambled he would not break his neck, and won.

Pico and the other posse leaders discussed the situation and were confident that the trio of outlaws had not actually broken out of the large net surrounding them. The posse retraced their steps; they would follow a safer route to the next canyon, Flores, and two other bandits were later spotted in Harding Canyon, north of Santiago Canyon. After a brief gun battle, the three outlaws surrendered, tossing down their guns and walked out of a cave. They were taken about five miles down the canyon to Teodocio Yorba's ranch (near present day Irvine Lake). There, they were tied up and locked in an adobe hut, with guards only a few steps away. Andres Pico and other members of the posse spent the afternoon celebrating and making plans to transport Flores and the others to Los Angeles for trial.

The hanging tree in Presita Canyon, where on the morning of January 30, 1957, banditos Juan Catabo and Francisco Ardillero were executed. *Photo Courtesy of Chris Jepsen.*

That night around midnight, Flores was able to overpower his guards and escape. Fellow bandits Juan Catabo and Francisco Ardillero were not as lucky. Pico did not take the news of Flores' escape well and his angry shouts echoed off the hills. Not wanting the two remaining criminals to escape, he ordered their immediate execution. A squad of men brought Catabo and Ardillero to a nearby arroyo called Presita Canyon. There Pico strode up to a large sycamore tree and oversaw the tying of nooses on two ropes, which were then tossed over a branch ten feet off the ground. Pico watched, while the two prisoners were hung, and as he turned to walk away, said, "Here are two, who will never get loose." He ordered their bodies to be left to sway in the wind as a reminder of frontier justice.

As to the eventual disposition of Catabo and Ardillero's bodies, Joseph Pleasants (local historian and caretaker of the Wolfskill Ranch) wrote:

Fort Moore Hill, circa 1883. *Courtesy of University of Southern California, on behalf of the USC Libraries Special Collections.*

> The bodies of the two bandits were left strung up to the sycamore for six months when some vaqueros who lived over in the Santa Ana Canyon cut them down and buried what was left of them in a shallow grave at the clump of sycamores. It was two years after that that I became foreman of the Wolfskill Ranch.... Two men, named Armento and Canyero, who were working for me, told me that they had helped cut down the bandit's bodies and bury them. The coyotes had dug into the shallow grave, and the bones of the two men were scattered around on the surface of the ground. I went to the place with Armento and Canyero, and we dug a new grave about four feet deep, gathered up the bones and put them in it. My remembrance is that one of the skulls was missing.

On Sunday, February 2, 1857, after nearly ten days on the run, Juan Flores was captured near the Simi Pass. He had stopped to water his horse, when he was apprehended by two soldiers. Initially, Flores told them his name was Juan Gonzales Sanchez, and he was traveling to Santa Barbara to purchase some horses. Suspicious of the story, the soldiers escorted him back to camp, where he was immediately identified as the fugitive bandit Juan Flores. He was brought back to Los Angeles under heavy guard to stand trial for the murder of Sheriff Barton and the others. Under interrogation, Flores admitted to the theft of a horse at Santa Ana, and later a second one at San Fernando. He

Near this location on February 14, 1857, Bandit Juan Flores was executed. The Fort Moore Pioneer Memorial Wall, downtown Los Angeles, dedicated in 1957.

denied ever being the leader of the "Los Manilas," or any involvement in the murders of merchant Pflugardt in San Juan Capistrano, or Sheriff Barton and his deputies. Flores was quickly tried by a citizen's court, found guilty, and sentenced to death. On Saturday, February 14, 1857, he was brought to Fort Hill (near present day downtown Los Angeles, the current site of the Los Angeles Board of Education complex) and hanged. It was estimated that nearly 3,000 citizens witnessed his execution. Addressing the crowd from the scaffold, one witness reported Flores' final words:

Barton Mound State Historical landmark #218 (near the I-405 and 133 interchange). Near here, outlaw Juan Flores and his gang ambushed Los Angeles County Sheriff James Barton and his small posse.

> He bore no malice, was dying justly, and that he hoped that those he had wronged would forgive him.

When his execution was carried out, his noose being too short, Flores died from strangulation rather than having his neck broken. After hanging some time, a physician examined the body and declared that there was no pulse. The body was kept hanging for about an hour and then handed over to friends for burial. Flores was only twenty-two years old, and was presumed to be buried in an unmarked grave at Fort Hill Cemetery.

In the aftermath of the carnage, the remainder of the "Los Manilas" gang dispersed throughout the region, and most were caught and executed. Pancho Daniel was captured on January 19, 1858, almost a year after the murders, near San Jose. The Santa Clara County sheriff found him hiding in a haystack. He had three trials, but through legal technicalities, managed to forestall conviction. A change of venue to Santa Barbara was eventually granted. On the morning of November 30, 1858, Daniel's body was found hanging from a beam across the gateway of the jail yard. Andres Fontes, who was supposed to have instigated the killing of Barton, escaped into Baja California, where he was later killed.

Sheriff Barton, Deputies Little, Baker, and Daly were buried together at the Fort Moore Hill burial ground; thousands lined the streets to witness the sad procession and honor the slain lawmen as it made its way to the cemetery. The Fort Hill Cemetery was closed in the early 1880s and the land was sold and zoned for residential usage but none of the bodies were removed. After decades of complaints, the city of Los Angeles agreed to removed all of the bodies, and rebury them at several area cemeteries, mainly, Evergreen, Angeles-Rosedale, and Hollywood Memorial Park. The reburial was completed in the 1940s. None of these cemeteries have records pertaining to the re-burial of Barton or the others. Where exactly Sheriff Barton and the others rest for eternity is a mystery. Part of Fort Moore Hill was demolished in 1949 to make way for the construction of the 101 freeway. The area is today memorialized by the Fort Moore Pioneer Memorial wall which was dedicated in 1957.

The Famous Duel of Terry and Broderick

(San Francisco area, 1859)

No record of the early crimes of California can be complete without mentioning the duels that were fought between men of business and politics in the name of honor. There were numerous meetings of duelists, where through a combination of poor marksmanship and good luck, serious injury was avoided. One of the greatest duels, one which ended in tragedy and created widespread attention throughout the state and nation was that fought between United States Senator, David C. Broderick, and Davis S. Terry, Chief Justice of the California State Supreme Court on September 13, 1859.

David C. Broderick was born in the District of Columbia on February 4, 1820. In his early years, he ventured to New York City, where he owned a saloon and dabbled in politics. Like many other fortune seekers, he left for California, arriving in San Francisco on June 13, 1849.

He again became active in local and state politics and was elected to the California State Senate in 1850, serving as its president until 1851. He was known as a political tyrant and virtually controlled all of San Francisco during the 1850s. He introduced into San Francisco, a modification of the vast political corruption with which Tammany Hall had controlled New York. Enriched by vast amounts of income earned from numerous shady backroom deals, Broderick used these funds and influence to be elected to the United States Senate in 1857.

U.S. Senator – David C. Broderick. *Courtesy of the Library of Congress, Prints and Photographs, Brady-Handy Photograph Collection, (LC-BH82-5107A).*

David S. Terry (1823-1899), California State Supreme Court Justice.

David S. Terry was born in Todd County, Kentucky on March 8, 1823. He came from a family of very distinguished military men. In his teen years his family moved to Texas and there he studied law. In December 1849, Terry came to California and after mining unsuccessfully in Calaveras County for a few months, began practicing law in Stockton. In September 1855, Terry was elected Chief Justice of the California Supreme Court. He was known for his fiery temper, and in 1856, during an argument, stabbed Sterling A. Hopkins, a member of the San Francisco Vigilance Committee. Because of his political connections, he was never tried for the assault on Hopkins. Justice Terry was an enthusiastic advocate of the extension of slavery into California, and this issue proved to be very divisive in the California Democratic Party.

Terry and Broderick were political allies and friends, but by 1859, that all changed. Like the rest of the nation, the issue of slavery was a hot topic in California. At that time, the Democratic Party of California was divided between pro-slavery and Free Soil factions. Senator Broderick led the Free Soiler's faction and Justice Terry was an advocate for the extension of slavery into California. Terry lost his re-election to the high court, and blamed Broderick for the defeat. In June of 1859, Terry, considered even by his friends to be very sarcastic and aggressive, made some inflammatory remarks toward Broderick at a party convention in Sacramento. Broderick took offense to these remarks, and sent his former friend, an equally malicious reply, which proclaimed Terry to be a "damned miserable ingrate, who was as corrupt as President James Buchanan and William Gwin, California's other U.S. Senator, I have hitherto spoken of him as an honest man, and as the only honest man on the bench of a miserable, corrupt Supreme Court, but now, I find I was mistaken. I take it all back. He is just as bad as the others." Passions escalated, and Terry feeling that he was left without any alternative but to demand the "usual satisfaction among gentlemen," and challenged Broderick to a duel.

On September 13, 1859, Terry and Broderick, both considered expert marksmen, met outside the city limits of San Francisco at Lake Merced for the duel. The pistols chosen for the duel had hair triggers, and Broderick's discharged on the count of one, firing prematurely into the ground, disarmed, he was forced to stand still as Terry on the count of two, fired, striking Broderick in the chest. After a deep spasm, Broderick sank to the ground, Terry stood like a statue with his arms folded, closely watching Broderick. Three days later on September 16, 1859, Broderick died from the wounds and an arrest warrant was issued for Terry. His trial for the murder of David C. Broderick was held in San Mateo County because it was widely thought he could not get a fair trial in San Francisco. The change of venue worked, and Terry was acquitted of the murder.

Sometimes fate has a way of making things right, and after the acquittal, Terry was practically ostracized in the community. In 1861, at the outbreak of the Civil War, he left California for Texas, where he joined the 8th Texas Cavalry. After the war, he came back to California to practice law, but was unable to re-enter politics. He became tangled in a strange divorce case in the early 1880s, in which a young woman named Sarah Althea Hill claimed that she was the legal wife of U.S. Senator William Sharon, a silver millionaire. Hill wanted a divorce and a share of Sharon's treasure. Sharon denied that they had ever been married. She lost her case and eventually married Terry. The newly wedded couple appealed the verdict.

A former friend of slain Senator David Broderick's, Stephen J. Field (an associate justice on the U.S. Supreme Court and senior justice of the Federal Circuit Court in California), presided over the case in 1888. He ruled against the Terrys in a final appeal, and jailed them both for contempt of court. David Terry vowed vengeance, and on August 14, 1889, assaulted Justice Field at a train station near Stockton, California. Field's bodyguard, U.S. Marshal David Neagle shot and killed Terry. The Marshall was arrested by local authorities on a charge of murder. The United States government secured the release of Neagle on a writ of habeas corpus. The issue was resolved by the landmark Supreme Court case In re Neagle, 135 U.S. 1 (1890); this United States Supreme Court decision determined that the Attorney General of the United States had authority to appoint U.S. Marshals as bodyguards to Supreme Court Justices, and that Neagle had acted within the scope of his authority by shooting Terry while protecting Field. David S. Terry is buried at Stockton Rural Cemetery in Stockton. Sarah Hill-Terry after which went insane, and spent the rest of her life at the Stockton State Hospital for the insane, where she died on February 14, 1937. She is buried in the same gravesite as her husband.

Sarah Althea Hill (1832-1937), wife of Senator William Sharon and Justice David S. Terry.

U.S. Senator William Sharon (1821-1885).
Courtesy of the Library of Congress, Prints and Photographs, Brady-Handy Photograph Collection, (LC-BH832-1272).

At the funeral of David C. Broderick, Edward Dickinson Baker, a future U.S. Senator from Oregon and congressmen from Illinois, and close friend of Abraham Lincoln, spoke and expressed the widely held belief that Broderick had been murdered because of his anti-slavery stance. Baker said: "His [Broderick's] death was a political necessity, poorly veiled beneath the guise of a private quarrel... What was his public crime? The answer is in Broderick's own words; I die because I was opposed to a corrupt administration and the extension of slavery." Some maintain that Broderick's death made him a martyr, and the episode represents yet another small contribution to the spiral towards civil war.

Stephen J. Fields (1816-1899), Associate Justice of the U.S. Supreme Court, 1863-1897. *Courtesy of the Library of Congress, Prints and Photographs, Brady-Handy Photograph Collection, (LC-BH832-29304).*

He was buried at Lone Mountain Cemetery (later named Laurel Hill), under a giant obelisk, erected by the state of California. Broderick lay undisturbed in his grave until 1942, when (for health purposes) the city of San Francisco ordered the removal of all remains from city cemeteries. Broderick was reburied with thousands of others in a mass grave at Cypress Lawn Memorial Park, Colma. His original memorial obelisk was destroyed, and the material was used to reinforce the sea wall of San Francisco Bay.

View of Laurel Hill Cemetery (circa, 1940). On the right is the David C. Broderick memorial obelisk. *Courtesy of the San Francisco History Center/ San Francisco Public Library.*

All for a Cluster of Fake Diamonds

(San Francisco, 1865- 1866)

In 1865, there resided in San Francisco, a young man named George Hill, who had inherited a comfortable sum of money from his parents. He was a flashy dresser and often wore a scarf, said to contain a cluster of diamonds worth a fortune. Hill had rented a room at the Mansion House on Dupont Street, and on February 15, 1865, he disappeared. Being that he had a wild and roving disposition, no significance was attached to this, by either his landlady or friends.

A few weeks after his disappearance, a gardener named Mr. McGloin was walking his dog on the beach near Fulton and Baker Streets. His dog began pulling on a piece of rope, which appeared to be fastened to something buried under the sand. He investigated and much to his horror, found that the rope was tied around the badly decomposed body of a man. McGloin immediately informed police of his discovery. The body was brought back to police headquarters for identification and there the coroner discovered a hole in the side of the head that apparently had been caused by blunt force trauma. All valuables had been removed from the body.

Owing to the advanced case of decomposition, it was very difficult to identify the body and authorities were about to bury the remains, when a newspaper reporter who knew Hill well, identified the body. Having identified the remains, police proceeded to Hills room at the Mansion House. The landlady stated that the day of his disappearance, a young man had come to the house, stating that Hill had gone to Contra Costa County to obtain money, but had met with an accident. She went on to say that the stranger produced a shirt, which had some blood on it. The young man told her that he was there to exchange the bloodied shirt for a new one. The landlady then admitted him to Hill's room, and after putting the bloody shirt in a trunk, retrieved a new shirt and some other objects, then left the boarding house. That same young man came back later, and appearing to be very anxious asked to retrieve the bloody shirt. Her suspicions being aroused, he was refused admittance to Hill's room.

One of the police detectives recalled that a person fitting the exact same description was already in custody on a charge of forgery. The landlady positively identified him as the same person who had attempted to retrieve the bloody shirt from Hill's room. His name was Thomas Byrnes, a butcher by trade and the son of the keeper of a roadhouse near Calvary Cemetery. During questioning of Byrnes and other witnesses, police learned that on the evening of February 15, 1865, George Hill had procured a two-horse carriage from Wright & Roden's livery stable on Kearny Street, near Pine, and in the company of Byrnes started for the Cliff House. About midnight, the horses returned alone to the stable causing the stable keeper to conclude that there had been a runaway and that the horses had broken away from the vehicle. Shortly afterwards, Byrnes returned to the stables alone, stating that he and Hill had met with an accident and that his partner had been seriously injured. He asked for a second team of horses, and before starting away with the second rig, asked for a shovel, stating that he wanted to dig the wheels of the other buggy out of the sand. It was observed by the stable man that Byrnes threw a piece of rope into the buggy. The stableman also told police that before Byrnes and Hill had started away from the carriage stable for the first time, Byrnes insisted on taking a monkey wrench, stating that it might be needed.

Byrnes confessed that he intended to kill and rob Hill of his valuables and when they arrived at the spot near where the body was found, he hit Hill on the head with the wrench. He then cut the horses loose to make it appear as if Hill had met death in a runaway accident. Determining that a runaway carriage would not account for the loss of Hill's property, he came up with the idea of burying the body. The rope was used to drag Hill's body to the beach, and the shovel was used to dig the shallow grave. He went on to tell police that he had attempted to pawn Hill's jewelry and then learned that the "diamond cluster" from Hill's scarf, which he thought was worth thousands was actually fake and worthless. Thomas Byrnes was tried and found guilty of the murder of George Hill, and after a futile appeal to the California State Supreme Court, was executed on September 3, 1866, at San Quentin prison.

Shootout on Center Street

(Anaheim, 1872)

Anaheim, a city steeped in history, was one of Orange County's earliest settlements. It was founded in 1857 by German immigrants; the city's name was derived from its proximity to the Santa Ana River, "Ana," and "heim," German for home. Early pioneers considered this their home by the river. Gunfights between gamblers, gunslingers, and lawmen in the old west were common. But such events were unheard of in Anaheim, a quiet vine-growing colony. One such gunfight which occurred in July of 1872, involved the first Anaheim law enforcement officer to be killed in the line of duty. Anaheim Town Marshal Charles F. Lehman did not have the same type of colorful background while serving as marshal as his predecessors, but unfortunately obtained his notoriety through his untimely death. He was elected town marshal on May 6, 1872; prior to his election, Lehman had served as an Anaheim constable and Deputy City Marshal from September 9, 1871 until May of 1872.

On Sunday evening, July 21, 1872, former town Marshal David S. Davies (a political rival of Lehman's), and a man named Horton were engaged in a spirited game of poker at Goldstein's Brewery-Saloon, located on Center Street (renamed Lincoln Avenue). Around 6 p.m., a dispute arose between the two card players as to the winnings; Horton seized the checks and Davies took the money. Harsh words were exchanged and tempers flared. Davies allegedly drew his revolver first, which prompted Horton to flee the saloon through the rear of the building. Davies followed and the gunfight continued into a vacant lot adjacent to the saloon and Macy's harness shop. Both Davies and Horton fired at each other from close range, both failed to injury one another. Marshal Charles F. Lehman rushed to the scene to investigate the commotion and while attempting to subdue the fight and arrest Horton, Lehman was shot in the abdomen, the ball entering in front an inch below the sternum. Horton immediately leaped onto a horse and rode away. He was pursued by an angry mob that soon captured him in Lorenz's vineyard and lodged him in jail.

Lehman was carried a short distance to Higgin's Drugstore and administered first aid. He was later transferred to Mrs. Brown's Boarding House, where he died at 7:30 p.m., Tuesday July 23, 1872. It had been suspected that Horton had fired the fatal shot, but on his deathbed, Lehman insisted that he was shot by Davies. On Wednesday, July 24, 1872 at 11 a.m., an inquest was held by John W. Clark, acting coroner. The results of which were printed in *The Southern Californian* on July 27, 1872, the following is an excerpt of the coroners findings:

Verdict of the Coroner's Jury – We, the undersigned, the jurors summoned to appear before the corner at 11 a.m., on the 24th day of July 1872, to inquire into the cause of death of Charles Lehman, having been duly sworn according to law having inspected the body and being present at the postmortem examination of Messrs. D'Assonville and Hardin, physicians of Anaheim, each and all do say: That we find the deceased was named Charles F. Lehman, was a native of Danzig, in Prussia, was aged about 44 years; that he died on the 23rd of July about 7:30 o'clock P.M. from the effects of a pistol shot received on the 21st of July, at about 6 o'clock P.M., near Goldstein's saloon, in Anaheim, during the discharge of his official duties of constable; the fatal shot having been fired by one if the two parties named – Horton and Davies, who are not under arrest and in court for examiner. All of which we duly certify by this inquisition in writing, by us signed the 24th day of July 1872, John Fischer, foreman, Peter Richards, J.B. Stone, L. Jandee, J.C. Hill and C.H. Smith.

These findings led to the arrest of Davies, who was charged with manslaughter of Marshal Lehman and taken to Los Angeles to stand trial. The sensational headline-grabbing trial was attended by many of Anaheim's citizens. At his trial, Davies was defended by Frank Ganahl, the leading criminal defense attorney in the County of Los Angeles. Eventually, Davies was acquitted of all charges and returned to Anaheim. As for Horton, he was detained for a short period of time, eventually gaining his release from jail; he quickly left Anaheim and was never seen again.

Grave marker of Sheriff Lehman at Anaheim Cemetery.

On his death bed, Marshal Lehman made a very strange request, he gave his infant daughter to the unmarried daughter of a friend, explaining that he felt that his wife was too young to care for their child. His funeral was one of the largest ever attended in the early days of Anaheim and his final resting place near the original entrance to Anaheim Cemetery, lay unmarked for over 100 years. In 1995, 125 years after the tragic events, Anaheim historical preservationists placed a memorial plaque at his grave.

As for David "Dye" Davies, he was a colorful character, a frontier gunfighter, gambler, and part-time lawman to whom the element of danger was unknown. His arrival in Anaheim and prior whereabouts are sketchy. What is known is that he was elected Anaheim's first town Marshal and Tax Collector on August 16, 1870, for which he was paid $50 a month to keep the peace. Early in 1870, an incident involving some citizens and the marshal developed. Davies was determined to disrupt a celebration of the French capitulation to the Germans in the Franco-Prussian war. This was due to Davies' allegiance to France. Apparently, some German citizens were planning to use some sort of fire torches to celebrate, but Davies forbade this in the public streets. The Mayor of Anaheim, Max Strobel, was appealed to, and overrode Davies' order, granting a permit for use of fire in the public streets. This angered Davies, who stated, "The first man who touches a match to that kindling is my prisoner." A man by the name of Fritz, struck a match, and was instantly hit on the head by Davies and rendered unconscious. Tempers flared, but cooler heads prevailed, and the celebrations were moved to private lots.

Another incident involving Davies resulted in the use of deadly force. Apparently, a woman had been severely beaten and mistreated by a male Indian acquaintance. At some point, several weeks after the attack, the woman had fully recovered from her injuries, and was able to identify her attacker. Marshal Davies was summoned; he went to the saloon where the Indian man was known to hang out. While attempting to arrest the culprit, a scuffle ensued; the Indian attempted to flee and was shot by Davies. The Indian man died of his wounds several days after the incident.

Davies was involved in yet another shooting incident, where an alleged horse thief was shot and killed. The suspected thief was rumored to be holding up in Soquel Canyon; a posse led by Davies tracked the thief and corned him in the canyon. Shots were fired and the horse thief was killed.

David Davies' career as a peace officer was short; he lost re-election to Talton T. Hill on May 1, 1871. He quietly blamed Lehman for his defeat and this caused much animosity between the two men, which most likely led to the shootout and death of Lehman at Goldstein's saloon on July 21, 1872. Despite his rough demeanor, Davies had many friends, and continued to live in Anaheim until his death on May 10, 1885.

Tiburcio Vasquez: The Last Great Mexican Bandit

(Central Valley, Coastal Areas & Southern California, 1854-1875)

Tiburcio Vasquez, one of the most notorious Mexican Banditos was born in Monterey, California on April 10, 1835. He came from a respectable family and received a fairly good education. He preferred to hang out with companions of questionable character, among them was a notorious outlaw named Antonio Garcia. One evening in 1854, Vasquez, Garcia, and Jose Guerra were attending a fandango in Monterey. A quarrel erupted between Garcia and Guerra, during which a constable named William Hardmont, attempted to quell. The combatants, fearing arrest, immediately turned their attention to him and shot Hardmont through the heart. Guerra was arrested and hanged for the murder. Vasquez and Garcia, fearing arrest, were able to escape, denying that they had any involvement. Vasquez would later claim his crimes were the result of discrimination by "White" Americans and insisted that he committed the crimes as a defender of Mexican-American rights. Vasquez and Garcia then played leading roles in Monterey County's murderous Roach-Belcher feud, which reached its apex when Garcia was lynched at the Monterey jail in 1857.

After the death of his friend and compatriot, Vasquez left Monterey and began to operate as a horse thief in Santa Clara, Merced, and Fresno Counties. In 1857, he was arrested and sentenced to five years in prison. While at San Quentin prison, he helped organize, and participated in, four bloody prison breaks which left twenty convicts dead. On June 25, 1859, he escaped after overpowering a guard making his way to Amador County, where he was again arrested for stealing horses. He was sent back to San Quentin, where he stayed until being paroled on August 13, 1863.

After his release from prison, Vasquez made an attempt at becoming a law-abiding citizen, but eventually returned to crime. He committed numerous burglaries, cattle thefts, and highway robberies in Sonoma County in 1867. He was captured on January 18, 1867, after a store burglary in Petaluma. He was sentenced to three more years in prison. Following his release on June 4, 1870, he organized a criminal gang, that included notorious bandits Juan Soto (known as the human wildcat), and Procopio Bustamante. From 1870 until 1875 Vasquez and his bandit gang roamed an area from Sonoma to Los Angeles committing robbery and murder. On December 26, 1873, Vasquez gained statewide and nationwide notoriety, when he and his gang sacked the town of Kingston in Fresno County. They robbed all of the businesses, making off with $2,500 in cash, jewelry, and provisions. A posse was dispatched by Governor Newton Booth, with a reward of $8,000 for his capture and $6,000 for his dead body. Sheriff John H. Adams from San Jose pursued the outlaws to Southern California but Vasquez escaped after a sharp gunfight.

Bandit Tiburcio Vasquez (1839-1875
Courtesy of University of Southern California, on behalf of the USC Libraries Special Collections.

Vasquez hid for a while in Southern California, where he was less well known. He was very popular in the Hispanic community, and had many friends. He was handsome, literate, charming, played guitar, and was a skillful dancer. Women were attracted to him and he had many love affairs. He enjoyed reading romantic Spanish novels and writing poetry for his female admirers. In May of 1874, it came to the attention of authorities that Vasquez was at the home of a man named "Greek George," near Los Angeles (located today at the northwest corner of Rancho La Brea, found 200 yards south of the present-day Sunset Strip in West Hollywood). Allegedly, Vasquez had seduced and impregnated George's niece; for a substantial reward (which he never received) George betrayed Vasquez.

On May 14, 1874, a posse that included Los Angeles Sheriff William R. Rowland procured a wagon and instructed its driver to proceed to George's house. The posse was concealed in the bed of the wagon and when they arrived at the home jumped out and surrounded the building. Vasquez attempted to escape through a window and was shot eight times. He then surrendered, but it was not thought he would survive his wounds. Vasquez beat the odds and recovered. He was indicted for murder and numerous other crimes and was held at the Los Angeles County jail for nine days prior to being transferred to San Jose for trial. During these few days, he had numerous requests for interviews but agreed to see only three individuals requesting: two from the *San Francisco Chronicle* and one from the *Los Angeles Star*. He told these reporters that he took to a criminal way of life because it was the only way that he could help return California to Mexican rule. He insisted that he was an honorable man, and reiterated that he had never killed anyone.

In late May, Vasquez was moved by steamship to San Francisco. He would eventually stand trial in San Jose, and there he became a celebrity. Hundreds of visitors flocked to his jail cell, many of them women. He signed autographs and posed for photographs. He sold photos from the window of his cell and used the money to pay for his legal defense. On January 5, 1875, the trial of Triburcio Vasquez began and during which, he admitted to being an outlaw, but denied ever killing anyone. On January 10, 1875, after six days of trial, Vasquez was found guilty and sentenced to hang for murder. After his conviction, he appealed for clemency, which was denied by Governor Romualdo Pacheco. On March 19, 1875, Vasquez calmly met his fate and was hanged in San Jose. He was asked, just moments before his execution, "Do you believe in an afterlife?" He replied, "I hope so... for then soon I shall see all my old sweethearts again." The only other word he spoke on the gallows was "pronto." With Vasquez' death the era of the Mexican bandito was at an end.

The Theft of Toby Rosenthal's "Elaine"

(San Francisco, 1875)

Toby Edward Rosenthal (1848 –1917) was an American artist. He moved to San Francisco with his parents in 1855, there he studied painting under Fortunato Arriola. In 1865 he went to Munich, where he was a pupil at the Royal Academy of Art. Among his more important works are: *J.S. Bach and his family at morning prayers*, *Who laughs last, laughs best*, *Trial of the escaped nun Constance de Beverly*, *Dancing Lesson During the Empire* and *Departure from the Family*.

No history of crime in California would be complete without mentioning the theft of Toby Rosenthal's famous painting, *Elaine – The Dead Steered by the Dumb*. Toby Rosenthal is perhaps one the greatest artists that California has ever produced.

While still a struggling artist, he was commissioned by Tiburcio Parrott of San Francisco to paint a subject from Alfred Lloyd Tennyson's famous poem, *Idylls*. Rosenthal developed and enlarged upon the theme suggested by Parrott, and when completed, sold the painting to Mrs. R.C. Johnson of San Francisco for $3,000.

On March 8, 1875, Mrs. Johnson exhibited the painting at the art gallery of Snow and May, on Kearny Street. The fame of the painting and of its artist, attracted thousands of visitors to the gallery. It remained on display for nearly a month, when on the morning of April 3, 1875, the painting was stolen. The famous canvas had been cut out of its frame in the night by thieves. Police detectives immediately began to theorize as to the motive for the theft. Was this the work of a thief, who desired a large reward for the return of the painting? Was it the work of an enemy of the gallery owner? Was it the work of an infatuated art lover, who desired the painting for their own collection?

Toby Rosenthal (1848-1917), American Artist.

While all these theories were being investigated, a witness came forward and told police that on the night of the theft, while standing in the vicinity of the gallery, he had seen four men surveying the building. He described all of them in great detail, with one in particular having a large scar on his face. One of the detectives immediately recognized three of the men, Cut-Face Donohoe, James Curran, and Tommy Wallace. Rounding up these suspect's police were first able to locate James Curran, who under intense interrogation, admitted to stealing the painting. Curran led police to a tiny shack in the rear of a lot on Langton Street, and there hidden beneath a bed was a cylinder marked "customs house official maps," inside the detectives found the missing painting.

The history of the theft and the motive that led to it was simple enough, Donohoe, Wallace, Curran and a man named Allen, broke into the gallery the night before the painting was to be removed from the city. They tried to take it from the frame but finding this impossible, Allen neatly cut the picture out of its frame, rolled it carefully and took it away. The whole heist took only fifteen minutes. The motive for the theft was the possibility of a large reward, with no questions asked for return of the painting. All four thieves were convicted of the theft and all served indeterminate amounts of time in state prison. Today, Rosenthal's painting of *Elaine – The Dead Steered by the Dumb* can be found on display at the Art Institute of Chicago.

Wheeler the Strangler & The Dawn of the Insanity Defense

(San Francisco, 1880-1884)

Before delving into the Wheeler case, it is necessary to explain a short history of the insanity defense. The earliest attempt to legally define insanity originated in England in 1843. It became known as the M'Naghten rule, after a paranoid schizophrenic, who was found not guilty after shooting and killing a politician. This rule stated that a person could not be held legally responsible for criminal actions committed while suffering a mental disorder that either, prevented them from understanding what he or she was doing, or prevented them from knowing his or her behavior was wrong. Some people in both the U.S. and England felt this law was too lenient, and that a person should not be excused of crimes as long as he or she is capable of controlling his or her behavior.

By 1840, most jurisdictions had refined the wild beast test to cognitive insanity and supplemented that with irresistible-impulse insanity. However, in 1843, a well-publicized assassination attempt in England caused Parliament to eliminate the irresistible impulse defense. Daniel M'Naghten, operating under the delusion that Prime Minister Robert Peel wanted to kill him, tried to shoot Peel, but shot and killed Peel's secretary instead. Medical testimony indicated that M'Naghten was psychotic, and the court acquitted him by reason of insanity (M'Naghten's Case, 8 Eng. Rep. 718 [1843]). In response to a public furor that followed the decision, the House of Lords ordered the Lords of Justice of the Queen's Bench to craft a new rule for insanity in the Criminal Law.

What emerged became known as the M'NAGHTEN RULE. This rule migrated to the United States within a decade of its conception, and it stood for the better part of the next century. The intent of the M'Naghten rule was to abolish the irresistible-impulse defense and to limit the insanity defense to cognitive insanity. Under the M'Naghten rule, insanity was a defense if: At the time of the committing of the act, the party accused was laboring under such a defect of reason, from a disease of the mind, as not to know the nature and quality of the act he was doing; or, if he did know it, that he did not know he was doing what was wrong. This was the theory often used by defense attorneys at the time and was used as a defense in the following crime story.

On the evening of October 20, 1880, a man by the name of George A. Wheeler entered the Central Police Station in San Francisco and in a matter of fact manner informed the desk Sergeant that he had killed his sister-in-law, Della J. Tillson. He told police that they could find her body at a lodging house at 23 Kearny Street and the body was hidden in an old trunk. The nonchalant manner, in which Wheeler spoke, caused police to think he was crazy. Reluctantly, Wheeler was placed into custody and officers were sent out to the boarding house to investigate. Officers located the trunk which Wheeler described, and much to their horror found that his statement was true. Inside the trunk, they found the dead body of a fully clothed and well-proportioned young woman. In searching the body police did not find any obvious signs of violence, but did find a small doll wrapped in the victims skirt. The coroner was immediately notified and investigators proceeded back to the station house to question Wheeler. During interrogation, Wheeler made the following statement about the crime:

> Della Tillson, the girl whose body you found, is my sister-in-law, regardless of any statement made to the contrary, and she was 21 years old a few months ago. I married her sister Mary in Massachusetts eleven years ago. Six years later I became intimate with Della, who lived in the same house as us. About a year afterward Della confessed to my wife that she was in a delicate condition and that I was responsible for it. To avoid scandal Mary protected Della and the child was born in our house, but died a few weeks afterward. Shortly after this the three of us came to San Francisco, and Della met a man named George Peckham, with whom she became intimate, according to a confession to me. By this time I had grown to love Della as much as I did Mary, my wife, and the three of us occupied one room. When Della made this admission I became furious, but forgave her with the understanding that she should cease her relations with Peckham. Tonight (the night of the murder) I went out on business and when I returned Della was in the front room with her hat and gloves on. I asked her where she had been. She sat on my knee and confessed that she had been in constant communication with Peckham. Furthermore she told me that she and Peckham had met that night and had agreed to go to Sacramento and live as man and wife. This admission crazed me and as she sat on my knee I strangled her. I then crowded the body into the trunk. My wife was out at the time.

Mrs. Wheeler, upon being interviewed denied that she had any prior knowledge of her husband's affair, stating "My husband and I have disagreed ever since we have been married. My sister has lived with me during the past three years. I was not aware that my husband had led her astray until recently."

After being incarcerated, George Wheeler said that he was willing to die for the crime, but later changed his mind, claiming that he was innocent by reason of insanity. During his trial (of which there were four), the court room was always thronged with spectators. The defense endeavored to prove a diseased condition of Wheeler's mind from the fact he had shown no remorse for the terrible crime, and showed no emotion when describing the details of the murder. The defense went on to state that there was no motive needed to explain the commission of a crime in cases where transitory mania exists. Expert testimony on insanity was introduced by the prosecution and defense. In the end, the jury did not believe Wheeler's defense of insanity and convicted him of murder in the first degree. He was sentenced to hang and was eventually executed at the county jail on January 23, 1884.

Postscript: Through the first half of the twentieth century, the insanity defense was expanded again. Courts began to accept the theories of psychoanalysts, many of whom encouraged recognition of the irresistible-impulse defense. Many states enacted a combination of the *M'Naghten* rule supplemented with an irresistible-impulse defense, thereby covering both cognitive and volitional insanity. The insanity defense reached its most permissive standard in *Durham v. United States*, 214 F. 2d 862 (D.C. Cir. 1954). The *Durham* rule excused a defendant "if his unlawful act was the product of mental disease or mental defect." The *Durham* rule was lauded by the mental health community as progressive because it allowed psychologists and psychiatrists to contribute to the judicial understanding of insanity. It was criticized for placing too much trust in the opinions of mental health professionals and within seven years of its creation, the rule had been explicitly rejected in twenty-two states. Today, it is only used in New Hampshire.

The Poetic Crimes of Black Bart

(Central Valley & Coastal areas, 1877-1888)

On August 12, 1877, the stagecoach running from Fort Ross to Russian River was held up by a lone highwayman wearing a mask and exhibiting a shotgun. There were no passengers on the stage and after obtaining $325 from the Wells Fargo strong box, the bandit very courteously bid the driver good-day and disappeared. On July 28, 1878, the stage running between Quincy and Oroville was held up by a robber whose general appearance and conduct indicated that he was the same individual who committed the Russian River robbery. On this occasion he obtained jewels and money valued at $600 from the Wells Fargo strong box. After the stage departed, he picked up a Wells Fargo waybill and dedicated the following verse to the company, which was afterward found at the scene of the crime:

> Here I lay me down to sleep, to wait the coming morrow, perhaps success perhaps defeat and everlasting sorrow. Yet come what will...I'll try it on, my condition can't be worse, and if there's money in that box 'tis money in my purse. Black Bart, the PO8.

Thus was the beginning of the legendary criminal career of Black Bart, and for nearly a decade (1877-1888), he evaded the authorities holding up more than two dozen stagecoaches on the different mountain roads of the state. He baffled detectives, who would have deemed it the proudest event of their lives to place him behind bars. Unlike bandits such as Joaquin Murrieta or Tiburcio Vasquez, Black Bart never shed a drop of human blood in the commission of his crimes. He was in fact more like the knight of Medieval times, who especially delighted in protecting the helpless. He was often known to assist with his ill-gotten gains by helping those in need. He invariably refrained from doing damage to stage coach passengers, and was particularly obliging and respectful of female travelers.

Very little is known about Black Bart, but historians agree that his given name was Charles Earl Boles. He was born in England around 1829, and came to the United States, and eventually California, sometime in 1849. Boles, like so many other fortune seekers, tried his hand at mining gold and for a brief time had limited success. But after a few months, tired of the lonesome and back breaking task, he left California for adventures elsewhere. In 1867, he returned to the western states to again attempt his hand at silver and gold mining. Failure again followed Boles, and some speculate it is during this time that he became a school teacher. His income being very meager, he quickly abandoned this profession in favor a life of crime.

Between 1877 and 1888, Black Bart robbed twenty-eight stagecoaches worth over $18,000 and left numerous poems at the scene of his crimes. Most of the robberies took place during the night, were quite sporadic, and he always acted alone. Law enforcement authorities were baffled at their inability to apprehend the poet-bandit. Citizens began to speculate that the lone bandit might be a ghost, because he appeared to vanish into thin air. Dime store novels were written about this strange robber, and his fame rose to legendary proportions.

Stage Coach Robber Black Bart. *Courtesy of the San Francisco History Center/ San Francisco Library.*

Eventually, as most criminals know, staying ahead of the law is very difficult, and on November 3, 1883, Black Bart's luck ran out. As the Sonora and Milton stagecoach rumbled over the mountains, Black Bart concealed his face and stopped the coach. The driver was ordered to throw down the strong box (which held over $4,000 in gold and coin). At this point, a young boy happened along the road carrying a rifle at which the driver beckoned him over and grabbed the gun. Black Bart having already secured the loot was on his way, when the stagecoach driver fired a shot at the bandit. The shot missed but in making his quick getaway Black Bart dropped his hat and a handkerchief. On this handkerchief was a laundry mark, which would be the clue that led police to his identity and whereabouts.

Police searched numerous laundries in San Francisco, and on Bush Street, they found a laundry where the markings matched the handkerchief. The owner recognized his mark and referring to his books, showed that the handkerchief belonged to C.E. Bolton, who occupied a room in the Webb House on School Street. Detectives waited outside of the Webb House and when Bolton approached, the laundry shop owner made a positive identification, C.E. Bolton, alias Charles Boles, alias Black Bart, was taken into custody without trouble.

After a search of Boles room, police found several half written notes that had been penned in the same hand as numerous other notes that had been left at previous stagecoach robberies. After several day of denying he was the infamous outlaw Black Bart, Boles confessed that he was indeed the notorious bandit. The jail where he was held was besieged with callers, who wished to see the famous outlaw. On November 21, 1883, in exchange for not going to trial and pleading guilty to one of the twenty-eight stagecoach robberies, Boles was sentenced to a light term of six years in prison. He was released from San Quentin prison on January 21, 1888; he was paroled from jail one year early due to his good behavior behind bars. Upon leaving prison, Boles told reporters that he would commit no more crimes and was asked if he would write anymore poetry. He replied, "Did you not hear me say I would commit no more crimes?"

Police kept a close eye on Boles after his release but he never seemed to venture far from San Francisco. As time went by, police observation lessoned and the bandit drifted away from the Bay area, and by 1889, Boles had vanished. In November of 1889, police suspected that Black Bart had come out of retirement, when a note was left behind at a hold-up: "Since here I've stood while wind and rain have set the trees a-sobbin' and risked my life for that damned box, that wasn't worth the robbin'." Police quickly deemed the note a hoax. The whereabouts of Boles was never determined and thus his legend grew. Newspapers continued to speculate that Black Bart was in hundreds of different locations robbing stages. It wasn't until 1895, when Wells Fargo closed its last stagecoach route that the rumors of Black Bart ceased. What eventually became of the infamous bandit has never been determined.

The Murder of the "Farmer King"

(Central Valley, Colusa County, 1883)

Dr. Hugh James Glenn, known as the "farmer king" was born in Augusta County, Virginia, in 1824. When he was a small boy his family moved to Monroe County, Missouri. There he was given every available opportunity at private schools, which included an education in medicine at McDowell's Medical College of St. Louis. Upon the break out of the Mexican War in 1846, he enlisted in the army, and participated in the battles of Taos and Moro. Later he received an honorable discharge, after which he found his way back to St. Louis, where he continued his medical studies and graduated with high honors. In April of 1849, he left St. Louis to seek his fortune in California. After an adventurous journey, he arrived in Sacramento and staked out a mining claim on the American River known as "Murderer's Bar." Glenn was mildly successful and remained at the site for a few months. With the little gold he found, he bought a small tract of land (which was later expanded) in northern Colusa County, where he raised horses, sheep, and cattle.

In 1865, Glenn and other associates purchased and began an agricultural operation at the "big ranch" in Yolo. It was here that Glenn began to cultivate wheat, managing the cultivation of nearly 6,000 acres of land in Colusa County; this made him the largest farmer in the state. The ranch was known as the Jacinto Ranch, and was one of the largest in the world, extending along the banks of the Sacramento River for almost sixteen miles. Glenn was the only wheat grower in America, who chartered his own ships, and sold by telegraph to Europe, dispensing with middle men entirely. Losses never disturbed him, nor did profits elate him. He was a very popular man in the state; his first foray into politics was as a member of the State Board of Agriculture. In 1879, with great reluctance, he accepted the nomination for Governor of California, under the New Constitution and Democratic Parties. He lost the election to George C. Perkins.

On February 17, 1883, Dr. Hugh J. Glenn, was murdered by an employee named Huron Miller at his Colusa County ranch. Glenn had discharged Miller a few days previously after an argument in which Miller (the ranch bookkeeper) was accused of being drunk. Miller called Glenn a liar and a physical altercation erupted. The next day Miller angrily sought out Glenn, finding the ranch owner standing on the porch of a hotel. Miller pulled a shot gun from underneath his coat, and firing the gun into the back of Glenn's head, killed him instantly. Miller attempted to flee the scene, but was quickly apprehended by S. M. Cochrane, foremen of the ranch. Miller was taken into custody after a short gun battle with Cochrane in which the former was wounded slightly in the leg; he was then taken to the town of Colusa to await trial for the murder of Glenn.

The trial of Huron Miller began in late June of 1883 and was a raucous and contentious affair. It was held before Judge Bridgeford at the Colusa County Court House. The defense attempted to prove that Miller was justified in shooting Glenn because, in his own drunken and impaired judgment, it was deemed necessary to kill Glenn in self defense. The prosecution argued that drunkenness was no excuse, and that Miller had prowled around town looking for Glenn with premeditation and malice. Prosecutor Joseph Hamilton stated, "Let it be telegraphed over the world that a jury in Colusa County had found that unlawful killing is murder."

On July 1, 1883, the jury deadlocked in its decision, nine men voting for murder in the first degree, three for murder in the second. Unable to agree on a verdict, a mistrial was declared. In a second trial, Miller was found guilty of second degree murder and sentenced to life in prison. On November 15, 1890, Governor Robert Waterman commuted Miller's sentence from life to fifteen years in prison. The following October 1891, Huron Miller was released for good behavior, after serving only eight years behind bars.

Historic Colusa County Court House, completed in 1861.

A Case of Deadly Infatuation

(San Francisco, 1886-1887)

A wild scene of confusion was present on the corner of Ash Avenue and Polk Street, which was just a block west of San Francisco's new City Hall. In front of a store on the northeast corner, a young girl lay in the throes of death. A stream of blood poured from a bullet wound over her right eye, her straw hat, lunch basket, and school books lay strewn about the scene. She was taken to a nearby house where she died. A half an hour later, the morgue wagon made its way through the gathered crowd and collected the body of the slain girl.

Nineteen-year-old Alexander Goldenson lived with his parents at 24½ Hayes Street. In the adjoining house lived a thirteen year old girl, named Mary Elizabeth Kelly, who was nicknamed Mamie, She lived with her mother and grandmother, and attended the John Swett Grammer School. Mamie left school on the afternoon of November 11, 1886, and walked home with a classmate. As she passed along Polk Street, a young man appeared, with whom Mamie stopped to speak. The young man was her neighbor Alexander Goldenson. What conversation passed between the two is not known, but a few minutes later, a loud gunshot attracted the attention of everyone in the vicinity. A witness saw a young man (Goldenson) running away from the scene carrying a pistol; he pursued the young man onto the grounds of city hall, and right into the police station. There Goldenson told the desk sergeant "Well, I've done it, lock me up, killed my girl, that's what I've done." He was then taken into custody.

Probably no crime excited more passion in the city of San Francisco then the senseless murder of Mamie Kelly. It sent a shudder of horror through every household, it was the topic of conversation throughout the community, and city newspapers ran daily headline accounts of the legal proceedings. The excitement caused by the murder brought loud and angry demands for the exercise of the lynch law. Mass meetings were held in the Metropolis Temple, and addresses were made from the steps of the U.S. Mint on 5th Street. An angry mob of over 1,000 people attempted to march to the jail on Broadway Street, where Goldenson was being held but were turned back by police.

Mamie Kelly's funeral was held on Saturday, November 13, 1886; as her body left her home on Hayes Street for the last time, thousands lined the street. Her service was held at St. Joseph's Church on 10th Street. Her coffin was placed at the front of the church; it was covered in white flowers. The service was conducted by Father Seanlan, who gave an eloquent eulogy and assured the crowd that justice would punish the murderer and insisted that the legal process be allowed to take its course. When the services had concluded, classmates of Mamie's were allowed to linger for one last goodbye. It was estimated that nearly 5,000 people lined the streets from the church to the cemetery. Mamie was laid to rest at Lone Mountain Cemetery (renamed Laurel Hill), where thousands more witnessed the burial.

In 1892, Laurel Hill Cemetery was closed to further burials. Beginning in 1939, and continuing through 1941, the bodies of nearly 35,000 people were disinterred and reburied in a mass grave at Cypress Lawn Memorial Park in Colma. Mamie Kelly was one of those reinterred. A giant monument adorns the top of the burial mound and memorializes the pioneers of San Francisco. Today, the area of the original cemetery encompasses part of the University of San Francisco, private housing, and other businesses.

On the morning of Mamie's funeral, Alexander Goldenson was arraigned on the charge of murder and pleaded not guilty. His trial was set to begin on Monday, November 22, 1886. A feeble attempt was made by defense attorneys for change of venue but this was quickly denied. The defense made it clear from the beginning that they intended to prove that Goldenson was not guilty by reason of insanity. They alleged that the defendant was the unfortunate victim of a genetic mental disease that caused him delusional thoughts and caused him to act irrationally. During the trial, Goldenson exhibited very unusual behavior, often acting out and refused to assist attorneys in his defense. The jury did not believe the defenses assertions that Goldenson was insane at the time of the murder; they found him guilty and sentenced him to death. The case was appealed to the California State Supreme Court but the verdict and sentence was upheld. His execution date was set for April 14, 1887.

Demand for invitations to Goldenson's execution was unprecedented. The Sheriff had received over 1,000 requests but only 500 tickets were available. The evening before his execution, Goldenson was allowed to see his family one last time, after which he threw himself on his cot and cried. It was his only display of emotion. The next morning, a priest was admitted to his cell and he made an odd request: that a photograph of Mamie (pictured in her first communion dress) be tied to his wrist. Alexander Goldenson had fallen in love with Mamie Kelly, he fantasized that they had been star-crossed lovers, who had intended to spend their lives together, marry, have children, and grow old together. All of which was a fantasy of his delusional imagination.

Mary Elizabeth Kelly, known as Mamie, first communion photograph (circa, 1885). A photo like this was affixed to the wrist of her convicted killer Alexander Goldenson at his execution.

As Goldenson was led to the scaffold; he turned and addressed the audience. In a loud and clear voice he said,

> I want to say a few words before I go. I have often reiterated that Mamie was my first and only love. I say now that she was, and I hope I will go to Heaven. I thank you all for your kindness to me. Goodbye. I die forgiving you all.

He shook hands with all around, lifted the picture of Mamie to his lips and kissed it. He then placed the noose around his own neck and a hood was placed over his head. The signal was given at 12:05 p.m., and the trap door was sprung. Alexander Goldenson's dead body slowly swayed to and fro on the gallows, and attached to his wrist was the photograph of Mamie Kelly. After the body had hung on the scaffolding for eighteen minutes, it was cut down by the deputies and placed in a rough wood coffin to be transported to the morgue. The coffin was loaded into the hearse outside the jailhouse door. Ten thousand people had stood in the streets outside the jail for the hanging and many of them followed the hearse as it drove rapidly to the morgue. An autopsy was conducted showing that death was instantaneous; the spinal cord having been severed and the second vertebrae fractured. An examination of the brain showed it to be normal. Once the examination was complete, Goldenson's remains were transported to his parent's home. It was written that, while his mother was moaning and crying over his body, newsboys paraded up and down in front of the house crying: "All about the Goldenson hanging."

On Sunday afternoon, September 16, 1888, Father Fassanotti arrived at the Goldenson's home to take charge of Alexander's burial at the Catholic cemetery, the same cemetery where Mamie Kelly had been buried. On the night before the hanging, Goldenson had been baptized into the Catholic faith. For some months, Goldenson and Father Fassanotti had discussed Goldenson's conversion to the Catholic faith, but it had been slow to happen for two reasons. The first was that Father Fassanotti believed in hell and Alexander did not. This was the subject of several heated arguments between the two. The second reason was that Goldenson's mother, Rebecca, had threatened to commit suicide if Alexander converted. When Alexander was baptized, he asked the priest to keep the information secret from his mother for as long as possible. So why did Goldenson convert to Catholicism at the eleventh hour? It wasn't his friendship with Father Fassanotti, or faith, but rather his desire to rest for eternity near Mamie Kelly. Goldenson made it clear that he believed he would regain Mamie beyond the limits of life and that the two would walk the endless paths of eternity hand in hand. Just prior to his baptism, Alexander revealed to Father Fassanotti that he intended to commit suicide prior to the hanging. He had in his possession a gelatin capsule containing ten grains of cyanide potassium, an amount sufficient to kill twenty men. The priest did not relieve the condemned man of the poison, but rather told him that based on his act of conversion, he would trust Goldenson's word that he would honor his faith. As we know, Goldenson did not take the poison, turning it over to the Sheriff and a jailer the morning of his execution.

After the execution, the Goldenson family refused to release the body to Father Fassannotti for Catholic burial and the permit for Catholic burial was withdrawn. The Goldenson's then made an application to the Jewish cemetery for burial, but those in charge would not permit the burial of the body in Jewish ground, as he had embraced the Catholic faith prior to his death. The family then secured a lot in the Odd Fellows cemetery. The burial took place without the benefit of service. Not Catholic, not Jewish, not Protestant. The cemetery was eventually closed and between 1929-1935, all bodies were removed from Odd Fellows Cemetery and reburied at Green Lawn Memorial Park in Colma.

In a twist of fate, Goldenson's body was returned to the family by Coroner Stanton minus the brain. During the autopsy, Stanton removed Goldenson's brain and kept it for investigation. He felt it was in the public interest to study the brain in order to refute any claim of Goldenson's insanity that might be made in the future. Both the City Attorney and District Attorney refused to defend Coroner Stanton. The court held it was the duty of the coroner to deliver the body to the family whole after the inquest. The brain was returned to the family, but there was no account of its burial. What this story doesn't tell us is how the Goldenson family discovered that the brain was missing almost two months after the body had been buried. The Goldenson's sued the City of San Francisco for damages alleged to have been inflicted on their property, they were awarded $3,725.70.

During his time in jail, Goldenson was known for creating many drawings and writings. Many people wanted his autograph and he was always eager to comply. Deputy Sheriff Robert McCord while on death watch asked Goldenson for his autograph. Goldenson did more he composed an original poem, Following is what he wrote:

> To Rob M'Cord:
>
> As now I live,
> My life is a death's annoy;
> But when I'm dead,
> My death will be a life's joy.
>
> ALECK GOLDENSON.
> SEPTEMBER 13, 1888.
> THE LAST MORNING

Much has been written about Goldenson's obsession with coincidences around the number 14; similar to Walter Sparrow, the character played by Jim Carrey in the 2007 movie, *The Number 23*. To have the matter stated correctly for posterity, Goldenson prepared the following;

> My first Sunday in jail was Sunday, November 14, 1886, add the letters of the Christian names Alexander and Mamie and you have fourteen, the same result is obtained by adding the number of letters in the surnames Kelly and Goldenson, the names of the attorneys who lost my case by deserting me each contains fourteen letters, I was fourteen months in solitary confinement, Mamie Kelly's age was 14 years *[he omits to say fourteen when he killed her]*, my trial commenced February 14, 1887, there are fourteen letters in the surnames Cook and Campbell, Jr., the names of the attorneys who defended me, Judge Murphy first passed sentence of death on me on April 14, 1887, I was finally sentenced to hang September 14, 1888, My name as I sign it contains fourteen letters.

This would account for Goldenson's reaction when sentenced to hang on September 14. He uttered an oath, leaned over to his attorney and said, "I told you so." In a cruel twist of fate, Goldenson was transferred to Cell 41 the day before he was hung. Fourteen backwards. In the end, why he shot Mamie was never discovered. Conjecture is that Mamie scorned his advances and being embarrassed and delusional, a "Romeo and Juliet" state of mind overcame him, in which he impulsively decided that if he could not have her, no one would.

The Foul Deeds of John Anschlag

(Orange County, 1888)

Among the hundreds of entries in the land title records of Garden Grove during the boom years of the 1880s, there is one entry which challenges the attention of anyone who has knowledge of the village. The grantor was Fred Anschlag and the grantee was A.J. Chaffee, administrator, dated January 20, 1888. It is part of the last chapter in the story of one of the most gruesome and shocking murders in the annals of Orange County history. Charles and Lois Hitchcock were prominent and well-liked early settlers of Garden Grove, who owned substantial ranch land in the area. On the night of Monday, January 23, 1888, they mysteriously disappeared.

John Henrich Fredrick Anschlag was a penniless drifter and petty swindler. He was born in Koeningberg, East Prussia on September 9, 1864. He had a very sad childhood; his mother died when he was very small, he suffered a severe head injury, and spent most of his youth in boarding schools. He immigrated to the United States in 1886, and like so many before, found his way to the west coast to seek a fortune in gold. Unfortunately, he was thirty years too late. While in San Francisco, he was unable to procure work, and to survive was thrust into a life of crime. Anschlag spent sixty days in the county jail for petty theft and while in jail; his criminal thoughts turn deadly. He hatched a plan in which he would murder a former neighbor for his property (a precursor of things to come).

Anschlag's plan was to kill Julius Fuge, a mildly successful Sacramento Valley area farmer and former acquaintance. Anschlag believed that he could kill Fuge, dispose of his body and procure his land for his own use. On September 1, 1887, Anschlag and Fuge went rabbit hunting. Anschlag shot him in the back of the head and buried his body in a shallow grave. Anschlag having second thoughts, and feeling that his foul deed would be discovered decided to flee the area.

Arriving in Southern California in January 1888, he tried to perfect his crime by procuring a legitimate land agent. Bracket, Beckett & Sanderson of Santa Ana brought Anschlag to Garden Grove to see some property. He professed to be a man of means from Northern California, who was seeking a ranch on which to settle. He was very attracted to the Hitchcock ranch which consisted of twenty acres, on the southeast corner of Nutwood Street and Stanford Avenue. It had been developed by the Charles and Lois Hitchcock, who had come to the area in 1876. After looking at several other properties, Anschlag decided to purchase the Hitchcock place. He paid a deposit of $25.00 and agreed to pay a total of $8,000 plus $150 for a team of horses. He was to pay the full amount when the deed was delivered. During the interval, while the deed was being drawn up, Anschlag moved to Garden Grove and hired a man to help him with work on the ranch. He knew he had no intention of obtaining the sum, and for the next few days in an attempt to appear genuine, stayed with the Hitchcocks, accepting their hospitality, while fiendishly trying to muster the courage to kill them.

The following is an excerpt of John Anschlag's confession (October 26, 1888) in his own words, about the sequence of events that occurred on the night of January 23, 1888:

Charles and Lois Hitchcock (undated photo).

> We ate supper together, and then sat reading for a short time, after which we (Anschlag and Mr. Hitchcock) started for the barn to water the horses. I had been drinking some wine in the evening to gain courage to commit the deed, I had premeditated. I had placed the hatchet during the day near the barn door, so I could get it easily. While Mr. Hitchcock was feeding the horses I placed myself in such a position that I could easily kill him. As he stopped to pick up a lantern I struck him on the head. Believing he was dead, I went to the house to kill Mrs. Hitchcock. Finding her standing in the kitchen, I entered the door with the hatchet in hand. She looked at me as I came in and then turned back to her work again. I approached her from behind and struck her on the head but did not kill her, and then struck her again knocking her over. Then I dragged her out doors near the wood pile. Then got the ax and cut her several times to be sure she was dead. I started for Mr. Hitchcock with the ax and gave him several more blows.

The Hitchcock's Home (undated photo).

Anschlag then procured a wagon from the barn, placed the bodies in the wagon and drove several miles to a secluded area (300 yards south of Dr. Henry W. Head's farm, near present-day Harbor Boulevard). There he dug a very shallow grave, in which he placed the bodies and his bloody clothes. Returning to the house, he acted as if nothing was out of the ordinary. He thought that no one would notice the Hitchcocks were gone. He assumed that because it was well known that he was buying the property and had signed the deed documents, he would be above suspicion. His plan quickly unraveled.

The next morning neighbors, many of who were close relatives, were astonished to find John Anschlag and a hired man in full possession of the

Hitchcock's property. Since he couldn't give a satisfactory account of the whereabouts of Mr. and Mrs. Hitchcock, City Marshal Finley arrested Anschlag and the hired field hand. A search for the Hitchcocks was commenced, which enlisted every able body man in the area. It was not until Thursday afternoon November 26, 1888, that the mystery was solved. The brutally bludgeoned bodies of Mr. and Mrs. Hitchcock were found in the shallow grave where Anschlag had hastily buried them several days prior.

The Old Los Angeles County Courthouse, 1861-1891. *Courtesy of the Security Pacific National Bank Collection/ Los Angeles Public Library.*

News of the discovery of the bodies spread throughout the community. All of Garden Grove and the surrounding area were aroused and it became necessary for Marshal Finley to hide Anschlag in a corn crib over night to evade a lynch mob, which had stormed the city jail. The following day, Anschlag was transported to Los Angeles to stand trial for the murder of the Hitchcocks. On April 13, 1888, after several months of headline grabbing proceedings, John Anschlag was found guilty of murdering the Hitchcocks and sentenced to death. On November 14, 1888, just two days before his date with the hangman, Anschlag escaped his prescribed punishment by taking some poison, which had been slipped into his cell with some tobacco. It was never discovered how Anschlag was able to procure this poison, but it was speculated in the press that relatives, fearing Anschlag's hanging would be a disgrace upon the family name, decided to have the murderer end his own life to preserve some resemblance of dignity.

The gravesite of Charles and Lois Hitchcock at Anaheim Cemetery.

A sad consequence of these tragic events was the untimely deaths of both Charles' mother and father and Lois' parents, Mr. and Mrs. Bradley. Overcome by grief, they survived their children by only a few months. The village of Garden Grove lost two well-respected citizens and the shock of their murders haunted the area for many years.

The Tragic Story of Effie Scholl

(Tustin, Orange County, 1889)

Effie Scholl is notoriously known for murdering her two young children, John (3 years old) and Eva (5 years old). In the fall of 1889, a recent divorcee, Effie was struggling to hold her life together. She lived in an age of religious repression and intolerance, in a society that frowned upon and ostracized divorce. The Scholls had been married for seven years, but those years were filled with great unhappiness. Their divorce was granted by default and Mr. Scholl left the county. Effie was left destitute with no income, and with no place to turn; she filed for public assistance. Mr. Scholl hearing of this, returned to Orange County. He was not fond of the idea of his children being raised in such squalled conditions, and immediately commenced proceeding to gain custody of his children. He believed Effie was an unfit mother and was in the process of having these papers drawn up when the horrific events of October 16, 1889 took place. Throughout the process, Effie had threatened to kill the children should Mr. Scholl ever get guardianship, but no one took her dramatic ranting seriously.

On the morning of October 16, 1889, Effie Scholl was very disturbed, and not in her right mind. She rationalized that there was no other course, preferring the children and herself to be dead rather than suffer the humiliation of her ex-husband gaining custody of the children. Effie reasoned that she and the children would be meeting their maker and would be in a much better place. As the tragic event unfolded, Effie used chloroform to subdue the children; she placed them in their beds, and cut their throats. Then in an attempt to kill herself, she ingested a large quantity of poison, a mixture of muriatic and carbolic acids. Fearing that this would not accomplish the deed; she took a knife, and cut her own throat. Effie lost consciousness, due to loss of blood but did not die. It was not until sometime later that she gained awareness of the events.

Effie Scholl's house, site of the double murder and attempted suicide (present day), corner of Pacific and 3rd Streets in Tustin.

Several notes were left at the scene; one of which was addressed to her mother, Mary Goodwin. It reads in part:

> This is the last blow of that cruel thing that calls himself a man. He can never have my sweet little ones to bring up in wickedness. I can say that he is a vile, wicked, depraved, devilish liar. My little ones will be in the arms of Jesus. I give up life everlasting that my little ones may gain it.

Reports of the crime scene were gruesome, the children were found in their beds soaked in blood, while Mrs. Scholl was found laying in her own vomit, covered in blood and unconscious. The planned effects of the poison were not immediately successful. Effie lingered in and out of a coma for two weeks. In lucid moments she was quite repentant of her evil act, and had a desire to reconcile with her maker. Effie finally succumbed to the effects of the poison, dying on the evening of November 2, 1889; having lingered near death for eleven days. The Scholl murders shocked the tiny hamlet of Tustin. Never before had the citizens of this small town witnessed such a heinous act of savagery. Effie Scholl was buried on November 4, 1889, in a simple ceremony at Santa Ana Cemetery. The location of her children's graves is unknown.

Effie Scholl's grave at Santa Ana Cemetery.

Murder at the Modjeska Ranch

(Orange County, 1892)

The following is the tragic story of William McKelvey and Francisco Torres, two people who are forever connected to the first and only incidence of vigilante mob violence in Orange County history. In the late 1800s, Orange County was a quiet and mostly peaceful community of rural farms and small businesses. Violence was not unheard of but was certainly not common place. William McKelvey was the much admired and adored foreman at famed Polish actress Madame Helena Modjeska's ranch in rural Santiago Canyon, a position he had held for several years. Francisco Torres, who often went by the nickname "Poncho" was a twenty-five-year-old Mexican drifter and migrant worker who was occasionally employed at the Modjeska ranch.

Madame Helena Modjeska. *Courtesy of the Library of Congress Prints and Photographs, (LC-USZ62-54156).*

At the Modjeska ranch and throughout the county it was customary to withhold $2.50 from laborers wages as a poll tax at the end of each month. Torres took exception to this and angrily sought out McKelvey on the early morning of Sunday, July 31, 1892. Torres found him attending to the morning rituals. Torres confronted him, and demanded to have his $2.50 returned. McKelvey refused, explaining that this was not his decision but was an order from the tax collector. This explanation did not satisfy Torres and angry words were exchanged. Torres continued to fume, stalking McKelvey throughout the ranch. Eventually, things came to boiling point. McKelvey entered a feed barn, Torres followed, picked up a pick axe, and hit McKelvey in the head, crushing his skull. In this frenzy of rage, Torres pulled out a knife and plunged it into the chest of his stricken victim. Believing McKelvey was dead, Torres then fled the scene.

An intensive man hunt for Torres ensued. Dozens of law enforcement officers were on his trail. A $200 reward was issued by the Orange County Board of Supervisors for Torres' capture, but even with this bounty on his head, he was able to elude capture for ten days. On August 10, 1892, Francisco was apprehended in the town of Rancheria in rural San Diego County. He was taken into custody by constables A. L. Wood and D.M. Knowles of Mesa Grande. Orange County Sheriff Theo Lacy was dispatched to Mesa Grande, and Torres was extradited back to Santa Ana to stand trial.

Madame Modjeska at her Arden ranch house in Santiago Canyon. *Courtesy of the University of Southern California, on behalf of the USC Libraries Special Collections.*

Francisco Torres was arraigned in Santa Ana Superior court on August 12, 1892, and charged with William McKelvey's murder. As the trial proceedings commenced, tensions began to run high in the community. Whispers of secret meetings and the possible lynching of Torres began to circulate throughout the city. On the early morning of Saturday, August 20, 1892, a masked group of men stormed the Santa Ana jail, subdued the jail guard, and forcibly extracted Torres from his jail cell, dragging him to the corner of Fourth and Sycamore Streets. Not a word was spoken between the masked men, only the sobs of Torres could be heard. There they bound Torres hand and foot. Tied a noose around his neck and hung him to the corner telephone pole. The body was discovered later that morning, attached was a note that read "change of venue." The identities of the vigilantes were never uncovered and no one was ever prosecuted for Torres' death. This was the first and only known lynching to occur in Orange County.

Francisco Torres. *Courtesy of the Santa Ana Reading Room/ Santa Ana Public Library.*

It must be noted that the descriptions and accounts of the aforementioned events of July and August of 1892 were reported through newspaper accounts of the day. These primary sources did not always use fair and balanced reporting techniques. They were often prejudiced, with unbalanced approaches to the facts. The racist attitudes of the time period were often an extension of the popular views of many. Although this attitude is unthinkable today, the reader must understand the events from a historical context.

The tragic tale of Francisco Torres and the murder of William McKelvey were reported in great detail in these sources. The newspaper industry during this time was very competitive and most used a brand of news reporting known as "yellow" journalism. This style of newspaper writing used bold, eye catching, and titillating headlines to grab the attention of potential readers. Torres was tried in these newspapers before he got a fair trial; he was convicted, and executed by the court of public opinion before having the opportunity to defend himself. With that said, even if the case had gone to a full trial, the outcome may already have been a foregone conclusion. The late eighteenth century was a time fraught with racial bigotry, hatred, and fear of minorities. Due to this attitude, a man like Torres had little chance of receiving a fair trial. The authorities were quick to point the finger of guilt at a person who could not defend himself. The question is: Did Francisco Torres murder William McKelvey? The evidence as presented in the newspapers and the preliminary trial proceedings, all point to his guilt. In reality there are only two people that know what happened on that early July morning in 1892, and neither is talking.

The old Rossmore Hotel on the corner of 4th and Sycamore Streets in Santa Ana. The telephone pole on the right was the scene of accused murderer Francisco Torres lynching on August 20, 1892. This was the first and only case of mob violence in Santa Ana city history. *Courtesy of the Santa Ana Reading Room/ Santa Ana Public Library.*

The Evans Sontag Gang & The Shootout at Stone Corral

(Central Valley, 1889-1894)

The Evans Sontag Gang, much like their contemporaries, the Dalton's and Butch Cassidy and the Sundance Kid, lived a life outside of the law. They choose to rob trains because of real and fanciful grudges against the railroad companies. They also found that robbing trains was easy business. The criminal career of the Evans Sontag Gang lasted from 1889 to 1894, their five-year criminal run brought misery and despair upon the owners of the Southern Pacific and consternation upon law enforcement agencies who failed to catch the allusive bandits. They also became folk heroes to the common man in and about the San Joaquin Valley region of California.

The Sontag Brothers, John and George, were born in 1861 and 1864 and were raised in the river town of Mankato, Minnesota. John (May 27, 1861) and George (April 10, 1864) were born to Maria (Bohn) and Jacob Contant. In 1867, their father died and their mother remarried to Matthias Sontag. George began his life of crime when, at 15, he was sent to the state reform school in St. Paul for stealing cigars from his employer, Nicholas Peterson. A few years later in Omaha, after another theft, he was given a sentence at the Nebraska State Prison.

In 1889, John Sontag joined up with Chris Evans of Visalia, California, and started his life as a train robber in what was to be known as the Sontag Evans gang. Two years later George became a member of the gang. They based their operations in Visalia, and during this period, most of their train hold-ups were in central California. The Sontag-Evans gang had a way of robbing trains that was simple but well thought out. Their method was to determine the place on the railroad track where they wanted to stop the train, tie up their horses, and walk back to the train station. When the train arrived they'd sneak aboard the engine and hide in the baggage car. After reaching the designated point, they would appear and order the engineer to stop the train. Using dynamite they would blow up the express car and gather up the money, then locate the horses and make their escape.

Back in Minnesota their exploits became known when, on July 1, 1892, George, along with Chris, attempted to rob the Omaha train between the Minnesota River towns of St. Peter and Kasota. They were not able to acquire anything during this hold up but their activities came under the eye of railroad officials and Pinkerton detectives. On August 3, 1892, after returning to California, they robbed a Southern Pacific train near their hometown of Visalia. This time, however, they were not as lucky as they had been with previous hold ups. Several days after the robbery, authorities following thousands of leads, arrived at the Evan's ranch and arrested George, while John and Chris escaped. After his arrest, George Sontag started singing like a canary. He told authorities all sorts of fanciful tales about the exploits of the gang. Until this confession, law enforcement had not connected the various train robberies to one criminal gang. In October of 1892, Sontag was tried in Fresno, found guilty, and sentenced to life in prison at Folsom Prison.

For ten months, John Sontag and Chris Evans evaded capture, finding refuge in the wilderness near what is now Sequoia National Park. This was rugged landscape, where men not wanting to be found could hide out. The place they settled upon was known as Stone Corral. Unbeknownst to the pair, a posse was hot on their trail. On May 28, 1893, luck ran out for the outlaws, suddenly and without warning, a rifle shot blasted the stillness of the forest. A posse of fourteen men had surrounded the robbers and opened fire. Evans was wounded in the leg and attempted to find shelter behind a haystack. Sontag was also wounded but the pair kept the posse at bay until early evening. Both Sontag and Evans were wounded and bleeding quite heavily. Sontag had six bullet wounds and did not have the strength to escape. Evans was able to muster enough strength to crawl six miles through the brush to safety. At dawn, the lawmen rushed Sontag only to find that he was near death. They stopped and had their picture taken before they carted him off to jail, where he died on July 3, 1893. Evans bloody trail was easy to follow and he was quickly captured. He was taken to the Fresno County jail, where he recuperated from his injuries and awaited trial.

Posse members pose with wounded train robber, John Sontag after the May 1893 Shootout at Stone Corral.

Evans was tried and convicted in Fresno on December 13, 1893 and sentenced to life in prison. Shortly after this, he was able to escape, and for a brief couple of weeks remained on the loose. He was eventually captured and sent to Folsom prison to serve out his sentence and was paroled in 1911. He died penniless in a Fresno County poorhouse in 1917. Having served fifteen years behind bars, George Sontag was given his freedom in 1907 and, with Opie Warner, wrote his autobiography called *A Pardoned Lifer*. He also began a speaking tour and lectured about the life of an outlaw. His talks were presented in such cities as Minneapolis and Milwaukee. He also gave a talk at the Opera House in Mankato, Minnesota, the town of his birth. Elaborating on his quest to warn the public about the dangers of becoming a criminal, he filmed the story of his outlaw career. The film was called *The Folly of a Life of Crime* and was filmed in Chico, California in 1915 (some sources say 1913). No copies of this movie are known to exist, but George is listed as having written and starred in it. When and where George Sontag died is not known. The last documented reference to him is in May of 1929, when his mother passed away and her obituary listed him as a survivor living in San Francisco.

The Demon of the Belfry: Theodore Durrant

(San Francisco, 1895-1898)

One of the most atrocious crimes ever committed in San Francisco was the murder of Blanche Lamont and Minnie Williams, which took place in the Emanuel Baptist Church on Bartlett Street in the month of April, 1895. Blanche Lamont was a wholesome girl who left her home in Dillon, Montana in 1894 for health reasons and came to San Francisco to continue her studies for the purpose of becoming a school teacher. She made her home with an aunt and uncle, Mr. and Mrs. C. G. Noble, at 209 Twenty-First Street in San Francisco. Blanche was very religious and attended the Emanuel Baptist Church. She seldom went to places of amusement, had a lovable disposition, and was well liked. On April 3, 1895, she mysteriously disappeared. Minnie Williams was also a member of the Emanuel Baptist Church, and she worked as a house servant. She had a very self-reliant personality that was made hard by years of difficulty. Her physique was frail and small and she suffered from many health issues.

Theodore Durrant was born in Toronto, Canada, in 1871 and while a small child moved with his parents to San Francisco. He was the product of a good education, and in 1895, was a medical student attending the Cooper Medical College. He was one of the most active members of the Emanuel Baptist Church and was well liked by all. His sister was famed actress/dancer Maud Allan; infamously known for creating a sensation in Europe with her "Vision of Salome" dance. She changed her name from Beulah Maude Durrant after the tragedy to escape attention.

On the morning of April 3, 1895, Miss Lamont left home as usual to attend the Boy's High School, at which she was taking a course. While enroute to the school, she was accompanied by Theodore Durrant, who after leaving her, went to Cooper Medical College. After Miss Lamont finished her studies at the high school, she left for the Normal School on Powell Street, where she was taking cooking classes. Shortly after 2 p.m., Durrant appeared in front of the school and waited for Miss Lamont to come out around 3 p.m.; they then walked to the Emanuel Baptist Church, arriving there around 4 p.m. The pair was then observed to enter the church. Around 5 p.m., church organist George King saw a disheveled and pale Durrant jump out from behind the piano. King asked Durrant if there was a problem. Durrant explained that he had been in the belfry fixing an electrical light and while up there became overcome by gaseous fumes. King then ran to a nearby drugstore, returning with a bottle of Bromo-Seltzer, which Durrant drank. During this time King was unable to detect any odor of gas.

Murder victim Blanche Lamont, pictured left, standing next to railing with her students at Heckla, Montana, 1893. *Courtesy of the Library of Congress, Prints and Photographs, (LC-USZ62-02132).*

That night, a prayer meeting was held at the church. Lamont not having returned home caused her aunt to worry. Thinking Blanche might have gone to the prayer meeting, Mrs. Noble also attended in hopes of seeing her niece. Durrant had a seat just behind Mrs. Noble and during the meeting said to her: "Is Blanche here tonight?" Mrs. Noble replied: "No, she did not come." Durrant then said: "Well, I regret that she is not with us tonight, as I have a book called *The Newcombs*, for her, but I will send it to the house." After a few days of suspense the Nobles contacted police to inform them of Lamont's disappearance. As Durrant was above suspicion, no one thought to mention the fact that he was seen with her the day of her vanishing. Durrant called on the Nobles to offer his services in the search.

On the evening of April 12, 1895, at 7 p.m., nine days after Lamont disappeared, Minnie Williams told her friends that she was going to a church member meeting at the home of a church elder T. A. Vogel, whose wife Mary had seen Theodore Durrant walking with Blanche Lamont the day she disappeared. A few minutes after 7 p.m., Williams was seen in a heated discussion with Durrant in front of the church. It was loud enough to alert a passerby who stopped to intervene and he later testified that Durrant's manner was not becoming of a gentleman and that the pair did calm down and entered the church together. At 9:30 p.m. Durrant arrived at Mr. Vogel's member meeting, he was a half an hour late, and witnesses stated that he appeared to be in a very agitated and excited state of mind.

On Friday morning, April 12, 1895, a horrific discovery was made by Minnie Lord and Katie Stevens. In a small closet, near the school library, in the church, they found laying on her back, covered in blood, the body of a young woman. Her right hand had almost been cut off and there was a horrible gash on her forehead. Some of her clothes had been torn from her body. Authorities quickly identified the girl as Minnie Williams, who was a Sunday school classmate of missing Blanche Lamont. The scene of the crime was a frightful mess; the body of Minnie Williams lay outstretched with horrific wounds to her hands and head. A piece of clothing assumed to be a part of her undergarments had been stuffed in her mouth and used as a gag. It was speculated by detectives that Williams had been surprised as she entered the church, and based on her wounds, had put up a good fight.

A detective named Barney Riehl, while searching the church for evidence, happened upon the church belfry. There in the semi-darkness, he discovered footprints in the dusty floor, and upon following the trail, found what he thought appeared to look like a white marble carving of a completely nude woman. Upon closer examination and much to his horror, it was found not to be a carving but a dead body. The body was nude, lying on its back with its hands folded across the chest, the head rested on a piece of wood. The body was identified as Blanche Lamont. An autopsy disclosed that Lamont had been strangled but further results were hampered by the advanced state of decomposition of the body. Police interviewed numerous witnesses, one of which was Charles Hill who stated that he saw Durrant and Williams enter the church around 8 p.m., the previous night.

The Emanuel Baptist Church, Bartlett Street, between 22nd and 23rd Streets in San Francisco, site of the murders of Blanche Lamont and Minnie Williams. *Courtesy of the San Francisco History Center/ San Francisco Public Library.*

Detectives ascertained that the two girls were both members of the church, and were friends. Both belonged to the same Sunday school class, and both had recently rebuffed romantic advances from Durrant, a medical student living with his parents in the city. He was the librarian at the church, and was the assistant superintendant of the Sunday school. He was familiar with the church and carried one of the few keys to its private doors. During a search of Durrant's room, police found Minnie Williams purse in a coat pocket. An arrest warrant was issued for Durrant. Police later learned that Durrant had left the city with the Signal Corp. of the state militia. On April 14, 1895, he was located near Walnut Creek, California, where he was arrested. He denied any knowledge or involvement in the crime and professed that he was at school when the murders occurred.

Theodore Durrant police booking photo.

Three friends of Lamont's were brought to the jail to identify Durrant as the man they saw walking with her on the day she disappeared. They positively identified Durrant, and also identified the clothing Lamont was wearing the day of her disappearance. It was later found that Durrant's alibi was unable to be collaborated. Informed by his defense attorney that physical evidence and eyewitness testimony all pointed to him as the murderer, Durrant appeared to be on the verge of a confession. He knew that nothing short of a miracle could save him from the gallows. Not withstanding, the tremendous amount of circumstantial evidence, Durrant was formally charged with the murders of Blanche Lamont and Minnie Williams and was ordered to stand trial.

His trial began on July 22, 1895, and lasted until September 24, 1985; during the proceedings nearly fifty witnesses were called to testify. As testimony and evidence was presented, the horrific events of April 1895 began to unfold. Although Williams was frightfully butchered and the room resembled a slaughter house, not one drop of blood was found on Durrant's clothes. It was alleged that Durrant was naked when he committed the crime. It was also alleged that he strangled Lamont in the library and then dragged her body up to the belfry to evade detection. Hairs from Lamont's head were found in splinters on the stairs.

As with many cases of such infamy, a certain class of woman takes advantage of the opportunity and leaps into the limelight. The more depraved and evil the deeds, the more woman shower attention on the defendant.

This case was no different, and as soon as the trial began, Durrant received numerous sympathy visits and gifts from admiring young woman. The trial was covered by major newspapers all across the United States. On September 24, 1995, the case was finally submitted to the jury, and after deliberating for an astonishingly short five minutes, brought in a verdict of guilty with the death penalty attached. The case was appealed to the California State Supreme Court which upheld the verdict and sentence. The date of execution was set for June 11, 1897. Durrant protested his innocence and remained unrepentant to the last, never confessing to the murders. He was granted a temporary reprieve in 1897, but the execution was eventually carried out on January 7, 1898 at San Quentin prison. Durrant was described by witnesses at the execution as being one of the most cool and collected murders who ever mounted the scaffold. When asked by Warden Hale whether he wanted the death warrant read to him, Durrant stated, "I will waive that right and spare you an unpleasant duty." As the rope was placed around his neck and just prior to the hood being placed over his head, Durrant asked to speak, in a slow and deliberate tone he said the following:

> Do you wish me to say anything? Well, I would like to say this. I have no animosity against anyone, nor even against those who have persecuted me and who have hounded me to my grave, innocent as I am. I forgive them all. I do not hold anything against the reporters. I do not look upon them as enemies. I forgive them as I expect to be forgiven for everything that I have done, but the fair name of California will forever be blackened with the crime of taking this innocent blood, and whether or not they ever discover the committers of this crime matters little to me now, for I before the whole world announce my innocence for the last time. I am innocent of the crimes charged to me before God, who knows the heart and can read the mind. I am innocent.

The hangman then gave the signal and the trap door was sprung. Durrant's body fell through the opening, fifteen feet breaking his neck instantly. In just eleven minutes, twenty-eight seconds, all signs of life had vanished and the one of the most infamous criminals of the nineteenth century was officially dead. After the execution, Durrant's parents took charge of his body. They feared grave robbers and decided to have the body cremated, but no San Francisco area crematory would accept the corpse. A Los Angeles mortuary, Kregelo & Bresee's accepted the corpse on January 13, 1898; the next day the body was moved to Reynolds & Van Nuys Mortuary in Pasadena, where the body was cremated. It is alleged that Durrant's remains are interred at Holy Cross Cemetery in Colma.

Part Two
The Sensational Crimes of the Twentieth Century
1900 – 1949

Crime is terribly revealing. Try and vary your methods as you will, your tastes, your habits, your attitude of mind, and your soul is revealed by your actions.

~ Agatha Christie (1890-1976)
English Playwright and Novelist

A Brief History of the State of California

1900 - 1949

In 1900, when the period covered by Part Two of this book begins, it was evident that California was entering a new era. The population of the state in 1900 was 1,485,053 and by 1950 had risen to 10,586, 223, a tenfold increase in just fifty years. The state's basic industries, agriculture, manufacturing, shipping, lumbering, and mining were expanding in both variety and volume. A rapidly growing demand for petroleum, stimulated in part by the use of fuel oil by the railroads and the continued discovery of new fields in central and southern California, promised to add another industry to the state's prodigal resources.

Interesting enough, four of the most revolutionary factors in the development of modern California, radio, the automobile, the motion picture industry, and aviation, were all looked upon as passing fads at the opening of the century. But what prophet, gazing down the decades from the vantage point of 1900, could foresee the revolutionary effect that these four inventions would exert upon the future he was seeking to envision?

California became an industrial power with the discovery of oil, the rise organized labor, the birth of Hollywood, and the post-war building boom in Southern California. In the 1850s, oil was collected and refined for the first time in California, both in Ventura County and the Los Angeles area, and in the 1860s, the first wells were dug. By the 1890s, numerous oil fields, including the Summerland Oil Field near Santa Barbara, the location of the world's first offshore oil wells, the giant Midway-Sunset field in Kern County, and several fields in the Los Angeles Basin were contributing to an oil boom that made California one of the largest oil producers in the nation. Oil during the period was the most profitable industry in the southern part of the state.

The first decades of the twentieth century also saw the rise of the movie studio system. MGM, Universal and Warner Brothers all acquired land in Hollywood, which was then a small subdivision known as "Hollywoodland" on the outskirts of Los Angeles. Soon, Americans from all over the country, especially the Midwest, were attracted to the mild Mediterranean climate, cheap land, and a wide variety of geography. By the 1930s, the show-biz population had extended its reach into radio, and by mid-century, Southern California had also become a major center of television production, hosting studios for major networks such as NBC and CBS.

During World War II, California's mild climate became a major resource for the war effort. Numerous air-training bases were established in Southern California, where most aircraft manufacturers, including Douglas Aircraft and Hughes Aircraft expanded or established factories. Major naval shipyards were established or expanded in San Diego, Long Beach and San Francisco Bay. San Francisco was the home of the liberty ships. After the war, hundreds of land developers bought land cheap, subdivided it, built on it, and got rich. Real-estate development replaced oil and agriculture as Southern California's principal industry. This is the back drop to the first notorious crime in twentieth century California.

The Great Shelby Smelting Works Heist

(San Francisco, 1901)

Smelting is a form of extracting metal from ore; this includes iron extraction (for the production of steel) from iron ore, and copper extraction and other base metals from their ores. Smelting involves more than just "melting the metal out of its ore." Most ores are a chemical compound of the metal with other elements, such as oxygen, sulfur, or carbon and oxygen together. To produce the metal, these compounds have to undergo a chemical reaction. Smelting therefore consists of using suitable reducing substances that will combine with those oxidizing elements to free the metal. Smelting works were popular at the turn of the century, as the industrialized cities of the world turned from mason, brick, and wood to steel for buildings.

Smelting works such as the Shelby Works on San Francisco Bay not only made steel but also melted gold into bar form; they were very busy and profitable. In their vault stood over a half a million in gold bars ready for transport to San Francisco.

On the early morning of August 5, 1901, between the hours of 12 and 5 a.m., the Shelby Smelting Works, located at the edge of San Francisco Bay, at Vallejo, California, was burglarized and $283,005 in gold bullion was stolen from its vault. The burglar committed the crime by digging a three-foot-wide tunnel under the building and up into the vault. A hole the size of a manhole cover was bored into the iron floor of the vault. The tunnel was estimated to have taken a week to complete. The thieves were very careful to cover their handy work and no suspicions were ever raised prior to the theft. A reward of $5,000 was issued by the Shelby Works for information leading to the arrest and capture of the thief.

San Francisco police detectives in cooperation with Private Pinkerton agents were initially baffled and numerous theories regarding the crime developed. Convinced that the burglary had to have been committed by someone with inside information, suspicion soon fell upon a former employee, John Winters, who owned a cabin about one quarter mile from the works. Upon searching Winters' cabin, detectives found various items such as a shovel, digging tools, and pieces of clothing with mud splattered on them, mud that was very similar to that which was found in the tunnel. Detectives had also found a cap in the tunnel, a cap which Winters was known to frequently wear. Several witnesses came forward to state that they saw a man fitting the description of Winters in the vicinity of the railroad tracks near the works several nights prior to the burglary. Winters was traced to San Rafael on August 7, 1901, at the home of Miss Ida Spencer, a friend of Winters.

Police found a letter she had written to him at his cabin. Police wanted to question Spencer to see if she knew of the whereabouts of Winters. They did not expect to find him there and immediately took him into custody.

Winters initially denied any involvement, but as circumstantial evidence began to mount against him, he felt no other avenues available to him but to confess to the crime. He told authorities that he had acted alone, and that the tunnel took him over a week to construct, and if daylight had not come so soon, he would have taken the whole lot. He then loaded the bars into a small boat and rowed to a secluded place not far from the works and dumped the bars in a shallow area near the shore of San Francisco Bay. He intended to retrieve the gold at a later date. Winters led detectives to the exact location where he had dumped the gold and police were able to recover every bar that was stolen. Winters was remanded to stand trial in Martinez, California, but pleaded guilty before any proceedings could start. On August 21, 1901, he was sentenced to fifteen years in prison. On November 24, 1908, after serving only seven years for his crime, Winters was paroled.

The Bakersfield Shootout: James McKinney, Last of the Old West Gunslingers

(Bakersfield, 1903)

In April of 1903, the sleepy little town of Bakersfield, California, located in the San Joaquin Valley, was the sight of one of the Wild West's last great shootouts. James McKinney was one of the most wanted outlaws at the turn of the nineteenth century. He was a killer and gunslinger, with a reputation for having a quick temper and even faster gun. Little is known about his early life, but his unlawful ways started twenty years earlier in Farmville, California, where he pistol whipped a teacher for trying to discipline his younger brother. He was found not guilty of the crime, but was never welcome in the town again.

McKinney drifted throughout the West for the next twenty years, always remaining outside of the law. It was rumored that he was wanted in several states for murder and it was also alleged that he rode with infamous outlaws Butch Cassidy and the Sundance Kid. In 1899, McKinney again found himself in Bakersfield, California, where an incident took place in which McKinney killed a local gambler, named Long Tom Sears. One night, McKinney was provoked into a fight with Sears by a woman who complained of ill treatment at the hands of Sears. What Sears had done to the woman is unknown. What *is* known is that it didn't take much to get McKinney worked-up. McKinney sought out Sears trying to provoke a fight, but Sears would have none of it. Knowing McKinney's temper and propensity for a quick trigger finger, Sears threw down his weapon and refused to fight; stating that if he wished to shoot him, he might as well get it over with. McKinney obliged shooting him down in cold blood. The gunshots were heard by Deputy Sheriff John Crawford, who ran to the alley where the stricken Sears lay mortally wounded. McKinney whirled and fired at Deputy Crawford, who narrowly escaped injury. McKinney was apprehended and stood trial for the murder of Long Tom Sears and assault on Deputy Crawford but somehow avoided conviction. McKinney's luck at avoiding the law would soon run out.

In April 1902, McKinney again found himself on the other side of the law. While visiting Porterville, California, and bored one night, he got drunk at a local saloon and began shooting at bottles behind the bar. The town marshal intervened; an altercation ensued with the officer getting shot in the face (the marshal survived the injury). McKinney fled the scene on horseback, riding to hide out with a friend named Al Hulse. The pair holed up at a Chinese joss house (a place of worship, which were common in Chinatowns across the American frontier) on L Street in Bakersfield.

On the morning of April 19, 1903, law enforcement discovered McKinney's location and with a posse of nine officers, surrounded the joss house. Town Marshal Jeff Packard and Deputy Sheriff Bill Tibbet went from room to room searching for the outlaw. Packard and Tibbet kick down one door and were immediately met by a barrage of gunfire from McKinney and Hulse. Both lawmen were seriously wounded. McKinney rushed for the nearest exit, and as he burst through the back door, he was intercepted by Deputy Bert Tibbet (brother of Bill Tibbet). Tibbet let loose with his double-barrel shot gun hitting McKinney in the upper body and head area. Mortally wounded, the outlaw staggered through the door and attempted to fire off a few more rounds before hitting the ground. Another Deputy finished McKinney off with a rifle shot through an open window. Hulse, fearing escape was hopeless, gave up and was hauled away to jail. Deputy Tibbet and Marshal Packard being seriously injured were carried to a local hotel for medical attention and shortly thereafter both lawmen died from their wounds.

Al Hulse alone stood trial for the murders of Deputy Tibbet and Marshal Packard, but jurors were unable to come to a verdict. A second trial was held, and in May of 1906, Hulse was found guilty of second degree murder and sentenced to life in prison. On October 15, 1906, while awaiting an appeal of his conviction, Hulse committed suicide. On April 22, 1903, McKinney was quietly buried at the Porterville Cemetery. There were few people present to mourn his death. The justice system had failed to end McKinney's trail of blood and mayhem. It unfortunately took a barrage of bullets and the tragic death of two more lawmen to finally bring down the notorious outlaw. Thus came to a finish the tragic story of one of the Old West's last outlaw gunslingers. James McKinney had died the way he lived, at the end of a rifle barrel. He had fought his last gun fight and lost. His bloody trail of death and mayhem was over.

San Francisco Graft Trials
The Political Crimes of Eugene Schmitz

(San Francisco, 1902-1912)

Eugene Edward Schmitz was born August 22, 1864, in San Francisco, California, "Handsome Gene" rose to the presidency of the Musicians' Union, which gave him entry into society, along with nominal membership in the labor movement. Perhaps because of this unique position, Schmitz came under the appraising eye of political "Boss" Abraham Ruef, who with minimum delay had installed the handsome and popular Schmitz as his newly-formed Union Labor Party's mayoral candidate. It was the fall of 1901 when Schmitz sprang into the political limelight as a candidate for mayor of San Francisco. Few San Francisco citizens had ever heard of him and even fewer paid attention when it was announced that he was a candidate. But San Francisco awoke one morning to find that Eugene E. Schmitz, the orchestra leader, was Mayor of the City. He became the first Union Labor mayor in United States history.

During this new regime, politics in San Francisco reached an all-time high water mark for venality and corruption. Schmitz was called "the smallest man mentally and the meanest man morally that ever occupied the Mayor's office." For five years the city's real overlord was Abraham Ruef. The Ruef-Schmitz combination began the prostitution of the city government as soon as Schmitz took office. In short time, the connection between the mayor's office and criminal underworld became notorious. This political machine began to extort tributes from reputable businesses and corporations as well as the usual sources of graft.

All went as planned for the "puppet mayor" until 1906 when two monumental events hit San Francisco: the Great Earthquake and Fire, and a massive crack down on city-wide graft and bribery.

Abraham Ruef (1864-1936). *Courtesy of the Library of Congress, Prints and Photographs, George G. Bain Collection, (LCB2-1148-15).*

Three men finally initiated an all out attack on the Ruef-Schmitz machine, Fremont Older, editor of the San Francisco *Bulletin*, Rudolph Spreckels, and James D. Phelan. On November 7, 1906, a new grand jury was seated, and this marked the beginning of the graft prosecutions. Soon after, Schmitz was indicted and implicated in twenty-seven counts of extorting payments legal services from the city's infamous French restaurants. Under the state's promise to recommend immunity, eighteen city supervisors confessed to wholesale acceptance of bribes.

The grand jury then returned sixty-five indictments against Ruef for bribery of city supervisors. On May 15, 1907, Ruef pleaded guilty and the next day began to confess before the grand jury, incriminating Schmitz. This led to Schmitz's conviction on June 13, 1907; he was found guilty of extortion and the office of Mayor was declared vacant. He was sentenced to five years in prison, the maximum sentence the law allowed. On December 10, 1908, Ruef was sentenced fourteen years for bribery. On August 23, 1915, having served a little more than four and a half of his fourteen-year sentence, he was released from San Quentin. He was not allowed to return to the bar. Before he went to prison, he had been worth over a million dollars; when he died on February 29, 1936, he was bankrupt.

Schmitz immediately appealed the verdict, and on January 9, 1908, the District Court of Appeals nullified his conviction. Two months later, the California Supreme Court upheld the Court of Appeals' ruling. Schmitz was released on bail, pending the resolution of other outstanding bribery indictments. He was brought to trial once more in 1912 on charges of bribery, but was acquitted. Freed of the legal stigma, he returned to politics and unsuccessfully ran for Mayor in 1915 and again in 1919. In 1921, he ran for a spot on the Board of Supervisors and won; he remained in that position until 1925, after which he was engaged in private business until his death in San Francisco on November 20, 1928. The San Francisco graft prosecutions helped to discourage subsequent instances of a similar nature and profoundly influenced the political uprising in California that led to the triumph of reform under the Lincoln-Roosevelt League and the Progressive Party.

The Murders and Other Crimes of Leon Soeder

(San Francisco, 1882-1907)

Very little is known about the early life of Leon Soeder; he was born in Lorraine, Germany, in 1865 and immigrated to the United States at the age of 17. He arrived in New York City on April 19, 1882, aboard the *Amerique.* By October 1882, he had found his way to California, and under the assumed name of Leon Seter, committed his first crime, a burglary in Alameda County for which he was sentenced to three years in state prison. Following his release from San Quentin in 1894, he wandered throughout the San Francisco Bay area taking on various jobs, primarily working as a railroad hotel cook. On January 29, 1894, he was again arrested for burglary. This time he stole from his employer, Johnson's Restaurant in San Francisco, and was sent back to San Quentin for three more years. Paroled around 1900, he found his way to Petaluma, California, where he met Pilar Mirander. They were married in 1901 and moved to Tesla, California. There Soeder found work as a cook and his wife as a waitress. Soon suspicious things began to happen around the Soeder home. Numerous animals, most notably the family dogs, began to die from mysterious illnesses, most likely poisoning. It was learned later that Soeder was using the animals in experimental work.

Soeder and his wife left the Tesla area in December of 1902, and returned to Petaluma, where Soeder purchased a $2,000 life insurance policy on his wife. Shortly after arriving, she died mysteriously, and for unknown reasons police did not investigate her death. Even stranger, a few days following his wife's funeral, Soeder proposed marriage to another woman, Lillian Justi, who rebuffed his advances. Then the restaurant at which he was working inexplicably burned to the ground. In another unusual turn of events, just a few days prior to the fire, Soeder had purchased a $2,000 insurance policy on the property, and outlandishly no one investigated.

In April of 1903, Soeder traveled to Alaska, and returned to the Bay area in September of that same year. He then told acquaintances of plans to travel back to Germany, where he was to inherit a large sum (estimated at $10,000). He proceeded to Germany to collect his inheritance. After spending several months in his hometown, he persuaded his sister's husband, Joseph Blaise (Blais), to accompany him back to the United States. The pair arrived in New York on November 28, 1903, and shortly after arriving, Soeder attempted to procure a life insurance policy on Blaise (without his knowledge) for $5,000. Because of a paperwork delay, Soeder lost patience and left for San Francisco without purchasing the policy.

On January 11, 1904, William Hogan, a laborer, was passing along Taylor Street, between Green and Vallejo in San Francisco, when he found a man lying at the bottom of a cliff. Upon closer examination it was found that the man was dead. There was a large wound on the back of the head and the right side of the throat had been cut. His clothes had been rifled through in attempt to make the scene look like a robbery. Soeder reported Blaise missing on January 12, 1904, the pair had shared a room at 827 Jackson Street. He told his landlord that Blaise had not returned home the night before and he feared that something had happened. The authorities were informed of Blaise's disappearance and they advised him that a body had been discovered. He went to the morgue, and appearing distraught, identified the body as that of his brother-in-law.

Police investigators soon found out that Soeder was an ex-convict with a long history of criminal acts. They also learned that he had taken out three life insurance policies each for $3,000 on Blaise. His apartment was searched and police found a large knife, on which human blood was found. Evidence began to mount against Soeder. A witness came forward who identified Soeder as the man seen carrying a body near the location where Blaise was found dead. Soeder was taken into custody and charged with murder. While in jail awaiting trial, a cell mate named John Cooper informed police that Soeder had tried to persuade him to find witnesses for an alibi. He also said that Soeder confessed that he had killed Blaise and his own wife. Cooper produced a diagram of the crime scene which had been written on a piece of newspaper. It was allegedly drawn by Soeder. It was written in great detail with names of streets, etc., and with such accuracy that it would have been impossible for a stranger with no knowledge of the crime to have drawn it. During his trial which began on May 8, 1904, this evidence, along with other expert testimony proved that Soeder had in fact killed Blaise. It was told that Soeder had stabbed Blaise in the throat, hit him over the head with a shovel, and pushed his body over the cliff in order to procure a life insurance policy. On May 23, 1904, after only twenty minutes of jury deliberation, Soeder was found guilty. He was sentenced to death and after several years of failed appeals was executed at San Quentin Prison on March 29, 1907. On the gallows, he collapsed but continued to profess his innocence, insisting that San Francisco police had railroaded and concocted the plot against him.

Tragedy in Auburn: The Weber Family Murders

(Auburn, 1904-1906)

On the afternoon of May 26, 1904, a masked man entered the Bank of Placer County in Auburn, California, and brandishing a hand gun, ordered everyone to their knees and demanded the teller hand over all of the money in the cash drawer. The masked robber got away with over $5,000 in gold coins, and then disappeared. At the time, circumstantial evidence pointed to the bank robber's identity as Adolph Weber, the twenty-year-old son of prominent retired brewery owner Julius Weber.

On the evening of November 10, 1904, a fire broke out at the Weber family home. A neighbor by the name of George Ruth discovered the fire, and broke into the house in an attempt to locate family members. He found the bodies of Mrs. Weber and her eighteen-year-old daughter, Bertha, in a room not yet reached by the fire. They had been shot and they apparently had been dragged into the room after being killed. It appeared as if an effort had been made to set their clothes on fire. The Weber's youngest son, eight-year-old Earl, an invalid, was found barely alive with a massive head wound, but succumbed to the injury soon after he was discovered by rescuers. The body of Mr. Weber was not found until the next morning, and he too had suffered a bullet wound to the head.

At the exact moment George Ruth was discovering the fire and bodies, Adolph Weber was seen in a store on Cohen Street purchasing a new pair of trousers. He was observed wrapping his old trousers in a paper bag, then leaving the store. He ran home, broke a window, and threw the paper bag into the flames. Suspicion was immediately placed on Adolph Weber, the only surviving Weber family member. His odd behavior in the days following the tragedy only fueled gossip. He exhibited no emotions and refused to attend his family's funeral.

On November 12, 1904, a coroner's inquest was held, at which Adolph was questioned and refused to admit any knowledge of the fire or shooting deaths of his family. A Weber relative, Mrs. Snowden, testified that Adolph knew a great deal about the crime, whereupon he (Adolph) flew into a rage and said, "Your turn will come next." Adolph Weber was arrested at the conclusion of the inquest, and remanded into custody to stand trial for the murder of his family.

The Auburn County Courthouse (present day).

Weber's trial, which began at the Auburn County Courthouse on February 6, 1905, lasted almost three weeks. Numerous witnesses testified, one came forward to say that he saw the defendant enter the washroom of the American Hotel on the night of the crimes and wash off what appeared to be blood from his hands. Police detectives also testified that they had found a 32-caliber revolver under the flooring of the Weber barn, the same kind of weapon used in the murders. On the handle of the gun was found clots of blood and some hair, all the bullets had been exploded. Henry Carr, a United States government gun expert, testified that this pistol was indeed the weapon used to murder the Weber family. A pawn shop owner in San Francisco also testified that he had sold Weber the exact pistol in July, 1904. The trousers that Adolph had tried to destroy in the flames were recovered, and upon closer examination, blood stains were found on them. Coroner Shepperd and other officers stated that while digging in the yard of the Weber home, they found a five-pound can filled with $20 gold pieces, which were evidently the proceeds from the bank robbery. All of this evidence, along with questionable and self-damning testimony by Weber himself, left little doubt to the outcome of the trial.

At 2 p.m., on February 22, 1904, after twenty-one hours of deliberation, the jury found Adolph Weber guilty of four counts of murder in the first degree and sentenced him to death by hanging. Numerous appeals were attempted; a stay of execution was even granted pending his examination for insanity, but in the end, all defenses failed. On the afternoon of September, 27, 1906, at Folsom Prison, Adolph Weber was executed. He remained stoic to the end, refusing to make any last-minute confessions or statements. On the gallows, he simply met his fate with little emotion and faced the crowd of spectators without flinching. Weber's relatives undoubtedly knew that Adolph had committed the bank robbery, and his motives for committing the murders, which have few parallels in the annals of crime, was probably for the purpose of forever sealing their lips and to gain possession of the Weber family fortune.

Entrance to Folsom Prison (present day).

The Bombing of the Los Angeles Times Building

(Los Angeles, 1910)

In the early years of the twentieth century, unionism and yellow journalism were at their height. Tension between these two titans came to a boiling point in 1910 with the bombing of the *Los Angeles Times* building in Los Angeles, California. In order to better understand the circumstances around this tragedy (which killed twenty-one people), a discussion of the history and events leading up to this event must be explored.

In 1886, the Iron Workers Union was formed but was weak and unorganized. Made up of mostly seasonal and unskilled laborers, it remained feeble and ineffective until 1902, when its members won a monumental battle against iron industry giant and industry leader, the U.S. Steel Corporation. This win by the union helped propel membership, brought signed contracts, and within the year almost all iron-producing companies were unionized. In 1903, management at U.S. Steel and several other iron manufacturers founded the National Erectors Association. This organization's goal was to break the unions. It promoted the open shop and assisted employers in union busting. Tactics such as spies, detective agencies, strike breakers, and violence were used to disrupt union organization. Law enforcement authorities cooperated with the Erectors Association strategy and often turned a blind eye to violent behavior against union members, refusing to prosecute. Tension rose, and violence became common place. In 1905, Iron workers elected Frank M. Ryan president and John J. McNamara secretary-treasurer. Both men were fervent unionist and advocated militant activities in order to promote unionism. The movement was a success for several years.

Union officials, desperate to keep their movement alive, felt a need to combat anti-unionist violence with more violence. In late 1906, Union leaders authorized a tactic of dynamiting. This was not meant to destroy plants or kill people, but was used as a method to scare companies to the union bargaining table. Between 1906 and 1910, the Iron Workers Union was responsible for blowing up 110 iron works, with only property damage reported; no other injuries were reported. On October 1, 1910, all of that changed.

Harrison Gray Otis, publisher of the *Los Angeles Times*, was a fervent anti-unionist. He was born on February 10, 1837 in Marietta, Ohio. A Civil War veteran, politician, and newspaper editor after the war, in 1876, he moved his family to Santa Barbara, California. There he purchased a small local newspaper and turned it into a success. In 1882, he took over editorial duties at the *Los Angeles Daily Times*, now the *Los Angeles Times*. Eventually, he was promoted to president and general manager of the newspaper (a position he held until his death in 1917). Known for his very conservative political views, these ideals were reflected in the newspaper, he is attributed with coining the phrase "you are either with me, or against me." A vehement anti-unionist, Otis used his newspaper as a vehicle to spearhead a twenty-plus year campaign to rid union activity from the city of Los Angeles. He was a hated man in union circles.

Harrison Gray Otis (1837-1917), 2nd publisher of the *Los Angeles Times* (circa, 1890s).

James and John McNamara were Irish-American union organizers. No information existed about their early life or when they came to the United States. The brothers became members of the Iron Workers Union, of which they both eventually rose to become high-ranking officials. They were advocates and helped develop the campaign of dynamiting against the steel industry. They became key players in the coming events of October 1910.

In a last ditch effort to stop the spread of unionism in Los Angeles, the city council on July 15, 1910, enacted an ordinance that prohibited picketing and public speaking (in loud tones). The penalty was jail imprisonment of up to 50 days with a $100 fine. Union members refused to obey this law, and hundreds of union activists were arrested. This new ordinance proved to be ineffective in stopping the union from organizing. On October 1, 1910, at approximately l:07 p.m., a bomb exploded at the *Los Angeles Times* building. The south wall of the building collapsed, which also caused the second floor and then first floor to collapse into the basement. The gas main exploded and a massive fire erupted, hundreds of workers were trapped inside the collapsed and fire-ravaged building. Twenty-one employees were killed in the blast, most burning to death.

The bomb was supposed to have gone off at 4 a.m., when the building was empty, but a faulty timing mechanism triggered the blast early. Sixteen sticks of dynamite had been placed in a suitcase and placed in the alley next to the building.

Bombed out remains of the *Los Angeles Times* Building. *Courtesy of the Security Pacific National Bank Collection/ Los Angeles Public Library.*

The bombers had not been aware of natural gas lines near the placement of the device. Unexploded devices were also found at the home of Harrison Gray Otis, the Los Angeles County Hall of Records, and at the Alexandria Hotel. Harrison Gray Otis condemned the bombing and its perpetrators as "cowardly murders, anarchist scum, and leeches." Leaders of the Iron Workers Union and Samuel Gompers, President of the American Federation of Labor all disavowed any involvement and condemned the bombing.

A reward of $25,000 was posted by the City of Los Angeles for the capture and arrest of the bombers. As weeks passed, no arrests were made and authorities became desperate to find the perpetrators. The City of Los Angeles hired well -known private detective William J. Burns to head the investigation into the bombing. For four years, Burns (known as the American Sherlock Holmes) had been investigating the wave of violence against the steel industry. Burns and his network of spies were able to infiltrate the Iron Workers Union and discovered that John McNamara was boasting privately that he had masterminded and carried out the *LA Times* bombing.

William J. Burns (circa, 1900-1920). *Courtesy of the Library of Congress, Prints and Photographs, George G. Bain Collection, (LC-USZ62-114566).*

On April 14, 1911, Burns, along with police officers from Detroit and Chicago, went to the Oxford Hotel in Detroit and arrested James McNamara and Ortie McManigal. A search of the hotel room found blasting caps and other bomb-making implements. The pair was taken to Chicago, and from April 13 to April 20, were held and interrogated against their wills. McManigal, in order to save himself, cut a deal and confessed to authorities that both James and John McNamara, Frank Ryan, and others were the masterminds and perpetrators of the bombing. On April 22, 1911, authorities burst into a meeting of the Iron Workers Union and arrested John McNamara, and Frank Ryan. The pair was extradited back to Los Angeles to stand trial.

National union leaders were outraged by the treatment of the McNamaras and others. They believed their arrest was made upon coerced information and their extradition was basically a kidnapping. Labor movement leaders even hypothesized that the whole bombing and arrest was a frame-up, and that Otis might have even planted the bomb himself in an attempt to convince the public that the unions were evil. Union leaders asked famed defense attorney Clarence Darrow (of the famed Scopes Monkey Trial, 1925) to defend the accused bombers. Reluctantly, Darrow agreed to head the team of defense attorneys. On May 5, 1911, the

McNamara brothers were arraigned in Superior Court and the actual trial began on October 25, 1911. As jury selection began, Darrow became concerned that the outcome of the proceedings might turn against the brothers. He learned that the prosecution had obtained massive amounts of evidence against the McNamaras. On November 17, 1911, the jury was finally seated.

Muckraking journalist Lincoln Steffens was convinced of the McNamaras' guilt. He visited the brothers in jail, and proposed to defend their actions as justifiable. Steffens argued that because of state-sponsored repression of labor and violence against the organization by employers, the public would stand behind the bombing as being warranted and righteous. The McNamaras admitted to Steffens that they had masterminded and committed the bombings. Darrow was stunned to learn that the brothers had met and confessed to Steffens without his knowledge or approval. Darrow and Steffens met secretly with newspaper publisher E.W. Scripps, in hopes of enlisting his support of the possibility of suggesting a plea arrangement with District Attorney John D. Fredricks. In exchange for light prison terms, the American Federation of Labor would end strikes in the Los Angeles area. Steffens met with Otis and was surprised when he proposed the plea deal; Otis agreed to speak with District Attorney Fredricks to bring about an end to the trial. At first Fredricks balked at giving the McNamara's a break. After much pressure from both sides, he agreed to compromise in which James McNamara would receive life in prison and John McNamara would receive 7-10 years in prison. This agreement was brought to the McNamara brothers, and at first they refused to accept the plea agreement. Darrow explained that the defense had very little chance of succeeding and long prison sentences were likely for both defendants. In order to settle the case with one of the brother's getting off lightly, both need to agree to the plea bargain. On December 1, 1911, the McNamara brothers changed their pleas in open court from not guilty to guilty. They admitted that they had deliberately placed

Clarence Darrow (circa, 1922). *Courtesy of the Library of Congress, Prints and Photographs, (LC-USZ62-11819).*

Lincoln Steffens (circa, 1894), American muckraking journalist.

a bomb outside of the *Los Angeles Times* building in attempt to gain public support for their cause. The pair were sentenced on December 5, 1911, with James receiving life in prison, and John fifteen years behind bars.

Los Angeles Times Bombing Victims Memorial at Hollywood Forever Cemetery.

Following their plea of guilt, it became known to the McNamaras that public sentiment had been on their side. They learned that Darrow and others had conspired to keep them isolated from this knowledge, and had they known the public was behind them in such a strong manner, they would not have made the deal. Following the trial and plea, the labor movement in Los Angeles collapsed and did not show signs of strength again in the city until the 1950s.

Frank Ryan was sentenced to seven years in prison, and Ortie McManigal received a sentence of two and half years. James McNamara died from cancer in 1941 at San Quentin Prison, and despite repeated attempts by numerous left-wing labor groups to gain his release, he refused to file parole papers on his own behalf. At the conclusion of the trail he is alleged to say, "You see…the whole damn world believes in dynamite." His brother John served his sentence, and upon release from custody, returned to active union organizing. He died on May 8, 1941 in Montana. Clarence Darrow would go on to become one of the most famous lawyers and civil libertarians in America. He would represent Leopold and Loeb at their infamous murder trial in 1924, and famously defended John T. Scopes at the Scopes Monkey Trial in 1925. Darrow died in Chicago on March 13, 1938. Harrison Gray Otis continued his fervent anti-union stance and remained in charge of the *Los Angeles Times* until his death on July 30, 1917; he is buried at Hollywood Forever Cemetery in Los Angeles. Nearby, a memorial was erected to the lives that were lost in the bombing. Eighteen of the victims are buried at the site.

Close-up view of the victim's plaque at the *Los Angeles Times* Victims Memorial.

The Battle of Tomato Springs

(Orange County, 1912)

Almost fifty-six years to the day, four miles from where Los Angeles Sheriff James Barton and his posse were gunned down by Juan Flores and his gang, another outlaw shot it out with law enforcement. On December 15, 1912, Joe Matlock (also known as Ira Jones) an out of work drifter, assaulted seventeen-year-old, Myrtle Huff, on her uncle's (William A. Cook) Irvine area ranch. Matlock then escaped into the foothills near Tomato Springs (near present-day Irvine). The sheriff's department was contacted and a posse consisting of Sherriff C.E. Ruddock, Santa Ana City Marshall Samuel Jernigan, Constable Calvin E. Jackson, Deputy Sheriffs Robert Squires and James Stacy, Jailer Theo Lacy, Leonard A. West, William Culver, and Al Prather, all made their way to the Tomato Springs area. By the time the posse had arrived, Matlock, heavily armed with a rifle, had found refuges in the western hills. As Deputy Sheriff Squires and Stacy were making their way up the steep ridge, Matlock suddenly appeared and opened fire. Stacy was shot through the shoulder, leg, and wrist, while Squires sustained a mortal gunshot wound to the head. The remaining members of the posse scrambled for cover, encircled the bandit, and returned fire. Feeling that his men were out gunned and not knowing how many outlaws were present, Sheriff Ruddock sent for reinforcements.

Slowly, under cover of the brush, members of the posse made their way to the injured lawmen. Stacy and the body of Squires were found in a nearby ravine and were carried to safety. As the rescue party made their way down the hillside, shots again rang out. This time, Al Prather sustained a non-fatal gunshot wound to the head and William Culver was shot in the left knee. At around 12 p.m., Captain Nathan Ulm, and 150 men of company L, of the California National Guard arrived at the scene and proceeded up the steep hillside. Creeping closer and closer to Matlock's position, the army men slowly encircled the bandit. Matlock seeing that his situation was hopeless, burst from the brush in a futile attempt at escape; rushing forward, he fired his rifle as he rushed down the embankment. The men of company L opened fire, hitting the on-rushing outlaw multiple times; Matlock fell dead from a massive gunshot wound to the head. The Battle of Tomato Springs was over; it was the last great Old West style manhunt and shootout to take place in Orange County.

Immediately after the gun battle controversy arose as to the true identity of the bandit. Numerous people came forward to allege that the bandit was named Ira Jones not Joe Matlock. The alleged father of the bandit, J.D. Matlock, of Eugene, Oregon, publicly denied that the deceased gunman was his son. According to some sources, he privately told Sheriff Ruddock that the dead man was, indeed, his son. According to these same sources, the body of the bandit was secretly set back to Eugene, Oregon with his father. There are no public records of this happening, and a review of burial records at Santa Ana Cemetery show that Joe Matlock is buried in an unmarked pauper's grave at the cemetery. Newspapers of the day make no mention of his burial. Could there have been a cover-up? Matlock's father was a very influential man and this might have allowed him to take his son's body back to Oregon for proper burial. Could the supposed grave containing the remains of the bandit, Joe Matlock, be empty? After almost 100 years, there are no living participants of the incident, and there is no actual written proof of a cover-up. The only thing that is certain is that Joe Matlock or Ira Jones is dead, and is buried somewhere.

Deputy Sheriff Robert Squires was the first Orange County Deputy Sheriff killed in the line of duty. His funeral on December 18, 1912, was the largest ever held in the city of Santa Ana. Pallbearers included Orange County Sherriff Ruddock, Los Angeles County Sheriff Hammel, Superior Court Judge Z.B. West, and Marshal Jernigan. He was buried with full honors at Fairhaven Memorial Park in Santa Ana, California.

Grave of Deputy Sheriff Robert Squires at Fairhaven Memorial Park, Santa Ana.

The Preparedness Day Bombing

(San Francisco, 1916)

With World War I raging in Europe in 1916, the United States found itself perched on the edge of entering the war. In the U.S., isolations and sentiment remained strong, especially on the West Coast.

On July 22, 1916, employers in San Francisco organized a march through the streets in favor of an improvement in national defense. Critics of the march, such as William Jennings Bryan, claimed that the Preparedness March was being organized by financiers and factory owners who would benefit from increased spending on munitions. The huge Preparedness Day parade was a target of radicals. A radical pamphlet of mid-July read in part, "We are going to use a little direct action on the 22nd to show that militarism can't be forced on us and our children without a violent protest." The Preparedness Day parade was the biggest such event ever held in the city up until that date. Over 50,000 marchers were included and thousands more line the parade route. Around 2 p.m., a bomb exploded on the west side of Steuart Street (near the ferry building). The giant blast tore a gap into the ranks of Company K, First California Volunteer Infantry Unit, veterans of the Philippine Insurrection. The time bomb was concealed in a suitcase; the bomb maker had added heavy metal sash weights to the bomb to act as shrapnel when the explosives detonated to increase the bomb's effect. Ten bystanders were killed and fifty were injured making it the worst terrorist act in San Francisco history. The list of the dead included; Mrs. Howard Knapp, George Painter, O.H. Lamborn, George Lawlor, Arthur Nelson, Harry Turnbull, Adam Fox, Pearl Seemann, Mrs. L.O. Wymore, and Mrs. Kingsley Van Loo.

Witnesses described seeing two dark-skinned men, probably Mexicans, carrying a heavy suitcase near the site where the bomb exploded. The Chamber of Commerce immediately offered a reward of $5,000 for information leading to the arrest and conviction of the dynamiters. Other organizations and individuals added to this sum and the reward soon reached $17,000. Offering such a large reward was condemned by the editor of the *New York Times* claiming it was a "sweepstakes for perjurers."

On the evening of the bombing, Martin Swanson went to see the District Attorney, Charles Fickert. He told Fickert that despite the claims that it was the work of Mexicans; he was convinced that Tom Mooney and Warren Billings, both well-known radical labor leaders were responsible for the explosion. Billings had been convicted previously for carrying dynamite on a passenger train, and had a reputation for enjoying direct action, and Mooney, a militant socialist, was suspected of using explosives himself in past conflicts. Moreover, Mooney's union had passed out pamphlets warning about using "violent propaganda" against the marchers.

The next day, Swanson resigned from the Public Utilities Protective Bureau, and began working for the District Attorney's office. On July 26, 1916, Fickert ordered the arrest of Mooney, his wife Rena Mooney, Warren Billings, Israel Weinberg, and Edward Nolan. Mooney and his wife were on vacation at Montesano at the time. When Mooney read in the *San Francisco Examiner* that he was wanted by the police, he immediately returned to San Francisco and gave himself up. The newspapers incorrectly reported that Mooney had "fled the city" and failed to mention that he had purchased return tickets when he left San Francisco. None of the witnesses of the bombing identified the defendants in the lineup. The prosecution case was instead based on the testimony of two men, an unemployed waiter, John McDonald, and Frank Oxman, a cattleman from Oregon. They claimed that they saw Warren Billings plant the bomb at 1:50 p.m., and Oxman stated that he saw Tom Mooney and his wife talking with Billings a few minutes later. However, at the trial, a photograph showed that the pair was over a mile from the scene. A clock in the photograph clearly read 1:58 p.m., and heavy traffic at the time meant that it was impossible for Mooney and his wife to have been at the scene of the bombing. Despite this, Mooney was sentenced to death and Billings to life-imprisonment. Rena Mooney and Israel Weinberg were found not guilty, and Edward Nolan was never brought to trial.

In 1917, the American government became concerned about the conviction and imprisonment of Tom Mooney and Warren Billings and the Secretary of Labor, William Wilson, delegated John Densmore, the Director of General Employment, to investigate the case. By secretly installing a recording devise in the private office of the District Attorney, he was able to discover that Mooney and Billings had probably been framed by Fickert and Swanson. The report was leaked to Fremont Older who published it in the *San Francisco Call* on November 23, 1917. There were protests all over the world about this miscarriage of justice and President Woodrow Wilson called on William Stephens, the Governor of California, to look again at the case. Two weeks before Tom Mooney was scheduled to hang, Stephens commuted his sentence to life imprisonment in San Quentin. Soon afterwards Mooney wrote to Stephens: "I prefer a glorious death at the hands of my traducers, you included, to a living grave."

In November 1920, Draper Hand of the San Francisco Police Department, went to Mayor James Rolph and admitted that he had helped Charles Fickert and Martin Swanson to frame Mooney. Hand also confessed that he had arranged for John McDonald to get a job when he began threatening to tell the newspapers that he had lied in court about Mooney and Billings. Mooney's defense team now began to search for MacDonald. He was found in January 1921 and agreed to make a full confession. He claimed he did see two men with the large suitcase but was unable to get a good look at them. When he reported the incident to District Attorney Charles Fickert, he was asked to say the men were Warren Billings and Tom Mooney. Fickert said that if he did this, "I will see that you get the biggest slice of the reward." Later, two witnesses, Edgar Rigall and Earl K. Hatcher, came forward and provided evidence that

Frank Oxman was 200 miles away during the bombing, and could not have seen what he told the court at the trial of Mooney.

In February 1921, John McDonald confessed that police had forced him to lie about the planting of the bomb. Despite this new evidence authorities refused a retrial. After the publication of this new evidence, it was generally believed that Charles Fickert and Martin Swanson had framed Mooney and Billings. However, Republican governors over the next twenty years, William Stephens, Friend Richardson, Clement Young, James Rolph, and Frank Merriam, all refused to order the release of the two men. The international campaign to free Tom Mooney and Warren Billings continued, and in 1937, a group of politicians asked President Franklin Roosevelt to intercede in the case. When Roosevelt declined, a resolution was introduced in the Senate calling on Governor Frank Merriam to pardon Mooney and Billings. In November 1938, Culbert Olson was elected Governor of California. He was the first member of the Democratic Party to hold this office for forty-four years and soon after gaining power, he ordered that Mooney and Billings should be released from prison. Rena Mooney, who welcomed her husband as he left San Quentin, was quoted as saying: "These twenty-two long years have been moth-eaten. Life to me has been something like a cloak. There is little left but the tatters."

The identity of the bomber (or bombers) has never been determined, but numerous historians believe that the conspiracy was led by Alexander Berkman, especially because of his extensive knowledge and involvement in other bombings and a rather suspicious one-year sojourn to San Francisco. However, whether he was involved in the conspiracy or not, Berkman was almost certainly not the person who constructed the actual bomb, since he was known to have little or no technical skills with explosives. Mooney, and especially Billings, both had prior knowledge of how to use dynamite (Billings was also familiar with clockwork timing mechanisms, and became a watch repairman after his release from prison), though they were by no means the only ones. Another suspect group included the Galleanists, radical anarchist followers of Luigi Galleani, particularly the elusive Mario Buda, who was a bomb-maker of deadly repute, and who was known to include heavy metal slugs in his dynamite time bombs to increase maiming and overall casualties. The Galleanists conducted most of their bomb attacks on the East Coast and Chicago, and were suspects in the later Wall Street bombing, though they were also active in San Francisco.

Mose Gibson: The Fiend of Fullerton

(Orange County, 1920)

In the early morning hours of July 15, 1920, an intruder attacked and killed prominent Fullerton rancher, Roy Trapp and seriously wounded his wife. Shortly after midnight, two men rode up to the Trapp ranch house. One held the horses as the other, armed with a pick axe, crept into an unlocked window in the rear of the house. Mrs. Trapp was awakened to sounds of someone in her bedroom. She awoke just in time to witness the horrifying murder of her husband. As Mr. Trapp slept, he was hit multiple times over the head by the intruder with the pick axe. She leapt from her bed and attempted to fend off the prowler as best she could, until she was felled by a blow to the head and left for dead. Unconscious for several hours, around 5 a.m., Mrs. Trapp regained semi-consciousness and crawled to a telephone. Phoning her nearest neighbor, Pete Nicholas, she shouted "Two Mexican's tried to kill us," then lost consciousness again.

It was first thought that the attacks were perpetrated by two Mexicans, seeking revenge because of a quarrel over employment as initially described by Mrs. Trapp. Police were quickly able to round up two men fitting the description. Under interrogation it was determined that they had nothing to do with the murder of Mr. Trapp and were released. Further investigation by police determined that the crime was more likely an attempted burglary gone horribly wrong.

The only other person present at the Trapp home the night of the murder was Eugene Chappella, the eleven-year-old nephew of the Trapps. He was able to escape injury by hiding under his bed. The young boy was able to give police valuable information on the crime and a description of the assailant. The boy told detectives that he heard his uncle say "Hold on a minute! Hold on a minute," then heard the clock strike midnight. Right after that, something heavy fell down the stairs and then he heard his aunt try to use the telephone. He also said he saw a lone black man wearing a blood-stained white shirt pacing back in forth in front of the house. With this new information, police determined that they were erroneously looking for two Mexicans and redirected their search for a lone black man. An all-points-bulletin with the following description was sent all over southern California;

> The Negro's description was given as 30 years old, 5 feet, 8 inches tall, of stocky build, high cheek bones, looks like a Mexican and speaks Spanish fluently.

A $500 reward for the capture of the murderer was posted by the Orange County Board of Supervisors.

Reports flowed in from all over the Southland; a witness came forward to detail that he saw a man fitting this description, wearing what appeared to be a white blood-stained shirt board a train at El Toro that was headed to San Diego. It was also reported that a man fitting this same account was seen at the San Diego train depot. A search of the train depot at El Toro uncovered a pair of blue overalls covered in blood. Loaded with this new information, Orange County Sheriff Calvin E. Jackson was determined that the suspect had fled to San Diego. He and a posse left Santa Ana on the evening of July 15, 1920, for San Diego in an attempt apprehend and to cut off the black man alleged to be the Trapp murderer from the Mexican border.

It was further determined that the man they were looking for was named Mose Gibson, a black man who fit the description of the assailant and was wanted in connection with several other crimes in the San Diego area that included perjury and burglary. As the man hunt for Gibson widened, the trail of the suspect led to the little California/ Arizona border town of Needles, California. Shortly after midnight, on Sunday, July 18, 1920, a San Bernardino Deputy Sheriff and an agent of the Santa Fe railroad depot arrested Mose Gibson with little resistance. A search of his possession found a quantity of jewelry that was reportedly taken from the Trapp home. Orange County law enforcement authorities arrived in Needles the next morning and transported Gibson under heavy guard back to Orange County.

Meanwhile, Mrs. Trapp was recovering at a Fullerton area hospital and had regained such awareness that she was able to identify Mose Gibson as her assailant and as the man responsible for murdering her husband. Under interrogation Gibson confessed to killing Roy Trapp and to the burglary of their home. His confession laid bare all the ghastly details of the crime; he told how he stole a horse at a place a quarter of a mile away from the Trapp's home. He drove to the Trapp home and tied the horse to a post. He then removed his shoes and walked up to the back of the house, gaining entrance through an unlocked window. He said he was drunk at the time. Once inside the house, Gibson made his way to the bedroom of the Trapps and began to ransack the bureau drawers. Mr. Trapp awoke, and fearing capture, Gibson struck him over the head with a pick axe. Mrs. Trapp then came toward him calling for help and he then hit her in the head. Gibson said he took some money and a few pieces of jewelry before fleeing the house; he mounted his horse and then hid in a local packing house, under the loading platform waiting for the next freight train to arrive. He hoped on the freight and rode it as far as El Toro, where he boarded a passenger train to San Diego. He spent one day in and around San Diego before boarding another train to Los Angeles, then going on to San Bernardino and eventually to Needles, where he was arrested. He confessed that the decision to burglarize the Trapp's was due to revenge. The day before the murder, he had asked Mr. Trapp for money. He felt slighted after being ordered off the Trapp ranch, and decided to rob them as retribution. During this initial confession, Gibson admitted to numerous other crimes that included hundreds of burglaries and one additional homicide that occurred around 1908 in Baton Rouge, Louisiana.

Once the grisly details of Gibson's crimes became public, it was decided that because of the massive amount of community uproar against Gibson, there was the possibility that he might be forcibly taken from the jail and lynched. Orange County law enforcement decided that the only way to secure his safety was to transfer him to the Los Angeles County jail to await trail. Gibson's hearing, trial, and conviction for the slaying of Roy Trapp took place on July 21, 1920, and he was sentenced to death. The whole proceeding lasted only two hours from start to finish and has the dubious distinction as being one of the quickest of such capital punishment cases ever tried in the history of the United States.

Gibson was quickly transferred to San Quentin prison to await his death sentence on September 24, 1920. Following his removal to prison, Gibson trying to clear his conscience confessed to numerous other crimes while awaiting execution. These crimes included hundreds of thefts and five additional murders: two in Louisiana, from 1908 to 1910, the killing of Mary Clark in Florida (1919), and the slaughter of Mr. and Mrs. Jacob Erhardt of Phoenix, Arizona in June of 1920. On the morning of September 24, 1920, only forty-two days after the brutal slaying of Roy Trapp, Mose Gibson with a firm step strode to the gallows at San Quentin Prison. Repentant for the crimes he had committed, he had studied the Bible continuously since his summer trial and conviction. As the noose was placed around his neck, he raised his eyes to the sky, and repeated the Lord's Prayer. In a moment, the trap door was released and Mose Gibson, the "Fiend of Fullerton," was dead.

Prohibition Era Violence in the Bay Area

(San Francisco and Santa Rosa, 1920)

The Eighteenth Amendment of the United States Constitution, along with the Volstead Act, which defined "intoxicating liquors" excluding those used for religious purposes and sales, established Prohibition in the United States. Its ratification was certified on January 16, 1919. The amendment reads in part:

> "Section 1 – After one year from the ratification of this article the manufacture, sale, or transportation of intoxicating liquors within, the importation thereof into, or the exportation thereof from the United States and all territory subject to the jurisdiction thereof for beverage purposes is hereby prohibited.
>
> Section 2 – The Congress and the several States shall have concurrent power to enforce this article by appropriate legislation.
>
> Section 3 – This article shall be inoperative unless it shall have been ratified as an amendment to the Constitution by the legislatures of the several States, as provided in the Constitution, within seven years from the date of the submission hereof to the States by the Congress.

The Eighteenth Amendment to the United States Constitution banned the manufacture, sale, and transport of alcohol, and almost overnight, organized crime took over as the provider of this most popular, but banned, beverage. The amendment was repealed by the Twenty-First Amendment on December 5, 1933. It remains the only constitutional amendment to be repealed in its entirety. The fourteen years from 1919 to 1933 in which this amendment was enforced was one of the most violent criminal periods in American history. Illegal profits from the sale of alcohol soared and crime increased. Organized syndicates of criminal gangs formed in all the major cities and battles over turf ensued.

San Francisco had its first taste of the Roaring Twenties on December 5, 1920, when two police detectives and the Sonoma County Sheriff were shot and killed by three members of the Howard Street Gang, a group of organized bootleggers operating out of a South-of-Market warehouse. The sad episode began on December 2, 1920 in San Francisco, when three members of the Howard Street Gang lured two young girls to a home, where they were "brutally assaulted." The three members, Terry Fitts, George Boyd, and Charles Valento, promptly left the city and headed to Santa Rosa, which they thought, would be the perfect place to hide out from the law.

Their trail was traced by two San Francisco Detectives to Santa Rosa. The detectives contacted Sonoma County Sheriff Jim Petray and they combed west Santa Rosa in search of the suspects. They were found at 28 West 7th Street and in a gun battle; Sheriff Petray and Detectives Miles Jackson and Lester Dorman were killed. The detectives, Miles Jackson and Lester Dorman, were the first officers to lie in state in the San Francisco City Hall rotunda. While the city mourned their passing, department investigators tracked their killers to Sonoma County. Acting on information provided by the San Francisco department, Santa Rosa police apprehended the three suspects and jailed them two days later.

Outrage over the death of the two officers was so great that an angry mob (estimated at over 200) stormed the Santa Rosa Jail that night. A mob of people disguised and masked, "overpowered" jail personnel and removed the three prisoners, who were being held for the murder of Sheriff James Petray and two San Francisco police detectives. The mob took the three prisoners to the Rural Cemetery on Franklin Avenue. An area fifty feet from the street was lit up by car headlights. The three bound prisoners were dragged beneath a locust tree and lynched. The leader of the vigilantes made everyone remain at the grisly scene until the three were dead.

Newspapers around the state denounced the lynch mob. *The Los Angeles Times*, December 11, 1920, in a headline declared:

> NO LYNCH LAW, the cause of justice has suffered in California by the lynching of the three supposedly despicable characters in Santa Rosa by a mob whose passions were aroused that they could not let the law take its course. The three victims were taken from cells in the county jail, where they were awaiting arraignment on charges... The evidence in the case was quite certain... No good purpose was served by the crime committed by the lynchers, while a precedent was established which may lead to the lynching at some future time of innocent persons.

The Santa Rosa episode was to be the second to last lynching in California. The last such event occurred in January of 1947 in Siskiyou County.

The Black Widow: Louise Peete

(Los Angeles, 1920-1947)

Born Lofie Louise Preslar on September 20, 1880 in Bienville, Louisiana, she became one of America's first female serial killers, and one of only four woman ever executed in California's gas chamber. She was the daughter of a socially prominent New Orleans newspaper publisher and attended the best private schools. While in school she became notorious for her sexual escapades, and was expelled for "inappropriate behavior." After this, she moved to Boston and worked as a high-class call girl. In 1903, at the age of 23, she married Henry Bosley, a traveling salesman and joined him on the road. In the summer of 1906, Henry caught his wife in bed with a local oilman. Grief-stricken, Bosley killed himself. Louise sold Henry's belongings and then moved to Shreveport, Louisiana, where she again found work as a prostitute.

The dramatic change of scene meant little to Louise. Her trade was still the same, and as a hooker making house calls, she became a favorite with the local gentry. On the side, she also pilfered jewelry from the absent wives of wealthy clients, selling off the pieces that she did not choose to keep herself. In time, she pushed her luck too far and was discovered. Threatened with exposure, she retired to Waco, Texas, where she wooed and won the affection of Joe Appel, an oil man, best known for the diamonds that studded his rings and belt buckles. One week after Appel met Louise, he was found dead, a bullet in his head, and his diamonds were missing. Called before a special grand jury, Louise admitted shooting Appel in self-defense, explaining that Appel had turn violent and had tried to rape her. It was then that she shot him in self defense. Members of the jury openly applauded as they set her free. The missing diamonds were never found.

By 1913, running out of luck and ready for more cash, Louise travelled to Dallas, Texas, and married local hotel clerk Harry Faurote. It was primarily a marriage of convenience for Louise, and she flagrantly indulged in numerous affairs. These illicit dalliances by his wife soon drove Faurote to commit suicide by hanging himself in the hotel basement. In 1915, moving on to Denver, Colorado, Louise married Richard Peete, a door-to-door salesman. She bore him a daughter in 1916, but Peete's paltry income did not measure up to her "standard of living," and she soon took off for Los Angeles.

In 1920, while shopping for a house to rent in Los Angeles, Louise met mining executive Jacob Denton. He had a house to rent, but was persuaded by Louise to retain the property himself. He hired Louise as a live-in companion. After several weeks of torrid sex, Louise asked Denton to marry her, but he refused. It was a fatal error. Smiling through rejection, Louise ordered Denton's caretaker to dump a ton of earth in the basement, where she planned to "raise mushrooms," Denton's favorite food, as a treat for her lover. No mushrooms had sprouted by the time Denton disappeared, on May 30, 1920, but Louise had numerous explanations for curious callers. First, she told all comers that Denton had quarreled with "a Spanish-looking woman," who became enraged and chopped his arm off with a sword. Although he managed to survive, she said, poor Jacob was embarrassed by his handicap, and so had gone into seclusion. Pressed by Denton's lawyer, she revised the story to incorporate an amputated leg; the missing businessman was scheduled to return once he was comfortable with an artificial limbs. Incredibly, these tales kept everyone at bay for several months, while "Mrs. Denton" threw a string of lavish parties in her absent lover's home. By September, Denton's lawyer grew suspicious, calling on police to search the house. An hour's spade work turned up Denton's body in the basement, with a bullet in his head. Louise fled Los Angeles and police detectives traced her back to Denver, Colorado, where she had resumed a life of wedded bliss with her estranged husband, Richard Peete.

Arrested and brought back to stand trial for the murder of Denton, Louise was convicted of first degree murder on February 5, 1921, and sentenced to life in prison. In the beginning, her husband, Richard Peete, corresponded faithfully, but absence failed to make Louise's heart grow fonder. In 1924, when several of his letters went unanswered, Peete committed suicide. It was reported that she liked to boast about the lovers she had driven to their deaths, and she especially cherished Richard's suicide, as proof that even prison walls could not contain her fatal charm. In 1933, Louise was transferred from San Quentin to the woman's prison at Tehachapi, and after eighteen years and in 1939 on her tenth attempt to win parole, she was released from custody. Her ultimate release was due, in no small part, to intercession from a social worker, Margaret Logan, and her husband, Arthur.

Louise Peete testifying during her murder trial, 1921. *Courtesy of the Los Angeles Times Photographic Archive/ University of California, Los Angeles.*

Paroled to the care of Mrs. Emily Latham, in Los Angeles, Louise was allowed to take the name "Anna Lee," after her favorite movie star. She became a housekeeper for numerous wealthy people.

In 1942, an elderly female friend, Jessie Marcy, was found dead; her home was discovered in a state of disarray. Police detectives interviewed "Anna Lee," the missing woman's closest friend, and they were told the woman had died of injuries sustained in a fall. In what may only be described as epic carelessness, police bought the story, never bothering to check out "Anna's" background or obtain a death certificate.

The kindly Mrs. Latham died in 1943, and Louise became the housekeeper for Margaret and Arthur Logan of Pacific Palisades. She then married elderly bank manager Lee Borden Judson in May 1944. On May 30, 1944, Margaret Logan mysteriously vanished without a trace. Immediately a suspicious mound of fresh dirt, marked with an array of colorful flower pots was found in the Logan's garden. Louise told Margaret's aged husband that his wife was in the hospital, unable to receive visitors. By late June, Louise had persuaded authorities that Arthur Logan was insane; he was committed to a state hospital, where he died six months later. With typical lack of feeling, Louise donated his body to a medical school for dissection.

Louise moved into the Logan's home with Judson, but all was not well in the household. In short order, her husband discovered a bullet hole in one wall, a suspicious mound of earth in the garden, and an insurance policy naming Louise as Margaret Logan's sole beneficiary. Still, he said nothing, and it remained for Louise herself to unravel the web of deception. By December 1944, Louise's parole officer had grown suspicious of the regular reports, submitted over Margaret Logan's shaky signature that contained such glowing praise for their charge. Police investigators searched the Logan home shortly before Christmas, prompting Lee Judson to voice his suspicions at last. Margaret Logan's body was unearthed in the garden, whereupon Louise offered another of her patented fables. In this story, feeble Arthur Logan had gone suddenly insane, beating his wife to death in a rage. Frightened of attracting suspicion due to her background, Louise had buried the corpse and had Arthur committed to an asylum. Police did not buy the story and Louise was arrested and charged with Margaret Logan's murder. Her husband was booked as an accessory. He was acquitted on January 12, 1945, and the next day, Judson took his own life, leaping from the thirteenth floor of a Los Angeles office building. Louise, it was observed, seemed pleased with the news of his death.

Louise Peete's trial began on April 23, 1946, and after a month of testimony, was convicted of first-degree murder of Margaret Logan and was sentenced to death. After numerous stays of execution and appeals, Louise Peete was put to death in San Quentin's gas chamber on April 11, 1947. She met her fate with no remorse for her victims, and remained cool and collected throughout the entire processes. When asked by the warden if she was ready, Peete stated, "I've been ready for a long time." She was the second of only four women to die in California's gas chamber. Peete's body was released to Mrs. Mima Snodgrass, a jail social worker; her remains were cremated and buried in an unmarked grave at Angelus-Rosedale Cemetery in Los Angeles.

San Quentin's warden, Clinton Duffy, once described Louise Peete as projecting "an air of innocent sweetness which masked a heart of ice." She died one of California's most notorious "Black Widows." Her decade's long saga of murder and suicide is unrivaled in the annals of California criminal history. Possessed of a cool and cunning charm, and an unusual attraction to men, Peete learned early on how to use her deadly talents to gain what she wanted.

Louise Peete on the witness stand during her murder trial, 1945. *Courtesy of the Los Angeles Times Photographic Archive/ University of California, Los Angeles.*

Fatty Arbuckle and the Tragic Death of Virginia Rappe

(San Francisco, 1921)

It is true that Roscoe "Fatty" Arbuckle was not "actually" murdered, but it can be argued that because of the sensational accusations of his involvement in the death of Virginia Rappe, and the headline grabbing trial, all unquestionably led to the demise of his film career and most likely caused his untimely death at age forty-six. A crime did take place, but not the type of misdeed you would suspect. This was a crime character assassination. It was the pilfering and slaughter of a promising film career for nothing more than political gain and to sell newspapers, all at the unfortunate and shameful expense of a troubled, young would-be actress, who wound up dead in the hotel suite of a famous celebrity.

Roscoe "Fatty" Arbuckle, the ground breaking comedic actor and mega-star of the silent film era was born March 24, 1887, in Kansas. The youngest child of William and Mollie Arbuckle, Roscoe was a very large baby, weighing in excess of thirteen pounds at birth. His father a slim man did not believe that the child could be his, and thus named the baby after a politician he despised, U.S. Senator Roscoe Conklin of New York. Roscoe's birth, the last of nine children, was very hard on Mollie, and resulted in chronic health problems the rest of her life; she died in Santa Ana, California in 1899. The Arbuckle family moved from Kansas to Orange County, California in 1896.

Young Arbuckle was a jovial child, who had a wonderful singing voice. His mother encouraged him to perform. At the age of eight, Roscoe made his first appearance on stage, playing the part of a wise-cracking kid for the Webster-Brown Stock Company at the Santa Ana Opera House.

After his mother's untimely death, his father, who always treated the young boy with disdain, refused to support his theatrical endeavors. So, after Mollie Arbuckle's death, William moved the family north to San Jose. There the young Arbuckle found odd jobs cleaning hotels and other businesses. He always had the habit of singing while he worked, and one day, he was overheard by a patron, who happened to be a professional singer. This contact led him to met Sid Grauman, who, in 1904, gave Roscoe his first professional singing opportunity. Arbuckle sang, danced, and did some clowning around which impressed audiences with his versatility. On August 6, 1908, he married Minta Durfree; she was a movie star of some early comedy films.

Arbuckle began his film career in July of 1909, when he appeared in *Ben's Kid*. He worked sporadically in single reel films until 1913, when he moved briefly to Universal Pictures, where he became a star in producer-director Mack Sennett's, *Keystone Cops* comedies. Although his large size was undoubtedly part of his comedic appeal, Arbuckle was self-conscious about his weight and refused to use it to get "cheap" laughs. Despite his massive physical size, Arbuckle was remarkably agile and acrobatic. Arbuckle disliked his screen nickname, which he had been given because of his substantial girth. "Fatty" had also been Arbuckle's nickname since school. "It was inevitable," he said. He weighed 185 pounds when he was 12. Fans also called Roscoe "The Prince of Whales" and "The Balloonatic." However, the name *Fatty* identifies the character that Arbuckle portrayed on-screen, not Arbuckle himself. He discouraged anyone from addressing him as "Fatty" off-screen, and when they did so, his usual response was: "I've got a name, you know."

In 1914, Paramount Pictures made Arbuckle a contract offer of $1,000 a day, plus 25 percent of all profits and complete artistic control to make movies, something that was basically unheard of it its day. These movies were so lucrative and popular that in 1918, they offered Arbuckle another contract, this time for three years, and $3 million dollars. His first full length feature was *The Round-Up* (1920), soon followed by other successful features such as *Brewster's Millions* (1921) and *Gasoline Gus* (1921). By September 1921, Roscoe "Fatty" Arbuckle was one of Hollywood's most successful and profitable film stars, second only to Charlie Chaplin. But tragic events were about to unfold that would topple his celebrity.

Actor Roscoe "Fatty" Arbuckle. *Courtesy of the Library of Congress, Prints and Photographs, George G. Bain Collection, (LC-B2-5545-9).*

Virginia Rappe was born on July 7, 1891 to unwed mother Mabel Rappe in New York City. Mabel died when Virginia was 11, and Virginia was then raised by her grandmother in Chicago. At age 14, she began working as a commercial and art model in Chicago. In 1916, she relocated to San Francisco to pursue her career as an artist's model, where she met dress designer Robert Moscovitz and they became engaged. Shortly after the engagement, her fiancé was killed in a streetcar accident and she moved to Los Angeles. In early 1917, Rappe was hired by director Fred Balshofer and given a prominent role in his film, *Paradise Garden* opposite popular screen star Harold Lockwood. Balshofer then hired her again to costar with film newcomer, Rudolph Valentino in *Over the Rhine*, for which she was awarded the title of "Best Dressed Girl in Pictures." This film was not released until 1920, when Balshofer recut it and released it under the title *An Adventuress* and later in 1922 as *The Isle of Love*. While working at Mack Sennett Comedies Corporation, Rappe had numerous sexual relationships with cast and crew members and gained a reputation as a party girl. In 1919, she began a relationship with director/producer Henry Lehrman; the two eventually became engaged. She appeared in at least four films for Lehrman: *His Musical Sneeze*, *A Twilight Baby*, *Punch of the Irish* and *A Game Lady*. Virginia Rappe and Roscoe Arbuckle's path's were about to cross at a luxurious San Francisco hotel. The tragedy and unfortunate circumstances that were about to unfold brought an end to the very profitable and promising film career of Arbuckle and resulted in an early grave for Rappe.

Virginia Rappe (circa, 1920). *Courtesy of the Library of Congress, Prints and Photographs.*

On September 5, 1921, Arbuckle took a break from his hectic film schedule and drove to San Francisco with two friends, Lowell Sherman and Fred Fischbach. The three checked into three rooms 1219 (Arbuckle & Fischbach), 1220 (empty) and 1221 (Sherman) at the St. Francis Hotel. They had rented room 1220 as a party room and invited several women to the suite (one of whom was Virginia Rappe). During the carousing, Rappe was found seriously ill in room 1219 and was examined by the hotel doctor. He concluded that her symptoms were mostly caused by intoxication; she was given a dose of morphine to calm her nerves. She was not hospitalized until two days after the incident. In fact, Rappe was already an ill woman. She suffered from chronic cystitis, a condition that flared up dramatically whenever she drank alcohol.

At the hospital, Rappe's companion at the party, Maude Delmont, told doctor's that Arbuckle had raped her friend. The doctor examined Rappe but found no evidence to substantiate the claim. Rappe died one day after her hospitalization of peritonitis, caused by a ruptured bladder. Delmont then told the police the fanciful story that Arbuckle had raped Rappe. A police investigation concluded that it was possible that Arbuckle's overweight body could have caused Rappe's bladder to rupture during sexual intercourse. Rappe's manager, Al Semnacker, accused Arbuckle of using a piece of ice to simulate sex with her, which led to the injuries. By the time the story was reported in newspapers, the object had evolved into being a Coca-Cola or champagne bottle, instead of a piece of ice. This rumor, however, was never proven. In fact, witnesses testified that Arbuckle rubbed the ice on Rappe's stomach to ease her abdominal pain. Arbuckle denied any wrongdoing but soon after was arrested and charged with murder.

The St. Francis Hotel, Union Square in San Francisco (present day).

Arbuckle's trial was a major media event; exaggerated and sensationalized stories in William Randolph Hearst's nationwide newspaper chain damaged his career. The newspapers portrayed him as a gross lecher who used his weight to overpower innocent girls. In reality, Arbuckle was a good-natured man who was so shy with women that he was regarded by those who knew him as: the most chaste man in pictures. The resulting scandal destroyed Arbuckle's career and his personal life, and studio executives ordered Arbuckle's industry friends not to publicly speak up for him.

The prosecutor, San Francisco District Attorney Matthew Brady, an intensely ambitious man, who planned to run for governor, made public pronouncements of Arbuckle's guilt. Brady at first used Maude Delmont as his star witness during the indictment hearing. Although the judge threatened Brady with dismissal of the case, Brady refused to allow Delmont, the only witness accusing Arbuckle, to take the stand and testify. Delmont had a long criminal record with convictions for racketeering, bigamy, fraud, and extortion. The defense had also obtained a letter from Delmont admitting to a plan to extort payment from Arbuckle. In view of Delmont's constantly changing story, her testimony would have ended any chance of going to trial. Ultimately, the judge found no evidence of rape. After hearing testimony from one of the party guests, Zey Prevon, that Rappe told her "Roscoe hurt me" on her deathbed; the judge decided that Arbuckle could be charged with first degree murder. Brady had originally planned to seek the death penalty. The charge was later reduced to manslaughter.

Maude Delmont. *Courtesy of the Herald Examiner Collection/ Los Angeles Public Library, (LC-USZ62-136850).*

Arbuckle was then arrested on the charges of manslaughter and the first trial began on November 14, 1921. At the beginning of the trial Arbuckle told his already estranged wife, Minta Durfee, that he did not harm Rappe; she believed him and appeared regularly in the courtroom to support him. The prosecutions first witness included Betty Campbell, a model, who attended the September 5th party and testified that she saw Arbuckle with a smile on his face hours after the alleged rape occurred; Grace Hultson, a local nurse who testified it was very likely that Arbuckle did rape Rappe and bruise her body in the process; and Dr. Edward Heinrich, a local criminologist who claimed he found Arbuckle's fingerprints smeared with Rappe's blood on room 1219's bathroom door. Heinrich's claim to have found fingerprints was cast into doubt after Arbuckle's defense attorney produced the St. Francis hotel maid, who testified that she had cleaned the room before the investigation even took place. Dr. Arthur Beardslee, the hotel doctor, testified that an external force seemed to have damaged the bladder. He admitted that Rappe had never mentioned being assaulted while he was treating her. The defense was furthermore able to get nurse Hultson to admit that the rupture of Rappe's bladder could very well have been a result of cancer, and that the bruises on her body could also have been a result of the heavy jewelry she was wearing that evening. The pathology experts testified that while the bladder had ruptured, there was evidence of chronic inflammation and no evidence of any pathological changes preceding the rupture; in other words, there was no external cause for the rupture.

Taking the witness stand, Arbuckle was simple, direct, and unflustered in both direct and cross examination. In his testimony, Arbuckle claimed that Rappe, whom he testified he had known for five or six years, came into the party room around midnight, and that some time afterward, Mae Taub asked him for a ride into town, so he went to his room (1219) to change his clothes and discovered Rappe vomiting in the toilet. Arbuckle then claimed Rappe told him she felt ill and asked to lie down, and that he carried her into the bedroom and asked a few of the party guests to help treat her. To calm Rappe down, they placed her in a bathtub of cool water. Arbuckle and Fischbach then took her to room 1227 and called the hotel manager and doctor. After the doctor declared Rappe was just drunk, Arbuckle then drove Taub to town. The courtroom spectators, most of whom were fans and supporters of Arbuckle, reportedly booed and jeered at Brady and most of the prosecution witnesses during the entire trial, and they also reportedly stood, cheered and applauded for Arbuckle after he testified.

The prosecution then presented medical descriptions of Rappe's bladder as evidence that she had an illness. In his testimony, Arbuckle denied he had any knowledge of Rappe's illness. The prosecution then noted that Arbuckle refused to call a doctor, and argued that he refused to do so because he knew of Rappe's illness and saw a perfect opportunity to kill her. After over two weeks of testimony, with sixty prosecution and defense witnesses, including eighteen doctors who testified about Rappe's illness, the defense rested. On December 4, 1921, the jury returned deadlocked after forty-four straight hours of deliberation with a 10–2 not guilty verdict, and a mistrial was declared.

The second trial began on January 11, 1922 with a different jury, but with the same legal defense and prosecution as well as the same presiding judge. The same evidence was presented, but this time one of the witnesses, Zey Prevon, testified that district attorney Brady had forced her to lie. Another witness who claimed Arbuckle had bribed him turned out to be an escaped prisoner charged with assaulting an eight-year-old girl, and who was looking for a sentence reduction. Heinsen took back his earlier testimony and testified that the case's fingerprint evidence was likely faked. Further, in contrast to the first trial, Rappe's history of promiscuity and heavy drinking was detailed. The second trial also discredited some major evidence such as the identification of Arbuckle's fingerprints on the hotel bedroom door. The defense was so convinced of an acquittal that Arbuckle was not called to testify. The defense barely made a closing argument to the jury. However, the jury interpreted the refusal to let Arbuckle testify as a sign of guilt. After over forty hours of deliberation, the jury returned on February 3, deadlocked with a 9–3 guilty verdict. Another mistrial was declared.

Roscoe "Fatty" Arbuckle on trial for manslaughter in San Francisco, November 18, 1921. Seated left to right; T.M. Smalevitch, Milton Cohen, Roscoe Arbuckle, and Arbuckle's brother. Standing left to right; Gavin McNab and Charles Brennan. *Courtesy of the Library of Congress, Prints and Photographs, (LC-USZ62-63393).*

By the time of the third trial, Arbuckle's films had been banned, and newspapers had been filled for seven months with stories of alleged Hollywood orgies, murder, and sexual perversion. The third trial began on March 13, 1922, and this time the defense took no chances and used aggressive defense tactics, tearing apart the prosecution's case. This time, Arbuckle testified and maintained his denials in his testimony about his version of the events at the hotel party. The defense also managed to use more evidence about Virginia Rappe's lurid past, and reviewed how the district attorney, Matthew Brady fell for the outlandish charges of Maude Delmont, whom defense attorney's described in his long, closing statement as "the complaining witness who never witnessed." Another hole in the prosecution's case was opened when its star witness, Zey Pevron, was discovered to have fled the country. On April 12, the jury began deliberations and it took only six minutes to return a unanimous not guilty verdict, five of those minutes were spent writing a statement of apology, a public apology unprecedented in American justice. The jury statement as read by the jury foreman stated:

> Acquittal is not enough for Roscoe Arbuckle. We feel that a great injustice has been done to him... there was not the slightest proof adduced to connect him in any way with the commission of a crime. He was manly throughout the case and told a straightforward story which we all believe. We wish him success and hope that the American people will take the judgment of fourteen men and women that Roscoe Arbuckle is entirely innocent and free from all blame.

Some experts later concluded that Rappe's bladder might also have ruptured as a result of an abortion she might have had a short time before the September 5, 1921 party. However, Rappe's organs had been destroyed and it was now impossible to test for pregnancy. Because alcohol was consumed at the party, Arbuckle was forced to plead guilty to one count of violating the Volstead Act, and had to pay a $500 fine. At the time of his acquittal, Arbuckle owed $700,000 in legal fees to his attorneys for the three criminal trials, and had lost his house and his cars to pay off some of the debt. Although cleared of all criminal charges, the scandal and trials had greatly damaged his popularity among the general public, and Will H. Hays, who served as the head of the newly-formed Motion Pictures Producers and Distributors of America, Hollywood censor board, cited Arbuckle as an example of the poor morals in Hollywood. On April 18, 1922, six days after Arbuckle's acquittal, Hays banned Arbuckle from ever working in U.S. movies again. He had also requested that all showings and bookings of Arbuckle films be canceled, and exhibitors complied. In December of the same year, Hays elected to lift the ban, but Arbuckle was not able to secure work as an actor for a long time. Arbuckle tried returning to filmmaking, but industry resistance to distributing his pictures continued to linger after his acquittal. He retreated into alcoholism. In the words of his first wife, "Roscoe only seemed to find solace and comfort in a bottle." Good friend, Buster Keaton attempted to help Arbuckle by giving him work on his films. In 1932, Arbuckle signed a contract with Warner Bros., under his own name in a series of two-reel comedies. These shorts constitute the only recordings of his voice. Roscoe Arbuckle had finished filming the last of these films on June 28, 1933. The next day he was signed by Warner Bros., to make a feature-length film. He reportedly said, "This is the best day of my life." He suffered a heart attack later that night and died in his sleep. He was forty-six. Arbuckle was cremated, and his ashes were scattered at sea.

Virginia Rappe was laid to rest on September 19, 1921, at Hollywood Cemetery (now known as Hollywood Forever). Her burial ceremony was brief and simple. A huge crowd of curiosity seekers attempted to gain entrance to the cemetery but was turned back at the gate. The chapel at the cemetery was filled with personal friends of the dead actress. Notable attendees were director Norman Taurog, actors Oliver Hardy, David Kirkland, and Frank Coleman. Maude Delmont did not attend the service but sent an arrangement of flowers; the card read, "To Virginia; you know I love you as though you were my sister." Rappe's grave is found along the lake in the Garden of Legends, she rest for eternity next to her fiancé, film director, Henry Lehrman.

Virginia Rappe gravesite at Hollywood Forever Cemetery.

The Mysterious Murder of Director William Desmond Taylor

(Los Angeles, 1922)

At 7:30 a.m. on the morning of February 2, 1922, the body of successful movie director William Desmond Taylor was found inside his bungalow at the Alvarado Court Apartments, 404-B South Alvarado Street, in the Westlake Park area of downtown Los Angeles, California, which was then known as a trendy and affluent neighborhood. A crowd gathered inside and someone identifying himself as a doctor stepped forward, made a cursory examination of the body, declared the victim had died of a stomach hemorrhage and was never seen again, perhaps owing to his own embarrassment. When doubts later arose, the body was rolled over and it was discovered the forty-nine year old film director had been shot in the back. In Taylor's pockets was a wallet holding $78, a silver cigarette case, a pocket watch, and an ivory toothpick. A two carat diamond ring was on his finger. A large but undetermined sum of cash which Taylor had shown to his accountant the day before was missing and apparently never accounted for. After some investigation, the time of Taylor's death was set at 7:50 p.m., the previous evening, February 1, 1922. While being interviewed by the police five days after the director's body was found, actress Mary Miles Minter said that, following the murder, a friend, director, and actor, Marshall Neilan, told her that Taylor had made several highly "delusional" statements about some of his social acquaintances (including her) during the weeks before his death. She also said Neilan thought Taylor had recently gone "insane."

William Desmond Taylor was born William Cunningham Deane-Tanner on April 26, 1872 in Carlow, Ireland. Taylor was one of four children of a retired British Army officer, Kearns Deane-Tanner, and his wife, Jane. He came to the United States in 1890, at the age of 18. He briefly pursued an acting career in New York City before marrying Ethel May Hamilton on December 7, 1901; they divorced in 1912. He then found himself in Hollywood, changed his name to William Desmond Taylor, and found work as an actor, appearing opposite actress Margaret Gibson in numerous films. Taylor made his directorial debut in 1914 with *The Awakening*. Over the next few years, he directed more than fifty films that included some of the greatest stars of the silent film era, including Mary Pickford, Wallace Reid, Dustin Farnum, and Mary Miles Minter (who starred in the 1919 version of *Anne of Greene Gables*).

The night of Taylor's murder, neighbors reported hearing a gunshot. During the inquest that followed, several witnesses came forward, reporting that they had seen a young, dark-haired man leaving Taylor's house the night of February 1, and one of them not only saw the man, but heard the shot that killed Taylor. Despite a long list of potential suspects, nobody

William Desmond Taylor, Motion Picture Director. *Courtesy of the Herald Examiner Collection/ Los Angeles Public Library.*

was ever arrested or tried for the crime. As an unsolved crime, Taylor's murder has continued to intrigue and tantalize people. Over the years, conspiracy theorists have drawn up a long list of potential suspects. Most seem fairly outrageous, but the continuing curiosity illustrates our enduring attraction with both crime and Hollywood.

What was the motive behind Taylor's murder? One interesting theory that came out at the inquest involved the woman Taylor was seeing at the time of his death, actress Mabel Normand. She was a cocaine user, and Taylor had gone to the federal government for help in stopping the pushers who were selling her drugs. Seeing their business threatened this scenario goes, the pushers decided to hire a hit man to "silence" Taylor. Taylor had been a prominent member of the Hollywood set, giving and attending parties where liquor was served (this was during Prohibition), so the press made much of his so-called wild personal life. Coming as it did on the heels of the Fatty Arbuckle scandal, Taylor's murder spurred Hollywood to clean up its act. Will Hays became president of the newly formed Motion Picture Producers and Directors Association, and a new age of censorship and studio control was born in Hollywood.

More than a dozen individuals were eventually named as suspects by both the press and the police. Newspaper reports at the time were both overwhelmingly sensationalized and speculative, even fabricated. Many inaccuracies were carried forward, but overall, most accounts have consistently focused on six people as suspects and witnesses, although hundreds of people came forward to either admit involvement or knew something about the crime. Most were dismissed by police.

Faith Cole MacLean is widely believed to have seen the killer. She was the wife of actor Douglas MacLean and the couples were neighbors of Taylor. She was the most cooperative witness and no one else seemed to have seen or heard anything. She told law enforcement authorities that she was startled by a loud noise around 8 p.m., and that when she went to her front door to investigate, she came face-to-face with someone emerging from the front door of Taylor's home. This person was described by Mrs. MacLean as looking "like my idea of a motion picture burglar. "She recalled this person paused for a moment before turning and walking back through the door, as if having forgotten something, then re-emerged and flashed a smile at her before disappearing between the buildings. She went on to state that this person "dressed like a man, but walked like a woman." She also revealed that she saw actress Mabel Normand leave the Taylor residence about ten minutes before the alleged gunshots and also saw Mary Minter Miles at the bungalow the same evening. It was alleged that Taylor was having an affair with both actresses at the time of his murder. There were even whispers of another mistress, actress Zelda Crosby, but she committed suicide before police could question her about Taylor's death. As the list of suspects began to swell, the tawdry underworld of William Desmond Taylor's life began to unfold like a dime store novel.

The first suspect in Taylor's murder was Edward Sands, who had prior convictions for embezzlement, forgery, and other crimes. He had worked as Taylor's valet up until seven months before the murder. While Taylor was in Europe, the summer before his murder, Sands had forged Taylor's checks and wrecked his car. Later Sands burgled Taylor's bungalow, leaving footprints on the film director's bed. Following the murder, Edward Sands was never heard from again and some accounts claim that his body was found in the Sacramento River in the early 1930s.

A second suspect was Henry Peavey, who was Sands replacement valet, and was the person who found Taylor's body the morning of the murder. He also had a criminal record, which included arrests for vagrancy and public indecency. Taylor had recently put up bail for him and was due to appear in court on his behalf. Peavey repeatedly accused Mabel Normand of the murder and was initially suspected of the crime himself. Eight years later, in 1931, Peavey died in a San Francisco asylum, where he had been hospitalized for dementia.

Mabel Normand, Actress. *Courtesy of the Library of Congress, Prints and Photographs, George G. Bain Collection, (LC-B2-6010-8).*

A third suspect was Mabel Normand, a popular actress and a close friend of Taylor. It was widely speculated that she and Taylor had a romantic relationship. It was also alleged that she and Taylor fought on the night of his murder. She was seen leaving his home around 7:45 p.m., and was the last known person to see him alive. The police quickly dismissed her as a suspect. Ironically, she had starred in several films with actor Fatty Arbuckle, the other famous Hollywood scandal at the time. By the time of the Taylor and Arbuckle scandals, her film career had already began to slow and her reputation had already been tarnished by revelations of drug use. Although she continued to make films throughout the 1920s, her movie career was never quite the same. She died from tuberculosis on February 23, 1930 in Monrovia, California.

A fourth suspect was Mary Miles Minter; she was a popular actress and teen screen idol whose career had been guided by Taylor. Coded letters found in Taylor's home suggested that a romantic relationship between the two had started when she was seventeen. Although Minter said Taylor had been against their romance almost from the outset and had often declined to see her, the letters (which she had written in 1919) were at odds with her screen image as a modest young girl. Minter was vilified in the press.

She made four more films for Paramount, and when the studio failed to renew her contract, she received offers from many other producers. Never comfortable with her career as an actress, she declined them all, left Hollywood, and for the rest of her life proclaimed her love for Taylor. She died in obscurity in 1984.

Mary Minter, Actress. *Courtesy of the Library of Congress, Prints and Photographs, George G. Bain Collection, (LC-B2-5411-2).*

A fifth suspect was Charlotte Shelby, Mary Minter's mother. Like many "stage mothers" before and since, she has been described as consumed by wanton greed and manipulation over her daughter's career. Mary Miles Minter and her mother were bitterly divided by financial disputes and lawsuits for a time, but they later reconciled. Shelby's initial statements to police about the murder are still characterized as evasive and "obviously filled with lies" about both her daughter's relationship with Taylor and "other matters." Perhaps the most compelling bit of circumstantial evidence was that Shelby allegedly owned a rare .38 caliber hand gun and unusual bullets very similar to the kind which killed Taylor. After this later became public, she reportedly threw the pistol into a Louisiana bayou. Shelby knew the Los Angeles district attorney socially and spent years outside the United States in an effort to avoid official inquiries by his successor and press coverage related to the murder. In 1938, her other daughter, actress Margaret Shelby (who was by then suffering from both clinical depression and alcoholism), openly accused her mother of the murder during an argument. Shelby was widely suspected of the crime and was a favorite suspect of many amateur sleuths who have speculated that Shelby was torn by feelings of maternal protection for her daughter and her own attraction to Taylor. Although (like Sands) Shelby feared being tried for the murder, she was never prosecuted. Almost twenty years after the murder, Los Angeles district attorney Buron Fitts concluded there wasn't any evidence for an indictment of Shelby and recommended that the remaining evidence and case files be retained on a permanent basis (all of these materials subsequently disappeared). Shelby died in 1957 and Fitts, in ill-health, committed suicide in 1973.

A sixth suspect was Margaret Gibson; she was a film actress, who worked with Taylor when he first came to Hollywood. In 1917, she was indicted, tried, and acquitted on charges equivalent to prostitution and changed her professional name to Patricia Palmer. In 1923, Gibson was arrested and jailed on extortion charges, which were later dropped. Gibson was in Los Angeles at the time of Taylor's murder, but there is no record of her name ever being mentioned in connection with the investigation. Soon after the murder, she got work in a number of films produced by Paramount Pictures, Taylor's studio at the time of his death. One of these films was among the last made by Mary Miles Minter. Gibson (in her words) "fled" the United States to the Far East in 1934, where she married her husband, who worked for Mobil Oil. However, she returned to Los Angeles in 1940 for medical reasons. Her husband, Elbert Lewis, died in a March 1942 Japanese attack on an oil refinery in Malaysia. It is alleged that on her death bed (October 21, 1964), Gibson confessed that she had shot Taylor. According to an account first published by the widely cited newsletter, *Taylorology* in 1999, on October 21, 1964, while still living in Hollywood, Gibson suffered a heart attack. A recent Catholic and sensing that she was dying, she asked for a priest and then confessed to neighbors that on the evening of February 1, 1922, she shot and killed Hollywood film director William Desmond Taylor. She may have made statements about a motive but in 1999, the only surviving witness to this incident, wrote that at the time, she was distracted by the immediate crisis of her heart attack and had no knowledge of who William Desmond Taylor was or what she was talking about. As a result, he could not remember further details about what Gibson said as she lay dying. The witness did recall Gibson, said she had been "nearly caught" and had "fled the country."

Gibson had apparently made similar remarks once before during the early 1960s. While watching a local television program which featured a short segment about the unsolved murder forty years earlier, Gibson "became hysterical and blurted out that she'd killed him and thought it was long forgotten."

At the age of 15, during the spring and summer seasons of 1910, Gibson worked as a stage performer in Denver, Colorado at a vaudeville theater owned by Alex Pantages. At that same time, Taylor also worked as an actor at a nearby theater. By the age of 18, she had appeared opposite William Desmond Taylor in four films, including *The Kiss.* As mentioned earlier, Gibson was in Los Angeles at the time of the murder but her name was never mentioned during the investigation and no surviving documentation refers to any association between her and Taylor after 1914.

Gibson's reported confession does not conflict with the known historical record. Given her documented arrest record along with Taylor's reportedly odd remarks in the weeks leading to his murder, the inferred motive would have been somehow related to blackmail in the wake of the Arbuckle scandal, during which the private lives of most Hollywood celebrities could easily fall under highly sensationalized public scrutiny. (The evening after Taylor's body was found, the *Los Angeles Evening Herald* carried news of Taylor's murder as a banner headline with an article about the ongoing Arbuckle trial immediately below.) Through a combination of poor crime scene management and apparent corruption, much physical evidence was immediately lost, and the rest vanished over the years. Various theories were put forward after the murder and in the years since, along with the publication of many books claiming to have identified the murderer, but no hard evidence was ever uncovered to link the crime to a particular individual. Margaret Gibson's thoroughly documented background and the report of her dying confession in the Hollywood Hills attracted the attention of film historians, but aside from circumstantial evidence, no independent confirmation has emerged.

Were the police actually unable to unravel the mystery? Or was there a cover-up? To this day, the murder of William Desmond Taylor remains unsolved. It was always said that around Hollywood the true identity of the killer was an open secret. Who really shot Taylor and why? This question most likely will never be fully answered, and today, the murder of William Desmond Taylor remains one of Hollywood's most enduring murder mysteries.

William Desmond Taylor's crypt at Hollywood Forever Cemetery.

Hollywood legacy: A spate of newspaper-driven Hollywood scandals during the early 1920s included Taylor's murder, the Arbuckle trial and the drug-related deaths of such stars as Olive Thomas, Wallace Reid, Barbara La Marr, and Jeanne Eagles, which prompted Hollywood studios to begin writing contracts with "morality clauses." This allowed for the dismissal of contracted stars who breached the clause. The 1950 film *Sunset Boulevard* with William Holden and Gloria Swanson featured a fictional, aging silent screen actress named Norma Desmond whose name was taken from Taylor's middle name and Mabel Normand's last name as a way to resonate with the widely publicized scandals of almost thirty years before. Gore Vidal's 1990 novel, *Hollywood*, features a fictionalized account of the Taylor murder. William Desmond Taylor directed or acted in over eighty films, most of which are believed to be lost. His former home and murder site is now a parking lot of a local discount store.

The Tiger Woman, Clara Phillips

(Los Angeles, 1922-1923)

Clara Phillips, after murdering her husband's latest lady friend whom she beat to death with a claw hammer, returned home clad in clothes still soaked with the blood of her victim. She threw her arms around her husband and said, delightedly: "I have killed the one you love most in this world. Now I'm going to cook you the best supper you ever had." Phillips, dubbed "Tiger Woman" by the Los Angeles news media was ultimately convicted in the grisly murder of her husband's paramour, Alberta Meadows, a beautiful, twenty-one year old widow.

During the early part of the 1920s, when oil wells were springing up across Los Angeles, Phillips' husband, Amour was beginning a career as an oil stock salesman. Charming and handsome, he bought expensive suits and a big house, all on credit for his 23-year-old wife, whom he had married when she was a teenager. As his credit began to dwindle and other problems arose, he started turning his attentions to a seductive bank clerk, Alberta Meadows. Clara Phillips had been a chorus girl, Santa Monica bathing beauty, and briefly in the employ of the Eclipse Film Company, and she began spending her days secretly following her husband. She soon found out who her husband had been seeing and decided what to do about it. She stopped by a dime store and bought a claw hammer. The next day, July 12, 1922, she told a friend, former chorus girl Peggy Caffee, of her pain and outrage over her husband's infidelities. The two women decided to drown their sorrows in alcohol at a Long Beach speak-easy, before catching a cab back to Los Angeles. By then, a bit unsteady on their feet, the two waited outside the First National Bank building at 9th and Main Streets in downtown Los Angeles for Meadows to finish work. When Meadows saw them, she recognized Clara, who coolly asked Meadows to drive them to the house of Clara's sister in Montecito Heights, then a new subdivision below a hilltop in northeast Los Angeles. At the end of Montecito Drive, then a winding dirt road, Clara angrily accused Meadows of having an affair with her husband Amour. Meadows pulled her car to the side of the road and then denied any inappropriate activity. Enraged by this denial, Clara then proceeded to punch Meadows in the head, knocking her out of the car. Fleeing down the hill, Meadows fell when the heel of her shoe broke; Phillips caught her, hoisted the claw hammer and brought it straight down into Meadows' face, over and over again. A police detective would later describe the condition of Meadows body as looking as if she had been mauled by a tiger. That statement along with sensational newspaper headlines would forever dub Clara Phillips as the infamous "Tiger Woman."

Amour L. Phillips, circa 1932. *Courtesy of the Herald Examiner Collection/ Los Angeles Public Library.*

Peggy Caffee, a key witness in the case against her frien[d] Clara Phillips, who brutally attacked and killed Alberta Meadows. *Courtesy of the Herald Examiner Collection/ Los Angeles Public Library.*

Following the murder, Clara Phillips calmly got back into Meadows' car and drove to her home on West 53rd Street. There she rushed into the house, crying out to her husband "I've killed the one you loved best. You'll never see her again." After calming down and cleaning up, it was decided by Amour that Clara needed to leave the area. He helped her to escape the following morning by purchasing a one-way train ticket to El Paso. After seeing his wife off at the train depot, guilt got the best of him and he went to the police, where he told them everything. Los Angeles police detectives issued an all-points-bulletin for Clara's arrest, at 11 a.m., she was apprehended at the Tucson, Arizona train depot. She was eventually extradited and returned to Los Angeles, where she stood trial for the murder of Alberta Meadows.

In a sensational headline-grabbing trial which lasted several months, Clara plead innocent by reason of insanity and her defense team engaged five psychiatrists, who testified that the hammer wielding 23-year-old woman had the mental capacity of an eight-year-old child, and that she was also susceptible to epileptic fits, which could account for her violent rages (apparently epilepsy was a viable murder defense in 1922). Clara gave her version of events from the witness stand. She said that it was her friend, Peggy, who had struck the fatal blow but was at a loss to explain the bruising to her hands and the fingernail scratches covering her arms and legs. Even with such damning evidence, public opinion began to sway in her favor. Some of the jurors were convinced by her story because, during their deliberations, they became deadlocked. Most of the eight men voted for acquittal, three of the four women voted for conviction. The jurors eventually reached a compromise decision, finding Clara guilty of second degree murder; she was subsequently sentenced to serve from ten years to life in prison. After the verdict Clara reportedly called her conviction an "unfair deal."

Clara Phillips the infamous "Tiger Woman" sitting in front of her jail cell, 1922. *Courtesy of the Los Angeles Times Photographic Archives/ University of California, Los Angeles.*

Los Angeles County Court House, 1891-1932. *Courtesy of the Los Angeles Public Library.*

In the early morning hours of December 5, 1922, while awaiting transport to San Quentin, in one of the boldest and most sensational jail breaks ever recorded, Clara Phillips escaped from the Los Angeles County jail. She cut the bars of her cell, squeezed through the tiny window, lowered herself by rope to the roof of an adjoining building, crossed the roof to a fire escape and then disappeared into the night. At least that was the story made available to the media. It was later learned that she had been aided in her escape by Jesse Carson, whose motives for assisting her remain unclear.

A self-described adventurer and South American revolutionary, Carson was more likely to have been a cattle thief and small-time criminal. In any case, Clara and Jesse made their way to Mexico where she was reunited with her younger sister, Etta Mae Jackson, and the threesome then headed off to Tegucigalpa, Honduras. There were dozens of "Tiger Woman" sightings from Mexico to Wyoming, none of which panned out. After being on the loose for over four months, Los Angeles police received a tip that Clara was in Honduras. Police were able to locate her hideout and she was arrested and returned to the United States. She was then sent to San Quentin to serve out her sentence.

Following her capture, Clara claimed that she had been the victim and that her so-called escape was actually a kidnapping. According to Clara, Carson had forced her to flee her cell at gun point. Carson was never held to answer for his part in Clara's escape. Ultimately, Clara Phillips would serve twelve years in prison, losing some of her good behavior time, when it was revealed that she and a male convict were exchanging graphic love notes. In 1938, she filed for a divorce from Amour, stating that she was in love with another man. Clara stated that she intended to remarry, but refused to divulge the name of her husband-to-be. She moved to the East Coast and vanished from public view.

Alberta Meadows was laid to rest in the Meadow family plot at Forest Lawn Glendale in a private service held on July 19, 1922. Today, her unmarked grave is found below the Great Mausoleum in the Slumberland lawn section.

On December 5, 1922, Clara Phillips, the so called "Tiger Woman," escaped from the Los Angeles County Jail, while awaiting transport to San Quentin after her murder conviction. The arrows show her escape route. *Courtesy of the Herald Examiner Collection/ Los Angeles Public Library.*

The Unexplained Death of Studio Mogul Thomas Ince

(Los Angeles, 1924)

William Randolph Hearst was beside himself at the newspaper headlines detailing the activities of his adored mistress, Marion Davies, and Hollywood screen icon Charlie Chaplin. The pair was in Paris, France, and competing newspapers had caught wind of Chaplin's romantic pursuit of Ms. Davies. The duo was spotted at local night spots dancing and gazing adoringly into each other's eyes. Hearst was humiliated by this; he had given Marion everything except a marriage proposal. But even he wasn't powerful enough to divorce his wife, who he also adored. He had created a newspaper empire that gave him more power than heads of state. He had just a few years earlier been instrumental in turning public opinion against popular actor, Roscoe "Fatty" Arbuckle.

In 1917, Hearst met a struggling young actress named Marion Davies. At the time, she had only made one film, *Runaway Romany,* but reviews were not favorable. Hearst was immediately infatuated with the blonde beauty and professed that he would personally make her into a star. Davies almost immediately began to live openly with Hearst at his hilltop mansion at San Simeon, California. The news of their love affair was suspiciously kept out of the press.

In 1919, Hearst made an arrangement with Adolph Zukor, head of Paramount Pictures to release Marion Davies' films. He invested thousands of dollars into these movies; all were lavish historical dramas and most never made a profit. Despite his enthusiasm for her films, it has been estimated that Hearst lost nearly seven million dollars producing her movies. He allowed Davies to spend free willingly and she often threw extravagant parties at San Simeon and at Hearst's beach house in Los Angeles.

By 1924, rumors began to swirl about a supposed romance between Davies and Charlie Chaplin. This was no secret to Hearst; he had hired a private detective to follow his mistress and the movie icon. Although, Hearst was jealous, he made no attempt to end the relationship. He loved Davies too much to jeopardize their affair and he also admired Chaplin's acting ability.

In 1924, Charlie Chaplin's life was in disarray, and Marion helped make his life a little more manageable. On the surface, Chaplin was the biggest name in Hollywood, but financially he was in trouble. He was also in legal trouble with allegations of statutory rape. He took solace in the arms of Davies and the pair met secretly, usually at Chaplin's home. They took every opportunity to get together and only occasionally were seen in public. Chaplin was in awe of his gorgeous blonde companion. The only time the pair was ever seen together publicly was in Paris, France. William Randolph Hearst had seen enough and set out to end the Davies/Chaplin tryst once and for all.

William Randolph Hearst (circa, 1906). *Courtesy of the Library of Congress, Prints and Photographs, (LC-USZ62-49253).*

Marion Davies, Actress. *Courtesy of the Library of Congress, Prints and Photographs, George G. Bain Collection, (LC-B2-5798-3).*

Charlie Chaplin, Actor (circa, 1910). *Courtesy of the Library of Congress, Prints and Photographs, George G. Bain Collection, (LC-B2-3766-11).*

On November 6, 1924, Chaplin received an invitation from Hearst to join him on his yacht, the *Oneida*, for a fun-filled cruise to San Diego and Baja Mexico to commence on November 15, 1924. Marion Davies was also invited on this little jaunt. The same invitation arrived at the home of studio head, Thomas H. Ince. He, like many of his Hollywood cronies, had begun his career as an actor but soon turned his talents to producing movies rather than act in them. Ince was born on November 6, 1882 in Newport, Rhode Island into a family of stage actors. Ince first appeared on the stage at age 6 and then worked with a number of stock companies. He made his Broadway debut in 1898 when he was 15. He met his wife, Biograph contract actress Elinor "Nell" Kershaw, when they appeared together in a roadway show, *For Love's Sweet Sake* in 1906. They were married a year later. With his stage career a failure, however, Ince felt he was headed nowhere as an actor. Through his wife's connections, Ince got a job with Biograph in New York.

In 1910, a chance encounter in New York with an old employee from his acting troupe led Ince to some work at the Independent Motion Picture Company. That same year he was given an opportunity to direct, when a director at IMP was unable to complete work on a small film. In a precocious moment of bravado he advanced the idea of working full time in that capacity to IMP's owner Carl Laemmle. Impressed with the younger man's pugnacity, Laemmle hired him on the spot sending him to Cuba to make films out of the reach of the Motion Pictures Patent Company (the trust that was attempting to crush all independent production companies and corner the market on film production). Ince's output, however, was small. Although he tackled many different subjects, he was strongly drawn to dramas. He wanted to achieve the sort of spectacular effects accomplished with minimal facilities that D.W. Griffith had done. This, he believed, could only be accomplished in Hollywood.

In September 1911, in an attempt to convey the appearance of a successful director by wearing a borrowed suit and a diamond ring he had also borrowed from a local jeweler, Ince walked into the offices of Charles O. Baumann, at the New York Motion Picture Company, which had recently decided to establish a West Coast studio to make westerns. The ruse worked, and Ince was offered $100 a week to go to California. He arrived at NYMP's small studio in November and began his first steps to revolutionize the filmmaking process as we know it today. He settled upon a 460-acre tract of land known as Bison Ranch located at Sunset Boulevard and Pacific Coast Highway in the Santa Monica Hills which he rented by the day. By 1912, he had earned enough money to purchase the ranch and was granted permission by NYMP to lease another 18,000 acres in the Palisades Highlands stretching 7.5 miles. It was here that Ince built his own studio (which he characteristically named "Inceville"). The studio was the first of its kind in that it featured stages, offices, labs, commissaries (which had to be large enough to serve hundreds of workers their noonday meal), dressing rooms, props houses, elaborate sets, and other necessities all in one location.

Ince gradually exercised even more control over the film production process as a director-general. In 1913 alone, he made over 150 movies, mostly Westerns, thereby anchoring the popularity of the genre for decades. Two of his most successful films were among his first, *War on the Plains* (1912) and *Custer's Last Fight* (1912), which featured many Indians who had actually been in battle. Even though he was the first producer-director and directed most of his early productions, by 1913, Ince ceased full-time directing to concentrate on producing.

By 1915, Ince was one of the best known producer-directors in Hollywood. It was around this time that he moved his "Inceville" Studios from the beach to Culver City and partnered with D.W. Griffith and Mack Sennett forming the Triangle Motion Picture Company. With Ince as its vice-president, Triangle announced that it would focus on feature-length epic and quality dramas. Triangle was one of the first vertically integrated film companies. By combining production, distribution, and theater operations under one roof, the partners created the most dynamic studio in Hollywood. They attracted the greatest directors and stars of the day and produced some of the most enduring films of the silent era. Though Ince had many credits as a director in this time period, he really only supervised the production of most of these pictures, working primarily as an executive and producer. For a short period of time Ince joined competitor Adolph Zukor to form Paramount Pictures. However, he yearned to go back to running his own studio.

On July 19, 1918, following Samuel Goldwyn's acquisition of the Triangle lot, he purchased a fourteen-acre property at 9336 West Washington Boulevard on an option basis from Culver along with a $132,000 loan. Thus was formed "Thomas H. Ince Studios," which operated there from 1919 to 1924. In his last years, Ince drifted away from westerns in favor of social dramas. He made a few more important films. One was a prestige version of *Anna Christie* (1923).

On Saturday, November 15, 1924, Hearst's lavish 280-foot yacht, the *Oneida*, set sail from San Pedro, California, and headed for San Diego. Among his guests that weekend were his mistress, Marion Davies, silent film star Charlie Chaplin, newspaper columnist Louella Parsons, and other assorted actors and actresses. Ironically, Ince, the guest of honor as it was his 42nd birthday, was late due to a production deal he was negotiating with Hearst's International Film Corporation and the yacht left without him. Ince finished up his business in Los Angeles and took a train to San Diego where he joined the guests the next morning.

At dinner that Sunday night, the group enthusiastically celebrated his birthday. Some time later, Ince suffered an acute bout of indigestion on the yacht. Determining that Ince was quite ill, the producer was taken from the yacht by water taxi and brought back ashore in San Diego, accompanied by Dr. Goodman, still a licensed, though non-practicing physician, then quickly put on a train bound for Los Angeles. However, while enroute, Ince's condition worsened. At Del Mar, he was removed from the train and taken to a hotel where he was promptly given medical treatment by Dr. T. A. Parker and a nurse. Ince informed them he had drunk liquor on the Hearst yacht. Afterward, he was taken to his home in Hollywood, where the next day, November 19, 1924, he succumbed to a heart disorder.

Less than forty-eight hours after leaving the *Oneida*, Ince had died at his estate in Benedict Canyon, officially of a heart attack. Dr. Ida Cowan Glasgow, his personal physician, signed the death certificate citing heart failure as the cause of death. The front page of the Wednesday morning Los Angeles Times, however, told another story: '"Movie Producer Shot on Hearst Yacht!" These headlines that mysteriously vanished in the evening edition. Without further ado, Ince's body was cremated, after which his widow, Nell, soon left for Europe. The first stories in Hearst's newspapers about Ince's death claimed the producer had fallen ill while visiting the Hearst Ranch in San Simeon and had been rushed home by ambulance, dying in the bosom of his family. The rumor mill in Hollywood immediately went to work. Several conflicting stories began circulating about the incident, often revolving around a claim that Hearst shot Ince in the head by mistake.

The story goes that Hearst suspected that Davies and Chaplin were secretly lovers. In order to keep tabs on the two, he invited them both on board the yacht. Supposedly, he found the couple in a compromising situation and went for his gun. Davies' screams awakened, Ince who rushed to the scene. A scuffle ensued, followed by a gunshot and Ince took the bullet for Chaplin. A second version of the story had Davies and Ince alone in the galley late Sunday night. Ince, who suffered from ulcers, was supposedly looking for something to ease his upset stomach when Hearst walked in. Mistaking Ince for Chaplin, Hearst shot him. A third version tells of a struggle over a gun below decks between unidentified passengers. The gun fired accidentally and the bullet ripped through a plywood partition straight into Ince's room where it struck him. Whether Ince was killed in a fit of jealousy or by accident, the story stuck. Many believed Hearst used his power and influence to cover up the incident.

One month after Ince's death, the rumors ran so rampant that the San Diego District Attorney was forced to take action. The D.A. only interviewed Dr. Goodman, who explained that once ashore, he and Ince caught a train heading back to Los Angeles. According to Goodman, Ince got sick on the train so they disembarked in Del Mar and checked into a hotel. Goodman then called a doctor, as well as Nell Ince. Concerned for her husband, Nell agreed to come to Del Mar immediately. Goodman, unclear whether Ince was suffering from a heart attack or indigestion, claimed he left Del Mar before Nell arrived. The D.A. quickly closed the investigation. Nonetheless, the rumors and suspicions continued to be fueled by the very people who celebrated with Ince that ill-fated weekend. Chaplin denied even being there, insisting that he, Hearst, and Davies visited the ailing Ince later that week. He also stated that Ince died two weeks after their visit. In reality, Ince was dead within forty-eight hours after leaving the *Oneida* with Chaplin attending the memorial services that Friday. Davies also added to the mystery in her attempts to deny the incident. She never acknowledged that Chaplin,

Parsons, or Goodman were aboard the yacht that weekend. She insisted that Nell Ince called her late Monday afternoon to inform her of Ince's death. When the *Oneida* sailed, Parsons was a New York movie columnist for one of Hearst's papers. After the Ince affair, Hearst gave her a lifetime contract and expanded her syndication. Hearst also provided Nell Ince with a trust fund just before she left for Europe. She refused an autopsy and ordered her husband's immediate cremation.

Despite all the excitement, the matter was eventually dropped. Hearst went on to live to the grand old age of eighty-eight. Marion Davies stayed by his side until the end. Four months after his death, she married for the first time. As for Nell Ince, she fared worse, the trust fund Hearst set up for her was wiped out in the Great Depression, and she ended up penniless. The circumstances of Ince's death tainted his standing as a pioneering filmmaker and diminished the way his role in the growth of the film industry was remembered. Even his studio could not survive his death. It shut down soon after he passed. As to whether Thomas Ince was murdered or died from a heart attack remains a matter of conjecture and speculation. No one is convinced of Hearst's story and only those involved know for certain what happened and all are dead now. Only the contradictory evidence remains, and too many unanswered questions ensure that, despite the official outcome, the death of Thomas Ince remains a mystery that might never be solved.

A Hollywood Love Triangle: The Tragic Death of Actor Ray Raymond

(Los Angeles, 1927)

Dorothy MacKaye, sometime actress and wife of actor and Broadway song-and-dance man, Ray Raymond, arrived home at their Hollywood apartment on the evening of April 16, 1927 to the house a wreck and her husband drunk, badly bruised, and bloodied. Raymond was a popular actor who made a name for himself in the *Ziegfeld Follies* of 1918 and 1919. He met and married MacKaye in 1920, while the two starred in *Blue Eyes* on Broadway. Dorothy MacKaye was born in Scotland and toured Britain's vaudeville circuit as a young girl. Primarily a comedic actress, she found her way to New York and was quite successful on Broadway where she appeared in nearly a dozen plays from 1917 to 1932.

MacKaye helped her badly injured husband into bed and despite his injuries and apparent drunken state, he was in good humor. He fell asleep but the next morning he didn't wake up. Two days later he was dead. Distraught and terror stricken, Dorothy called a personal friend, Dr. Walter Sullivan. He knew that a scandal would destroy her career. He attested that Ray had died from complications of past illnesses that included kidney trouble and cerebral hemorrhage, due to his alcoholism. That is how the official death finding would have stood, if police detectives had not questioned Ethel Lee, the Raymond's maid. She revealed that Raymond been involved in a fist fight with fellow actor Paul Kelly, several nights before his death. MacKaye had conveniently forgotten to report this little detail and suddenly, police were investigating a possible homicide.

Paul Kelly was born on August 8, 1899, in Brooklyn. His father owned Kelly's Café, a saloon that lay in the shadow of Vitagraph Studios. Paul's mother convinced a casting assistant to help her son get small acting roles. He was a cute kid, with red hair and freckles. In no time, he went from a $5-a-day extra to featured juvenile roles in silent comedy shorts. Kelly appeared in dozens of short films from 1910 to 1916. He matured into a handsome man, tall, and athletic with a thick mane of auburn hair. Kelly moved to Los Angeles and graduated to adult roles. He starred alongside actress Mary Miles Minter in *Anne of Green Gables* (1919), which was directed by the ill-fated William Desmond Taylor. Kelly became part of a fast-moving, heavy-drinking crowd of Hollywood types that included actress Dorothy MacKaye and her husband, Ray Raymond. Soon, Kelly and MacKaye developed a habit of sneaking off together until dawn. Rumors began to swirl that MacKaye and Kelly were lovers. Raymond warned Kelly to stay away from his wife, but Kelly showered MacKaye with love notes. He finally declared (to Raymond) his true love for MacKaye on the evening of April 16, 1927.

Kelly was very drunk when he arrived at the Raymond home that early evening in April. Almost immediately, Raymond (also drunk) confronted Kelly about the alleged affair with his wife. A heated discussion quickly turned violent. Raymond was really no match for the burly Kelly, who was taller and heavier. Kelly grabbed him by the throat, slapping his face over and over and slammed Raymond's head against a wall. The short fight was over, but the damage had already been done, Kelly quickly left, leaving Raymond bloodied and lying helpless on the living room floor.

Dorothy MacKaye may not have been an actual witness to the fight, but law enforcement believed she was concealing material information to protect her lover, and was considered a star witness for the prosecution. She told investigators that just before Ray died, he awoke and begged her not to let Kelly's name get dragged into things. He told her "I've had lots of fights in my life; this thing was just another stupid brawl and was as much my fault as his. So keep Paul's name out of it." This is the story she stuck to as the investigation heated up, but when Kelly was finally arrested and charged with Raymond's murder, MacKaye and Dr. Sullivan were also arrested and charged with feloniously concealing material facts of a murder.

Jurors and the public were anxious to learn about her feelings between her deceased husband and her movie star lover. Before official proceedings could begin Kelly had his charges reduced from murder to manslaughter, and his trial began in late May of 1927. MacKaye was determined not to help sway the jury by her feelings for either man, and she was resolute not to add to the scandal. She purposely remained distant during the entire court proceeding but what the public really wanted to know was she really in love with Paul Kelly? Extensively questioned by prosecutors as to her true feelings for Kelly, she responded matter-of-factly that he (Kelly), was nothing more than a good friend. Although, MacKaye did admit that she "partied around" with Kelly and did not think this was improper behavior for a married woman. She explained that "Hollywood is different; we accept violation of convention because it is alright for us. Professional people are less conventional, more sophisticated." With these words she found herself in a lot of trouble. The defense tried to control the harm made by these statements but the damage was already done. During the week long proceedings, numerous witnesses came forward to tell of outlandish and tawdry behavior of MacKaye and Kelly in the weeks leading up to Raymond's death. One such witness an employee of Kelly's described a "pajama party" at Kelly's home, in which he served the pair breakfast in bed. Other damning evidence that was admitted were dozens of "love letters," found under MacKaye's mattress. In these letters, Kelly professed his affections and love for MacKaye. As this and other facts began to mount, it became very clear that Kelly was going to be found guilty. On May 25, 1927, the jury brought back a verdict of guilty; he was convicted of manslaughter and sentenced to one to ten years, to be served at San Quentin Prison. MacKaye was not present when the verdict was read; she was giving a press conference at her hotel. When informed by her attorney of the judgment, she was quoted as whispering, "Well, that's that." Kelly did not attempt to appeal the conviction, stating, "I just want to get this over with."

With Kelly's conviction, MacKaye's troubles were only just beginning, her trial for obstruction of justice began in early June, and after a very quick trial, she was found guilty of the charges and sentenced from one to three years in prison. MacKaye stated after the verdict, "Because I kept my promise to my dying husband, a jury convicted me of compounding a felony." She was sent to the same prison as Kelly, but the two were never able to see one another. MacKaye was paroled for good behavior after serving less than a year of her sentence. Kelly kept his nose clean behind bars and he hoped to resurrect his film career with an early release. After serving a little over two years of his sentence, Kelly was also paroled for good behavior. Upon his release from prison, MacKaye was waiting, and the two eventually married in 1931. With sheer determination, Kelly was able to revive his film career and appeared in numerous B-movies, ironically, often played thugs, policemen, or prison wardens. In 1947, he won a Tony Award for his Broadway performance in *Command Decision*. He also starred alongside John Wayne in 1954's, *The High and the Mighty*.

Kelly and MacKaye were both quite successful in the years following the scandal, and their marriage and careers blossomed. Tragedy struck in early January of 1940, when MacKaye, while driving home late one night, lost control of her car, skidded off the road and ended up in a ditch. She had suffered severe internal injuries and died on January 5, 1940. She had no funeral and nothing was written about her passing in the newspapers. Her remains were quickly cremated and she was interred in an unknown and unmarked grave at Oakwood Memorial Park in Chatsworth, California, Paul Kelly quickly putting things behind him, married actress Claire Owen in 1941. He died from a heart attack on November 6, 1956 at his Beverly Hills home; he was fifty-seven. Ray Raymond's unassuming grave is found at Forest Lawn Memorial Park in Glendale.

The Murder of "Sunshine" Mabel

(Oakland, 1927)

Practically unknown in the annals of California's most heinous crimes is the dreadful story of the unsolved murder of teenager Mabel Mayer. This tragic tale panicked the citizens of Oakland for several weeks in the summer of 1927. The crime was so atrocious and mysterious, and struck so much fear into the community that for weeks following the crime parents were afraid to let their children out alone. The fear was amplified when law enforcement could not find the culprit, and this served to spread panic among the public. The clues were plentiful but they led nowhere and witnesses came forward with conflicting accounts of strange people who were seen with the dead girl hours before her killing. All of these stories conflicted with the evidence of the crime, and Guy H.B. Logan, prolific British writer of crime during the 1920s and 1930s, hauntingly wrote, "But the killer of Sunshine Mabel was never caught."

Fifteen year old Mabel Mayer lived with her parents, Mr. and Mrs. John Mayer at 2008 Eighty-Sixth Avenue in Oakland. On the morning of her slaying, July 2, 1927, Mabel left her parents home for a dentist appointment and a music lesson. After, she proceeded to Berkeley, to have dinner with the family of her uncle, Christian Mayer. It was arranged that she would stay the night there and was to be picked up the following morning by her father. All went off as scheduled until around 8 p.m. when Mabel's father phoned and suggested that she join him and her brother William, at a family friend's house to play cards. She agreed, and stated that she would come by train. Her brother William was to meet her at 10 p.m. at the Blanche Street train station. Mabel never arrived. Mr. Mayer was not unduly alarmed by this, and he thought that she had changed her mind and stayed at her uncle's for the night.

At 8:45 p.m., Mabel was dropped off by her uncle at the train station, but it was learned that the train had already left. She asked to be driven by her uncle to the street car terminal, where she boarded a street car for Oakland. It was 9:30 p.m., and upon leaving the street car at 9:45 p.m., witnesses stated they saw the girl walk up Eighty-Sixth Street in the direction of her home. She was never seen alive again.

Early the next morning, July 3rd, two workmen, L.C. Hall and C.M. Wilcox, came upon a frightful sight in the back yard of a vacant house located at 1738 Eighty-Sixth – the body of a young girl. The victim was found lying in a flower bed on her back, with her legs spread apart, and her clothes rolled up under her waist. Her head and face had been battered; blood was everywhere. They hurried off to phone police. After a careful investigation, in which the deceased was identified as Mabel Mayer, it was determined that the struggle had taken place in the back yard of the vacant house, and the weapon used in the murder (which was found near the body) consisted of two pieces of wood about three feet in length with a nail at the end. The body of the girl had been dragged from the sidewalk up the drive way of the house and into the vacant lot. A bloody imprint of a hand was found on a fence post near the house. Mayer's head had been crushed, her face had many lacerations, and her jaw and left forearm were fractured. It was determined that she died from a concussion, shock, and hemorrhage. Further investigation determined that Mayer had not had not been sexually assaulted, and that her clothing had gathered up after being dragged to the location, where her body was found.

Robbery and molestation were quickly ruled out as motives for the murder. Witnesses, clues, and possible suspects poured in to police but no solid information led to an arrest. Wild theories abound but police were baffled as to why the crime took place. Many believed that the killer was a crazed homeless tramp, but no evidence was found to validate the story. Soon the trail of the murderer went cold, newspaper headlines disappeared, and life in Oakland eventually returned to normal. Police continued to follow lead's for years after the crime, but nothing tangible ever developed. To this day, some eighty plus years after the terrible crime, the murderer of Mabel Mayer, still has not been identified and the case remains unsolved and open.

The Kidnapping and Murder of Marion Parker

(Los Angeles, 1927)

On December 15, 1927, Marion Parker, the 12-year-old daughter of Perry Parker, a prominent banker in Los Angeles, was abducted from her school. That day, a man appeared at the principal's office of the Mount Vernon Junior High School in the Lafayette Square section of Los Angeles, and told school registrar, Mary Holt, that Perry Parker (Marion's father) had been seriously injured in an accident, and wished to see his daughter. The man was posing as an employee of the bank where Perry Parker worked.

Letters demanding money for her safe return were sent to her father for several days. All the communications, which often taunted the parents, were signed with names such as, "Fate," "Death," and "The Fox." Negotiations with the suspect continued until a price was agreed upon and a meeting was set. A first attempt to deliver the ransom was ruined when kidnapper saw police in the area. Continued communications from the kidnapper set up a new meeting to exchange ransom on December 19, 1927, at the corner of 5th Avenue and South Manhattan Street in Los Angeles. Mr. Parker arrived alone at the place with the ransom money, $1,500 in $20 gold certificates. Mr. Parker handed over the money to a young man who was waiting for him in a parked car. When he paid the ransom, he could see his daughter Marion sitting in the passenger seat next to the suspect, wrapped up to her neck and apparently unable to move. As soon as the money was exchanged, the kidnapper drove off, pushing Marion's body out of the car at the end of the street. The coroner later testified that she had been dead for about twelve hours. Her arms and legs had been cut off and she had been disemboweled and stuffed with rags. Her eyes were wired open so as to make her appear alive. It was believed that Marion was still alive when the killer began to dismember her body. The arms and legs were later found in Elysian Park wrapped in newspaper.

A massive manhunt for her killer began with hundreds of police officers and thousands of volunteers. A reward of $50,000 was offered for the identification and capture of the killer, dead or alive. Suspicion quickly settled upon a former employee of Mr. Parker named William Edward Hickman. Several years before the abduction, Hickman was arrested on a complaint by Mr. Parker regarding stolen and forged checks. Hickman was convicted and did prison time. Police traced a laundry mark on a shirt found with Marion's body to an apartment house in Los Angeles, where they questioned a man named Donald Evans who matched Hickman's description. Evans allowed the police to search his apartment, but they found no evidence and left. Evans then disappeared but was later identified as Hickman. The getaway car used at the ransom exchange had been found by police, and it was identified as having been stolen weeks before. Investigators had Hickman's fingerprints on file owing to his previous arrest and incarceration, and they matched them to prints found on ransom notes and on the getaway car.

Only a week after the kidnapping/murder, two police officers, Tom Gurdane and Buck Lieuallen found Hickman in Echo, Oregon, and recognized him from wanted posters. He was extradited back to Los Angeles, where he confessed to another murder and numerous robberies. Eventually, Hickman confessed to over a dozen armed robberies. He boasted to detectives, "This is going to get interesting before it's over." Hickman later would state, "He and Marion were good friends, and really had a good time when we were together, and I really liked her. I'm sorry that she was killed." Hickman confessed that he had cut up the body with the intention of disposing of it, but later realized that the father would want to see his daughter before paying, the ransom. He then attempted to reconstruct and disguise the body to make it appear alive and cut off her legs. Hickman pleaded insanity as his official motive for the crime, although he had initially told police that he needed the $1,500 to go to a Bible college. Hickman also told his defense attorneys that he had killed Marion on the directive of a supernatural being called Providence. Evidence against his insanity defense included prison guards from Oregon who testified that Hickman had asked "how to act crazy."

Mary Holt, the school registrar, testified that she would never have let Marion go, but for the apparent sincerity and disarming manner of the man. Prosecutors, however, speculated that he wanted revenge against Mr. Parker for testifying against him in his earlier trial for theft and forgery. There is evidence that he did it in part for the notoriety because he told a reporter, he wanted as much press coverage as high-profile killers Leopold and Loeb. Though his attorneys attempted to plead insanity for Hickman, the jury wouldn't buy it and he was convicted of murder and sentenced to hang. Hickman was executed at San Quentin prison on October 19, 1928.

The Marion Parker case shocked America and inflamed the public's feeling for vengeance against child abductors. The case subscribed to a pattern of kidnappings during that era and intensified the dread that parents felt toward the possibility of losing their own children. But the most famous child kidnapping case was still yet to come. The victim was the son of a true hero, a man who was revered throughout the entire world and who became one of the icons of American culture. The baby's name was Charles A. Lindbergh Jr.

The Vineville Chicken Coop Murders

(Los Angeles & Riverside County, 1928)

In March of 1928, Christine Collins was raising her son, Walter, by herself in Los Angeles. Her husband, Walter Collins, Sr., was serving a term in Folsom Prison for robbery. On March 10, 1928, Christine thought Walter was playing in the neighborhood. When he did not return by the evening, she made a report with the police. She would never see 9-year-old Walter again. Police worked on the theory that Walter had been kidnapped as part of a revenge plot against his father. The elder Collins was a "straw boss" in the prison, and was in charge of several other inmates. Police surmised he had made enemies of those he was in charge of. They began searching for inmates who had been recently released. In addition, they followed up on reports of a gas station attendant who had seen a car with a "body wrapped in newspaper" in the back seat. A young friend of Walter's also reported that a stranger had been in the neighborhood, inquiring about the Collins residence. None of the leads went anywhere.

Walter's disappearance received nationwide attention and numerous leads were received by law enforcement but the boy was never found. The trail suddenly went cold, and police were under intense pressure from the public, the media, and Mrs. Christine Collins (the boy's mother) to solve the case.

In August of 1928 law enforcement authorities in Illinois discovered a young boy near the town of DeKalb. He resembled photos of the Collins boy that had been distributed nationwide. At first, the boy denied being Walter, but following "gentle" questioning, he admitted that he was, in fact, Walter. He was then returned to the Los Angeles.

Murder victim Walter Collins. *Courtesy of the Herald Examiner Collection/ the Los Angeles Public Library.*

Police were baffled when Christine stated that the boy was not her son. Detectives insisted that the boy was Walter but relented to have the boy undergo a series of tests. He had, allegedly, directed authorities to the correct home, and knew information about other homes in the neighborhood. Still Mrs. Collins disagreed, and though she stated the boy did closely resemble Walter, he did not act the same as her boy. Authorities tried to convince her that his kidnappers had "altered the aisles in his brain" during his captivity, which accounted for his odd behavior. As the final point, it was determined that the boy was in fact Walter; the police noted that Walter's pet dog, a black spaniel, immediately took to the young boy. When Mrs. Collins still refused to accept that the boy was in fact her son, public sentiment (fueled largely by statements from LAPD Captain J. J. Jones, in charge of the Juvenile Investigation Unit) turned against Christine. Based entirely on Jones' say-so, Christine was committed to a psychopathic ward. She spent ten days in the unit, until "Walter" finally recanted.

Under additional police interrogation, it was learned that the boy was not Walter, but was in fact Arthur Hutchins, Jr. He was a young runaway from Iowa, working in Illinois at the time of Walter's disappearance. He told reporters and police that he took what little he knew of the case from newspaper reports. When asked why he had perpetrated the hoax, he told authorities he had "always wanted to see Hollywood." Los Angeles police, trying to avert a scandal, had created an even bigger one for themselves and the Collins disappearance case was re-opened.

Gordon Northcott might have gone on raping and killing indefinitely, but in the summer of 1928, he visited the Riverside District Attorney's Office, complaining about a neighbor's "profane and violent" behavior. The outbursts reportedly upset his nephew, who was "training for the priesthood." Under investigation, the neighbor recalled seeing Gordon beat Clark on occasion, and he urged detectives to "find out what goes on" at Northcott's ranch. Immigration officials struck first, taking Clark into custody on a complaint from his Canadian parents, and the boy regaled authorities with tales of murder, pointing out newly-excavated "grave sites" on the ranch. Detectives dug up blood-soaked earth, unearthing human ankle bones and fingers on September 17. They also found a bloodstained ax and hatchet on the premises that Clark said had been used on human prey, as well as chickens.

Before police could arrive at the scene, Gordon and Sarah Northcott had fled to Canada, but on September 19, 1928, they were located and extradited back to California. Sarah initially confessed to all four murders, most likely in an attempt to save her son. On December 31, 1928, she was convicted of the murder of Walter Collins and sentenced to life in prison; she was paroled after only serving twelve years, and died in 1944.

It was reported that prior to his trial; Northcott took law enforcement authorities on a trek through the Mojave Desert in search of victim's remains.

During that time, he allegedly stated that he had killed "Walter Collins, the Winslow boys, and several others." He also hinted to police that it was possible another four boys had been murdered at the ranch. All was this was an attempt to manipulate, forestall, and possibly evade the hangman's noose. His trial began in January of 1929. During which the jury heard horrific details of torture and murder. Sarah Northcott incoherently testified that she was not actually Gordon's mother, but his grandmother. Christine Collins also testified during the trial. On February 8th, 1929, Gordon was found guilty of the murders of the unknown Mexican boy and the Winslow brothers. He was not charged with Walter Collins murder because the body was never found. He was sentenced to hang.

While marking time at San Quentin, Northcott alternated between protestations of innocence and detailed confessions to the murder of "18 or 19, maybe 20" victims. A pathological liar, he cherished the spotlight, several times he offered to point out remains of more victims, always reneging at the last moment. The night prior to the execution, Christine and the mother of the Winslow boys confronted Gordon after he sent them telegrams stating he would tell the truth of what happened to their children. Instead, Gordon proclaimed his innocence, blaming his mother and his nephew.

Gordon Northcott's trial in Riverside County, (Northcott is seated 2nd from right).
Courtesy of the Herald Examiner Collection/ Los Angeles Public Library.

On his last morning, October 2, 1930, Northcott began screaming and trembling. His hands shook fiercely as they were strapped together. "Will it hurt?" he asked softly. Told that no one had ever complained, he asked for a blindfold, so he would not have to see the gallows. He was dragged into the gallows room, pleading with guards, "Please – don't make me walk so fast." Northcott had to be hauled up the gallows steps. Seconds before the trap was sprung, he screamed, "A prayer, please, say a prayer for me."

Sanford Clark was never tried for murder, because the Riverside District Attorney strongly believed that he was innocent, was the victim of Northcott's death threats and sexual abuse, and that he was not a willing participant in the murders. Christine Collins never stopped believing that Walter might still be alive, as no solid evidence of his death was found at the farm. Christine's treatment at the hands of Captain Jones and his officers resulted in Jones' four-month suspension without pay. She was awarded over $10,000 in a lawsuit settlement against Jones. It was assumed by law enforcement that Walter had been killed by Northcutt, and his body disposed of in an unknown location, but Christine Collins did not believe that her son was dead, and vowed to use every cent of the settlement to find out what really happened. She never did. Christine Collins died December 8, 1964. Shortly after the conviction of Gordon Northcott, the city of Wineville changed its name to Mira Loma, in attempt to disassociate itself from the heinous crimes that had occurred within its community. In 2008, Angelina Jolie starred in *The Changeling*, a mildly successful fictionalized account of the Wineville murders; the film was directed by Clint Eastwood.

The San Diego Stalker

(San Diego, 1931-1936)

A serial killer is typically defined as a person who murders three or more people over a period of more than thirty days, with a cooling off period between each murder, and whose motivation for killing is largely based on psychological gratification. Other sources define the term as a series of two or more murders, committed as separate events, usually, but not always, by one offender acting alone or, including the vital characteristics, a minimum of at least two murders. Often, a sexual element is involved with the killings, but the Federal Bureau of Investigation states that motives for serial murder include anger, thrill, financial gain, and attention seeking. The murders may have been attempted or completed in a similar fashion and the victims may have had something in common; for example, occupation, race, appearance, sex, or age group.

Between the years 1931 and 1936, San Diego and its surrounding area (with a population of only 300,000) witnessed a murder surge. During this time, seven women and children, between the ages of ten and thirty-five, were murdered. It has been loosely speculated that several of these murders, if not all, could be related, and although there are many striking similarities between these crimes, no concrete evidence has ever been produced to substantiate the claim that these slayings were perpetrated by one person. Some have even gone so far as to claim that the murder of Elizabeth Short (the infamous "Black Dahlia"), might be linked to the San Diego Stalker case. Even though there have been many suspects and numerous arrests, no one has ever been convicted of these crimes. After 1936, the murders mysteriously and abruptly ended. Today, all seven murders remain unsolved and open.

The first murder that has been allegedly attributed to the "San Diego Stalker," is the case of Virginia Brooks. On the morning of February 11, 1931, ten-year-old Virginia Brooks was abducted on her way to school. She left her home at 5602 University Avenue with her lunch, library books, and a bouquet of flowers for her teacher. The walk to the Euclid Avenue Elementary school was approximately a mile and a half. Immediately, law enforcement set out to find Virginia, but there were no witnesses and very little evidence. On the morning of March 10, 1931, almost a month after the disappearance of Virginia Brooks, a badly decomposed body was found in a shallow grave by George Moses (a goat herder), near Camp Kearney Mesa, a rural area of San

Diego County. With the remains were found a red coat and a burlap bag full of books. Although the body was not initially identified as Virginia Brooks, an autopsy removed any doubt. Law enforcement officials concluded that she had been killed either the day of the abduction, or a few days following and because the body was so badly decomposed, it was never conclusively determined how Virginia was killed. Although the head had been severed from the body, it was impossible to determine whether this injury was the cause of death or was inflicted post-mortem. Police went on to speculate that the body was most likely placed at the location of its detection only a few days prior to the discovery. Virginia was laid to rest on March 21, 1931 at Mount Hope Cemetery in a plot provided by the city; six classmates bore her casket as honorary pall bearers, and nearly 4,000 spectators jammed the cemetery to witness the funeral proceedings. As the days, weeks, and years passed, police continued to investigate the slaying and numerous suspects were questioned. A few were arrested, but no one was ever charged in Virginia Brooks' murder.

A little over a month after the burial of Virginia Brooks, another dead girl was found. On April 19, 1931, the partially nude body of seventeen-year-old Louise Teuber was found dead, hanging from a tree limb in Black Mountain Park. Her body was found by Tony Martinez, who was searching for a picnic area for his family. It was determined that the young girl had been dead for about eight hours before being discovered. She was wearing only dark stockings and shoes, the rest of her clothing (including a light blue silk skirt, white silk blouse, black fur-trimmed coat, and underwear) were found nearby in a bag. The body was positioned half-seated with the heels of her shoes barely touching the ground, a noose (tied in a sailor's fashion) was tied around her neck and the body had been hoisted-up from a sitting position. A coroner's inquest was held on April 27, 1931; at which seventeen witnesses were questioned. Louise's father, William Teuber, testified that he had argued with his daughter a few days before her murder. The cause of death was determined to be strangulation. Police theorized that Teuber knew her attacker and struggled to fend off the attack, and that she was drugged prior to her death. She was hit on the back of the head to render her unconscious, then the noose was tied around her neck, and she was hoisted to a position where she strangled to death. It was assumed that the attacker had knowledge that Louise had planned to run away from home, and her body was intentionally left to look like a suicide. In the weeks following the crime, nearly three dozen suspects were questioned, including several boyfriends, and a local commercial photographer but no one was ever charged with the murder.

On April 23, 1931, only four days after the murder of Louise Teuber, another woman was found slain. Dolly "Diamond" Bibbens was found in her downtown San Diego apartment sprawled across her bed, partially clothed in blue silk pajamas, with a towel knotted around her neck. She had been last seen alive on April 15th. When neighbors became suspicious, they contacted the building manager. He entered the apartment and found her body. There was evidence a tremendous struggle and Bibben's apartment had been ransacked. Little is known about Bibbens; she was estimated to be around 35 years old, and kept to herself. She was often seen at the horse races in Agua Caliente and in Tijuana, Mexico, where she wore fashionable clothing and expensive jewelry. It was theorized by police that she may have been marked for robbery because of her assumed lifestyle. No jewelry was found at the scene of the murder. It is believed that she was killed on the same day that she was last seen alive, April 15, 1931. Several suspects were questioned in the apparent murder/robbery, including a known associate named H.C. Yardley, but like the previous two homicides, Dolly Bibbens murder also remained unsolved.

A few weeks later, on May 3, 1931, beautiful, 20-year-old Hazel Bradshaw was found stabbed to death in Balboa Park. Her fully clothed body was found about noon in an abandoned Indian village by a group of Boy Scouts, who had been camping in the vicinity. Bradshaw had been stabbed seventeen times in the upper torso. It was learned that the victim had left her home at 4510 Alabama Street around 6 a.m., on the morning of May 2, 1931, to report to work. She was employed as a telephone operator at the San Diego and Arizona Railway offices, and when she failed to arrive home that evening, relatives became alarmed and contacted police. A boyfriend of Bradshaw's, Moss Edward Garrison was arrested and brought to trial for the murder, but he was eventually acquitted. No other suspects were ever arrested in Bradshaw's murder and the case remains open and unsolved.

On March 4, 1934, nearly three years after the first murders, Mary Adams' lifeless body was found alongside a road in Mission Valley. Adam's had quarreled with her husband, Wesley Adams, the night of her alleged death (Saturday, March 3, 1931). Upset, she left her home at 1733 First Street, for a night of partying with friends at the "Fleet Café," a bar located in the gas lamp district. She was known to have a reputation as a drinker and was a well-known "party girl." Witnesses at the café noted that before leaving the bar around 12 midnight, Adams was observed to be in a very intoxicated state. Who she left with and where she went after leaving the bar is unknown.

She was found dead alongside Adobe Falls Road in Mission Valley by a local hunter early Sunday morning. There were no obvious signs of foul play, and an autopsy proved to be inconclusive as to the cause of death. There were multiple bruises on the body but none were considered to have been life threatening in nature. It was noted that she was heavily intoxicated but not to the extent that would have caused her death. How she died, and why she ended up dead alongside the road in rural Mission Valley remained a mystery. Police detectives questioned and detained numerous acquaintances but all were eventually exonerated. Like the other murders previously discussed, the trail of the killer went cold and the case remains open and unsolved.

In late summer of 1934, pretty 16-year-old Celia Cota went for an evening walk in her neighborhood (against the wishes of her mother), and was never seen alive again. Her blood-spattered body was discovered in the back yard of her home, beaten and strangled to death. Police discovered Celia's body hidden behind a shed and beneath a trunk in the back yard of the Cota home in the early morning hours of August 18, 1934. Detectives theorized that Celia was ambushed as she walked toward her home and was struck in the head, pulled to the yard, and then sexually assaulted. It was determined at autopsy that Celia had been sexually violated and that the blow to her head and strangulation were the causes of her death. Police questioned numerous suspects and several were arrested, but like the other aforementioned murder cases, no one was ever brought to trial and convicted. Celia Cota was laid to rest on September 3, 1934 at Holy Cross Cemetery.

The final victim of the so called "San Diego Slayer" was Ruth Muir; the 35-year-old was found beaten to death in La Jolla on September 1, 1936. She was a native of San Antonio, Texas, and was a Vassar College graduate; she had been employed for several years as an executive secretary at the Y.M.C.A., in Riverside. She was vacationing in La Jolla with her parents at the time of the murder. Ruth was known to take late night walks on the beach. When she failed to return by midnight to the beach cottage she shared with her parents, police were notified. Muir's body was discovered in some weeds at the base of an arroyo near the beach around 11 a.m. the following day by two women, who were walking their dog. Muir apparently had been attacked while sitting on a bench overlooking the beach. Her body was found crumpled up in some weeds in a pool of blood. There was evidence of a great struggle, her jaw had been broken and her skull was fractured.

Four days after the murder, Donald J. Hazell, a local transient was arrested; he was overheard by numerous witnesses mumbling about the slaying and other unsolved San Diego murders. He was remanded to the Patton State Hospital for observation. There he confessed to killing Muir, stating that "at times psychic spells come over me and compel me to take a life," and pertaining to the Muir case said, "I killed her with a beer bottle." Psychiatrists and other medical personnel expressed doubt that Hazell had actually committed the murder; he was deemed to be insane and delusional. He was questioned by police but was quickly ruled out as a suspect because of his mental condition. In the weeks and months following Muir's murder, numerous suspects were questioned, but none were ever charged with the slaying.

Following the Muir murder, the rash of killings (1931-1936) abruptly ended in San Diego County. What became of the murderer is unknown; he or she was never brought to justice. It must be noted that there are numerous similarities between the killings, but there is more contradictory evidence. The likelihood that all or any of the murders were committed by one person is very doubtful. Because investigative techniques and forensic evidence at the time were rudimentary, police were often at a disadvantage. If the suspect was not caught right away, the trail of the killer often went cold very rapidly and San Diego law enforcement was not equipped to handle such a surge in murder cases that enveloped their city during this time period. Today, seventy plus years after the last murder, all seven cases remain open and unsolved in San Diego County. As the years roll by, the probability that the San Diego Stalker or other killers, will ever be identified and brought to justice is quite doubtful.

The San Diego Sack Murder

(San Diego, 1933)

In the early morning hours of October 15, 1933, the mutilated body of a woman was found floating in San Diego Bay. First evidence of the murder was discovered by a shore boat crew of the USS *Trenton* around 8:40 a.m.; they noticed a duffle bag floating on the water. Inside the bag was a severed head and upper torso of a woman. Several hours later another duffle bag was found containing the lower extremities. The body was identified by three neighbors, as Laura Ella Straw, a fifty-year-old wealthy benefactress, who resided at 1204 Eighteenth Street. When police searched Straw's home they found evidence of the murder and mutilation. There was no obvious sign of a struggle, but two bloody mattresses, a hatchet, hammer, and bloodstained butchers' saws were found at the scene. Detectives theorized that Mrs. Straw was struck in the head with the hatchet, her body was cut into pieces, packed into the duffel bags, and then the bags were dumped into the bay. Autopsy evidence suggested that Straw might still have been alive prior to her dismemberment.

Suspicion immediately pointed to Thomas Jones, a roommate of Straw's. He was an ex-convict, who Straw had befriended several months prior to the murder. Jones was homeless, and living in a downtown park when Straw took pity on him. She gave him a place to stay, while he looked for employment. Several nights before the murder, neighbors heard Straw and Jones loudly quarrelling.

An arrest warrant was issued for Jones and in the months following the crime, police received numerous tips of the whereabouts of the fugitive (whose actual name was Tully McQuate). He was finally apprehended in Los Angeles on the night of May 27, 1934, when Los Angeles police arrested him during an attempted robbery. He was quickly identified as the fugitive who was wanted in the San Diego slaying. Upon his arrest, McQuate told officers, "I'm glad to get it over with, it's been on my conscience; I'm ready to face the music." He was transported under heavy guard back to San Diego to stand trial.

McQuate's trial for the murder of Laura Ella Straw began on June 2, 1934; he admitted that Straw was killed for money, and that he attempted to conceal the crime by cutting up her body, and disposing of the remains. On June 4, 1934, he was found guilty and sentenced to death by hanging. He accepted his sentence with indifference and resignation stating, "It's so foolish, I did it; let 'em sentence me and get it over with. If I hang, I hang. That's all there is to it. They can only hang me once."

He was only the second man in thirty-five years to be sentenced to death from San Diego. In the first case, Manuel Chavez was convicted of murdering his wife during a fit of jealousy in rural San Diego County; he was hung on December 16, 1898 at San Quentin Prison. On August 10, 1934, Tully McQuate, alias Thomas Jones, met the same fate at Folsom State Prison for the murder of Laura Ella Straw.

Murder or Suicide? The Mysterious Death of Actress Thelma Todd

(Los Angeles, 1935)

On the morning of Monday, December 16, 1935, actress Thelma Todd was found dead in her car inside the garage of her lover and business partner, Roland West. The garage door was closed and the engine of the convertible (top down) was running. In the front seat, Todd was slumped over, face down and dead. Her teeth had been knocked out; blood covered her face, dress, and mink coat. West's house was approximately a block from the topmost side of Todd's restaurant. Her death was determined to have been caused by carbon monoxide poisoning. Todd had a wide circle of friends and associates as well as a busy social life; police investigations revealed that she had spent the last night of her life at the Trocadero, a popular Hollywood restaurant, at a party hosted by Paramount Studios. At the restaurant, she had a brief but unpleasant exchange with her ex-husband, Pat DeCicco. However, her friends stated that she was in good spirits, and were aware of nothing unusual in her life that could suggest a reason for committing suicide. Police detectives questioned neighbors but no one seemed to have seen, or heard anything out of the ordinary. There was no suicide note found, and Todd had everything to live for; she was in the middle of shooting a new film, *The Bohemian Girl* with Stan Laurel and Oliver Hardy.

Thelma Todd, the vivacious blonde actress, was born on July 29, 1905, in Lawrence, Massachusetts. She excelled in school and initially became a teacher, but when she realized that her beauty could earn more money, she took to modeling. While modeling, she attracted the attention of numerous Hollywood talents scouts. Unlike many other would-be actresses, Todd did not end up on the streets of Hollywood, disappointed, disillusioned, and desperate. There were way too many good looking girls seeking fame and fortune in Hollywood, but finding only a good pair of legs, an hour-glass figure, and a pretty face were not enough to get their names on a movie contract. Todd was determined that things would be different.

Paramount Studios felt that Todd had the makings of a movie star and, in 1925, put her under contract. The studio did not want to push their budding starlet too fast, and they eased her into movie roles. After nearly a year of learning how to walk, dance, and sing, Todd was ready for her first role, a small part in *Fascinating Youth* (1926). When Al Jolson spoke on film for the first time in *The Jazz Singer*, the motion picture industry was revolutionized.

Thelma Todd, Actress, publicity photo from the motion picture Corsair (1931).
Courtesy of the Herald Examiner Collection/ Los Angeles Public Library.

Suddenly, some of the biggest names in movies disappeared. For Thelma, the coming of sound allowed her to develop her wise-cracking screen persona, and with the demise of so many veteran screen actresses, room was made for a whole new generation of movie stars, who were theatrically trained.

In 1929, Todd was approached by producer/ director Hal Roach, who featured her in a successful series of feature films. Roach's films concentrated on story, and appealed to sophisticated audiences. She was a favorite of Laurel and Hardy and the Marx Brothers, appearing in many of their films. Todd proved to be a great comedic actress and asset for Roach, where she personified the wise-cracking, cynical blonde. She was highly regarded as a capable film comedienne, and Roach loaned her out to other studios. During her film career, she appeared in 119 movies; many of these were short films in which she was sometimes publicized as "The Ice Cream Blonde." In 1931, she was given her own film comedy series, teaming with Zasu Pitts.

This was Roach's attempt to create a female version of Laurel and Hardy. When Pitts left the series in 1933, she was replaced by Patsy Kelly. In these shorts, Todd was often cast as a working girl having all sorts of problems, and trying her best to remain poised and charming despite the embarrassing antics of her sidekick.

While Todd's film career was hitting a high; her private life was a mess. She had, for a brief period, been married to Pat DiCicco, and after her divorce had had numerous affairs. In 1931, Todd became romantically involved with married director Roland West, and starred in his film *Corsair*. West had earned the respect of Hollywood. His output as a director was small, but his work was highly appreciated. In August 1934, she and West opened a successful cafe in Pacific Palisades, called Thelma Todd's Roadside Rest Cafe; the restaurant attracted many famous friends and became a popular tourist attraction. Todd and West had living quarters above the café, and West had an even larger home perched atop a cliff, just a few steps from the restaurant.

It seemed that Todd's affair with West was beginning to wane by 1935. She was only 30 and he was 48. She still had a zest for life and planned to make the best of whatever youth she had left. She drank heavily, took pills, and cheated on West. Whatever vices she may have had, she did not want any part of the underworld activity. California had not yet been overrun by gangsters, but was on the brink. Lucky Luciano was making attempts to penetrate California with illegal gambling enterprises. Money was flowing in and he was constantly on the lookout for establishments from which he could run illegal gambling and Todd's café seemed to be the perfect front. When Luciano paid Todd a visit, and proposed that the upstairs of her restaurant be turned into a gambling hall, Todd turned out to be as gutsy off screen as on, when she turned him down flat.

Thelma Todd's Roadside Rest Café. *Courtesy of the Herald Examiner Collection/ Los Angeles Public Library.*

On the evening of December 15, 1935, Todd attended a party at the Trocadero. The party was thrown by Paramount Studios for its newest starlet Ida Lupino. The party had all the classic ingredients for an explosive event. Todd's ex-husband, Pat DiCicco, was there with actress Margaret Lindsay. A drunken Todd and DiCicco exchanged heated words during the evening.

As the party swung into the early morning hours of Sunday, December 16, Todd had had enough and had her driver take her home. She left the Trocadero nightclub about 3 a.m., in a chauffeur driven car, arriving at her café at about 3:45 a.m., where she was last seen alive. Her body was later found by her maid, Mae Whitehead, slumped over the passenger seat of her convertible, which was parked in a two-car garage above her café. Police detectives at first concluded that Todd's death was accidental, the result of her either warming up the car to drive it or using the heater to keep warm. Other evidence, however, pointed to foul play. It was believed that she might have been the target of extortion, but refused to pay. It is also possible that she was locked in the garage by her assailant after she started the car. Blood from a wound was found on her face and dress, leading some to believe that she was knocked unconscious and placed in the car so that she would succumb to carbon monoxide poisoning.

It was not uncommon for suicide to be affected by the use of car exhaust fumes. If Todd had killed herself, how did she come to have her teeth knocked out, and have blood all over her face? Those who commit suicide almost always leave a note but none was ever found. Why would she have come home by limousine, then climb those steps up to West's garage, just to kill herself when it was well known that she kept a plentiful supply of pills on hand, for which she could have easily overdosed on? Some of these questions were covered in a relatively quick investigation by the Los Angeles County District Attorney's Office and the case was quickly closed with a verdict of suicide. The verdict was then rapidly overturned in favor of a finding for accidental death, and on December 21, 1935, the investigation was closed. Since her body was cremated, a second, more thorough autopsy could not be carried out. Todd's death certificate states her cause of death was accidental carbon monoxide poisoning. Initially, Todd's remains were interred at Forest Lawn, Glendale, but after the death of her mother, Gertrude Todd, in 1964, Thelma's cremated remains were placed in her mother's casket and re-buried at Bellevue Cemetery in Lawrence, Massachusetts.

In Todd's last film, Laurel and Hardy's comedy, *The Bohemian Girl*, all of her scenes except one were cut from the film. It was believed that to keep them in would be morbid. It was ironic that the famous "Ice Cream Blonde's" last on-screen film appearance would in a dark wig.

Although the case had been wrapped up as far as the law was concerned, too many questions remained unanswered. But Hollywood had its own style of retribution. The industry already had proven that it could terminate the career of those in its employ. Now Hollywood closed its doors on Roland West. He never worked again. Not everyone believed that West was responsible for Todd's death. But in private, it was strongly believe that mobsters, principally Lucky Luciano were responsible for her demise. However, no one in Hollywood would ever claim directly that this occurred. They figured if it could happen to Todd, it could happen to them.

The Duchess: Juanita Spinelli

(San Francisco and Sacramento, 1940)

The first woman to be executed legally in California was Juanita Spinelli, the cold-blooded "Duchess" of a Bay Area robbery gang. A grandmother and ex-wrestler, she had a reputation for being able to pin a poker chip with a knife thrown at fifteen paces. She was convicted in the murder of a gang member she feared would inform on her. Spinelli's entire life was a lie, but she had the talent to influence the young and dumb to do her bidding. She was born Ethel Leta Juanita Spinelli on October 17, 1889, in Kentucky. Very little is known about her past and whether she gave herself the nickname "the Duchess" or it was coined by her alleged Purple Gang connections – nobody will ever know for sure.

What *is* known is that she materialized in San Francisco sometime in the late 1930s, with three kids and a hoodlum named Michael Simone. Spinelli was a haggard, toothless woman who looked twenty years older than the 50 years she claimed to be. She asserted that she was an informer for Detroit's very violent Purple Gang and had to leave the city in a hurry. The Purple Gang was a Jewish organized crime outfit that was basically wiped out by internal disputes by 1935, so Spinelli's story is questionable. She was supposedly married to bank robber Anthony Spinelli, who was killed while smuggling contraband across the Mexican border. Information on Anthony is also sketchy and limited.

The Duchess rounded up a handful of malcontents, eighteen-year-old Robert Sherrod, 21-year-old Gordon Hawkins, and 24-year-old Albert Ives. Together with the 33-year-old Simone, the gang knocked off gas stations and rolled drunks. Spinelli's teenage daughter, Lorraine, was used as a sex lure. Her street name was Gypsy, and she would approach drunken men with a promise of easy sex. Once alone, Spinelli's thugs would rob the man. Juanita Spinelli thought of herself as the brains of the outfit, and when she wasn't planning small time robberies, she cooked and cleaned for her troupe of young criminals. Acting as a teacher, she instructed the boys in the fine art of robbery, assault, and car theft. She taught them that it was smarter to commit a steady stream of small crimes than one big one like robbing a bank. She explained that the police would go all out to find a bank robber, but would more than likely shrug at a man who woke up on the street with his wallet missing. Providing them with the mother figure that they may not ever have had, Spinelli delegated jobs for the gang, and doled out their cut of the money, as if it were an allowance.

The end of the Spinelli gang occurred on a very foggy night in San Francisco on the evening of April 8, 1940, when gang member Albert Ives shot *Barbeque* stand owner Leland S. Cash, while attempting to rob him of the day's receipts. The 55-year-old Cash was deaf and did not hear Ives when he demanded the money. Cash reached into his pocket to turn on his hearing aid, but Ives shot him before he had a chance to reply, leaving Cash to die in the parking lot of his diner at Lincoln Way and La Playa in the Sunset District of the city. Upon hearing the news, Spinelli panicked and packed up the gang and fled to Sacramento in a stolen car, robbing a gas station on the way out of San Francisco. Settling at a cheap motel in the seedy side of town, the gang drank whiskey and planned to make quick money rolling drunks in Sacramento.

Much to the dismay of the gang, the dim-witted Sherrod kept reliving the murder of Cash, asking the Duchess and others if they thought Cash had died right away or if he lingered. The hooligans sent Sherrod on an errand, so that they could discuss how to silence their companion. It was agreed upon that Sherrod had to die before he talked too much. Ives suggested that they shoot him the head and make it look like an accident, but the Duchess vetoed the idea. She did not want the boy to suffer. Knowing that Sherrod was a weak swimmer, they decided to have a picnic along the Sacramento River. After the cook out, they would go swimming in the river, where they would push Sherrod into the swift running current.

The next day, the hapless gang piled into their cars and drove about ten miles south of Sacramento near Freeport Bridge with the intent to drown Sherrod, but he refused to get near the river for fear of drowning. Rebuffed in their attempt to kill their loose-lipped compatriot, the gang drove back to Sacramento with Sherrod babbling about the Cash murder all the way. Fearful that Sherrod would go to police, Simone and Spinelli decided on a better plan, which they would implement the next day April 13, 1940. After several of the younger children went to bed, the Duchess had a get together in her room. Sherrod was anxious for a drink, and she poured him one laced with choral hydrate, popularly known as the knock-out drug. Sherrod quickly downed the drink and became groggy. After he became unconscious, the gang loaded him into the car and drove back to the Freeport Bridge. At the bridge, Ives dragged Sherrod's body to the edge of the bridge and tossed him of over into the icy water. Little did the gang know but Sherrod was already dead before he hit the water from an overdose of the knock-out drug.

The next day it was decided that the gang would head to Reno. They needed a fresh town full of money and drunks. They planned on robbing hitchhikers and motorists along the way. The real plan was to kill the simple-minded Ives before he too started running off at the mouth. Ives was getting full of himself, bragging about the two murders that he committed. The plan was to kill him in the High Sierra and dump his body off a tall cliff, where he would never be found. Sometime during the ride, Ives saw Simone give Hawkins a knowing glance. At a gas station near Grass Valley, he overheard the gang talking about a 700-foot cliff. Ives was not as stupid as everyone thought, and he ran into a nearby diner, through the kitchen, and out the back door and hid. He waited until the gang had left before he ran to a nearby California Highway Patrol Post, where he told the stunned officers his story about the gang. Later that day, the Duchess and her crew were pulled over by police near Truckee. Spinelli pulled her innocent mother routine, but after the police found a cache of weapons, the jig was up. They were all brought back to Sacramento to face charges of Robert Sherrod's murder, and quickly the gang turned on one another. Ives turned state's evidence first, and told the authorities about every robbery, car theft, and the two murders. Gypsy, who was pregnant, claimed that she had been attending high school in San Francisco and was too busy with school work to know about her mother's criminal deeds and was released from custody. The City of San Francisco waived its right to the prisoners, and the gang was tried in Sacramento County for the murder of Robert Sherrod, all of which were eventually found guilty of first degree murder and sentenced to death in the gas chamber.

About the Gas Chamber

The gas chamber was first used in California in December of 1938. On that day Robert Lee Cannon and Albert Kessell were executed for taking part in a Folsom Prison riot in which the warden and a guard were killed. Cannon and Kessell spent their last night playing records, singing, and shouting to each other in the adjoining death cells behind the gas chamber. Ten minutes before the scheduled time, they smoked a cigar and took a shot of whiskey. Cannon, barefoot with his arms strapped to his sides, walked first into the chamber and was cinched into a seat. Kessell then was brought in by guards and strapped down in the second chair. "Quite a congregation here," Kessell said quietly. Nearly forty witnesses looked on. The 1930s was the busiest decade for executions in California, with 107 men put to death, so the execution spectacle was commonplace. But the gas chamber was a curiosity. Kessell avoided looking up at the observers. When the faintly visible plume of death gas began to rise, Cannon looked through the windows and mouthed the words, "Nothing to it." Another phrase was forming on his lips when his face contorted into a look neither smile nor grimace. His eyes rolled and his head dropped.

The law forbade using gas on anyone condemned to hang, so the gallows at San Quentin was used one last time on May 1, 1942. Convicted murderer Raymond James Lisenba, alias Rattlesnake James, had kept himself alive on death row with appeals for several years. When his date with the executioner came up, the gallows had to be spruced up and a new holding cell built. He was the last man executed by hanging in California.

After being held at the woman's prison in Tehachapi, Spinelli was driven to San Quentin two days before her date with the gas chamber. About thirty prisoners signed a petition protesting the execution of a woman, and offered to draw straws among themselves to select a replacement. The governor granted her two stays. But the day after Thanksgiving, November 21, 1941, her time came. The *Los Angeles Times* reported that she wore a short-sleeved green dress and clutched a white handkerchief in her left hand. Photos of her children were tied over her heart. She was being walked into the chamber when the warden noticed that the 100 or so witnesses were not in place. The Duchess stood outside the gas chamber and chatted about the weather as the witnesses filed in. The *Times* story said "her face, minus dentures, looked sunken as the gas began to rise. She coughed; her head dropped forward, and then whipped back, streaming her long gray hair over the chair back. The Duchess coughed again, and then blew out her breath with a sound like that a horse sometimes makes with his lips." After five minutes, a prison official barked: "That's all, boys."

Spinelli was the first female put to death in San Quentin's gas chamber. One week later on November 28, 1941, Simone and Hawkins were gassed simultaneously in San Quentin's double seat gas chamber. Ives was found not guilty by reason of insanity and was sent to live out his life at the Napa State Asylum for the Insane.

The Unsolved Murder of Socialite Georgette Bauerdorf

(Los Angeles, 1944)

Georgette Elise Bauerdorf was a 20-year-old oil heiress from New York, who was found strangled on October 12, 1944 at the El Palacio Apartments on 8493 Fountain Avenue, West Hollywood, California. Her murder has often been connected with the infamous "Black Dahlia" unsolved murder of Elizabeth Short in 1947. Bauerdorf worked as a junior hostess at the Hollywood Canteen, where she danced with enlisted men. She had been living alone in the apartment for several weeks before her death.

On the morning of October 12, 1944, a house maid entered the open door to Bauerdorf's apartment and heard water dripping. She went upstairs into the bathroom and saw Bauerdorf floating face down in the bathtub. Bloody water was overflowing onto the bathroom floor. She leaned over and carefully turned off the faucet and then ran down stairs to get the building manager. It is believed that she was attacked by a man who was lying in wait for her. Detectives found that an automatic night light over the outside entrance of the apartment had been unscrewed two turns so it wouldn't go on. The murderer was thought to have stood on a chair to reach the light bulb nearly eight feet from the floor. Fingerprints were found on the bulb. The theory of someone lying in wait was reinforced by an empty string-bean can and some melon rinds, found by officers in the kitchen waste basket. Investigators think Bauerdorf may have eaten a snack before retiring upstairs to her bedroom. Examination of her stomach revealed that she had eaten string beans about an hour before her death.

Bauerdorf's jewelry and other valuables were not stolen, although almost $100 was taken from her purse. There was a large roll of $2 bills and thousands of dollars worth of sterling silver lying in an open trunk. A Pontiac 1936 coupe, registered in the name of her sister, Connie Bauerdorf, was missing. When the car was located several days later, there was a dent in one of the fenders. Mechanics said the damage was recent and may have been the result of a collision with another car. The Pontiac was discovered abandoned on East 25th Street just off San Pedro Street in Los Angeles, where it apparently ran out of gas.

An examination of Bauerdorf's body by Los Angeles County coroner found abundant bruises and scrapes. It was determined that Bauerdorf must have put up a great struggle with her killer. The knuckles on her right hand were smashed and bruised; there was a large bruise on the right side of her head and another on her abdomen, perhaps the result of blows from fists.

She had been strangled with a piece of towel, which had been stuffed down her throat. Her right thigh showed a bruised imprint of a hand.

A reconstruction of the murder scene gave investigators the idea that the killer perhaps entered Bauerdorf's apartment by key and lay in wait downstairs, until she got ready for bed. Another possibility is, he rang the doorbell after she went to sleep. It was determined unlikely that she would have been accompanied home by a serviceman. She might have met someone at the canteen and been driven home and he might have returned later to kill her. A neighbor, who requested anonymity at the time, told police that he was awakened by screams around 2:30 a.m. He first heard a scream which made him sit upright in bed. This was followed by a female voice yelling "Stop, stop, you're killing me." He said the screaming soon subsided. Thinking it might be a family argument, and being sleepy, he went back to bed. A date book diary was found in the bedroom containing the names of servicemen. Army authorities joined with the Los Angeles police detectives in a search for clues. A sailor was questioned in Long Beach, California, but was determined not to have been her attacker. Authorities hoped that someone who saw the young woman leaving the canteen, accompanied by an escort, would come forward. Numerous letters received by Bauerdorf were scrutinized by investigators.

The day before her murder, Georgette had cashed a $175 check and purchased an airline ticket to El Paso, Texas for $90. She told friends that she was going there to rendezvous with her soldier boyfriend. On October 11, 1944, Private Jerome M. Brown, an antiaircraft artillery trainee from Chicago, Illinois, was identified by Fort Bliss authorities as the man Bauerdorf was going to visit before she was slain. Brown told Army officials he met Bauerdorf at the Hollywood Canteen on the night of June 13, 1944 and that he left California a few days afterward. June Ziegler came forward to say that she had been with Georgette at the Hollywood Canteen the night prior to the murder. She told the police that Bauerdorf dated a serviceman who was 6'4" less than a month before her murder. He was a buddy of another serviceman whose name was frequently mentioned in the diary. According to Ziegler, Bauerdorf remarked that the tall soldier was very much taken with her. However, she did not return his interest and quit going out with him. The soldier was sought for questioning by officers. Newspaper reports indicate Bauerdorf went directly home after leaving the Hollywood Canteen around 11 a.m., the night of her murder.

At a coroner's inquest on October 20th, a jury of nine men found that Bauerdorf's death was a homicide and proposed a thorough investigation to apprehend her killer. During the hearing, Fred Atwood, janitor of the apartment building, provided new evidence for police detectives. He said he heard woman's heels clicking back and forth on the floor, followed by a loud crash, like a tray dropping on the floor. He was awakened by this noise around midnight on October 11, 1944. He recognized the sounds as coming from Bauerdorf's apartment. He said there was no one with her. Atwood also said he entered the apartment the next morning about 11 a.m., accompanied by his wife. They found Bauerdorf's body lying semi-nude in her bathtub. Two of the deputies confirmed the janitor's testimony that Bauerdorf was alone before her slayer evidently lured her to her darkened door. Atwood said he discovered the night light bulb being screwed around a couple of turns. He responded that he had never seen this happen before. Officers testified that the apartment showed no indication of a struggle. In contrast to the autopsy showed that Bauerdorf had put up a good fight. The sole and key clue other than the light bulb and physical injuries, was a bit of elastic bandage wedged down her throat as a gag. Officials hoped that by tracing it, they might solve the murder, they never did.

A Crime of Passion: The Bay City Nurse Slayer

(San Francisco, 1945)

On October 4, 1945, Annie Mansfeldt, the 45-year-old wife of prominent San Francisco physician John H. Mansfeldt, shot and killed Vada Martin. It was alleged that Martin, a 36-year-old nurse at Sutter Hospital was having an affair with Dr. Mansfeldt. At 10 a.m., Mrs. Annie Mansfeldt (the 1915 Fresno Raisin Festival Queen) walked into Central Emergency Hospital, dropped a pearl handled .32 caliber revolver on the counter and announced: "A woman is dying in the front seat of my automobile!"

Martin was already dead when hospital attendants reached the car. Frozen by shock and hysteria, Annie Mansfeldt stood quietly as the body was wheeled into the hospital. She whispered to no one in particular, "I shot her, I shot her." When asked why she shot Martin, Mansfeldt stated, "I accused her of being infatuated with my husband. She told me it was my imagination... and that she had never been intimate with him. She told me that with her dying breath, and now I believe her...and it is too late!"

When interviewed by police homicide detectives, Mrs. Mansfeldt stated that for over a year she had harbored doubts as to whether husband had been faithful. On Thursday, September 27, 1945, a week before the fatal shooting, things came to a boiling point, when Mrs. Mansfeldt traced her husband to French Hospital. There she saw an attractive women, whom she identified as Martin, sitting in the front seat of her husband's car. On Thursday, October 4, 1954, having not slept in six days, Annie Mansfeldt seethed with jealousy and, in a frenzied and unstable state of mind, traced Martin to her home on Geary Street. Before going to the address, Mansfeldt telephoned Martin to arrange a face-to-face meeting. Upon arrival at Martin's address, the pair got into Mansfeldt's car and began to talk. Things immediately got heated when Martin was accused of being infatuated with Mansfeldt's husband, which was vehemently denied. Not believing what Martin was saying, she decided to scare the woman with the revolver. Martin continued to profess her innocence and stated again that she had never been intimate with Mansfeldt's husband. Enraged by these denials, Mansfeldt attempted to strike Martin in the face with the butt of the revolver (which she thought was loaded with blanks). Tragically, the gun discharged with live ammunition, hitting Martin in the chest.

The next day, Mrs. Mansfeldt was transferred to the city jail after spending the night in protective custody at the hospital. Her husband, who was wanted for questioning about the alleged affair, was nowhere to be found. Forty-eight hours after the shooting, Dr. Mansfeldt was found dead in his car near the

Shelter Cove resort in remote San Mateo County. Apparently, he had taken a fatal dose of poison. There was no suicide note and there was no doubt that the doctor had been dead for at least two days. With Dr. Mansfeldt and Vada Martin now dead, it was never made clear whether Mrs. Mansfeldt was right in her supposition that they had had an intimate relationship.

Annie Mansfeldt was arrested and charged with murdering Vada Martin; her trail began on November 26, 1945. The defense contended that Mrs. Mansfeldt did not intend to kill Vada Martin, but her death was the result of a tragic and misfortunate accident. She was portrayed as a good wife and devoted mother of three young children. On December 19, 1945, the jury of six men and six women found Mansfeldt guilty of manslaughter, for which she was sentenced to one to ten years in state prison. On January 5, 1946, she was transferred to the custody of the California State Penitentiary for Woman at Tehachapi where she served out her prison term. How long she served or when she was released from custody is unknown.

The Battle of Alcatraz

(San Francisco, 1946)

One of the most violent escape attempts in Alcatraz Prison's history occurred, May 2-4, 1946. Many historians mark this date as the most significant event in the island's twenty-nine-year history as a Federal penitentiary, and it was appropriately christened the "Battle of Alcatraz." In the wake of the conflict, fourteen guards and one inmate were left injured, while two correctional officers and three inmates lay dead from bullet wounds. A bank robber from Kentucky named Bernard Paul Coy, who was serving out a twenty-six-year sentence for committing a holdup using a sawed-off shotgun, devised a forceful escape strategy with five accomplices. Coy had carefully studied the habits of various guards over a period of several months. Then on May 2, 1946, aided by accomplice Joseph Cretzer, Coy smeared axle grease over his chest, head, and extremities, and started climbing the West End Gun Gallery from the juncture at Times Square and Michigan Avenue. Climbing hand over hand, he scaled the barred cage until he reached the top. Clenched in his teeth was a small cloth bag containing a crudely fashioned bar-spreader device that had been fashioned from toilet fixtures in one of the prison workshops. Coy set the device firmly between two bars (which were approximately five inches apart), and using a small wrench, he was able to exert enough force to effectively spread the bars and create an opening nearly ten inches in width. It is believed that Coy had also been limiting his intake of food in order to reduce his body mass. With Crezter eagerly watching his progress from below, Coy painfully squeezed his body through the opening, and made his entrance into the West Gun Gallery.

Coy quickly secured a riot club and positioned himself in a low crouch, so that the officer on duty couldn't see him when looking through the door's access window. Waiting in ambush, his accomplices lured the officer out. As the unsuspecting guard passed through the doorway, Coy forcefully hurled the steel door forward, throwing the officer off balance, and brutally clubbed him, forcing him to the floor. He then strangled him into unconsciousness with his necktie. Working swiftly, Coy lowered firearms and riot clubs to his partners below, and searched for keys that would provide access to the recreation yard. The convicts were now fully armed, and were able to capture nine unarmed guards and lock them into cells #404 and #403, located at the juncture of Seedy Street and Times Square.

But their escape plan soon began to crumble, as they were unable to locate the key that would unlock the door leading to the recreation yard. The key had been concealed by a brave correctional officer named Miller, who had surrendered all of his keys to the convicts except the most critical one, which he was able to quietly hide in the toilet of the cell where he and the other correctional officers were being held hostage. Meanwhile, Coy and Cretzer had released three other accomplices from their cells. Clarence Carnes, Sam Shockley, and Miran Thompson were all serving sentences for violent crimes. When the breakout was discovered, the distress sirens of Alcatraz wailed, indicating grave trouble at the prison, and the sound could easily be heard from the shores of San Francisco. The Coast Guard and the Marines were mobilized to furnish the support of demolition and weapon experts, and all the off-duty correctional officers were brought in to help take back the cell house from the armed and desperate convicts.

Since the takeover had occurred after lunch, the majority of the prison inmates were in the Industries, and the cellblock was largely empty. Marines assisted correctional officers in assembling all of the industry workers into the recreation yard, and helped to gather blankets and jackets for the inmates who were unable to return to their cells. Meanwhile inside the cellblock, a battle was raging. The escapees, realizing that they were unable to gain access to the recreation yard, had become desperate. In a violent rage, and cheered on by inmates Shockley and Thompson, Joseph Cretzer took his revolver, and leaning against the bars of cell #403, started unloading rounds into the cramped cell. Officers fell in the hail of gunfire, some critically wounded.

The "Rock," Alcatraz Federal Penitentiary, San Francisco Bay.

Back at the Administration Office, Warden Johnston had called together his lieutenants, and they had formulated a plan to send in strike teams to rescue the guards who were being held captive. Lt. Phil Bergen was assigned to lead the first team into the cell house through the West End Gun Gallery. As the team approached, two guards first fired several rounds to clear the corridor. The team then rapidly made their entry into the Gallery, and mounted the stairs to the first level. As one of the inmates fired rifle rounds at the assault team, Bergen worked feverishly to rescue the officer who had been ambushed by Coy.

Harold Stites was one member of Bergen's team who courageously returned fire, attempting to suppress the convict's barrage. Stites was no stranger to this type of scenario. In 1938, three inmates had rushed him while he was on post in a guard tower. In an attempt to stop them from securing firearms, he was forced to shoot two inmates, one of them fatally. The 1938 escape attempt was one of the most violent in the island's history, and resulted in the death of a correctional officer, who was fatally assaulted with a hammer by inmate named Rufus Franklin. As Bergen provided medical care to the downed officer, Stites continued to spray rifle fire into the cell house. Then suddenly Stites was struck by a bullet, and yelled out that he'd been hit. Three other officers were also hit by gunfire during this assault. Stites was carried unconscious out of the Gun Gallery and laid onto a couch. He was quickly examined by the prison's physician, and pronounced dead, he would be the first casualty of the "Battle of Alcatraz."

Bergen and four other officers returned to the Gun Gallery, and communicated with the prison staff via one of the Gallery phone lines. It appeared that an inmate was running from cell to cell, firing random shots into the Gallery. Around 10 p.m., the Associate Warden took a group of fourteen officers and burst into the cell house, hoping to rescue their colleagues. The team fell under heavy gunfire from the inmates, who had positioned themselves on top of cell block C. One of the officers was able to close the D block access door, but then was immediately struck in the shoulder by gunfire. The escapees realized that their chances of escape were fading, and Shockley and Thompson retreated back to their cells to contemplate how to explain their involvement in the plan.

Not knowing the origin of the barrage of gunfire, the marines started bombing D block with explosives as the cellblock filled with dense smoke. Coy, Cretzer, and Hubbard retreated in the utility corridor as the bombing continued. The Marines drilled holes in the ceilings, lowering hand grenades attached to wire and then detonated them. The concussions were fierce and the prisoners in D block hid behind soaking-wet mattresses with little protection. The barrage of gunfire, mortars, and teargas was ceaseless. Water from the broken plumbing started flowing from the tiers and flooding D block.

Robert Stroud (the Birdman of Alcatraz), made efforts to end the battle. At 56 years of age, he climbed over the railing of the third tier and lowered himself to the second tier, then dropped onto the floor of D block. In what seemed to be a valiant move, he started closing the front solid steel doors of the six isolation cells to protect the helpless men. Stroud yelled up to Bergen, explaining that there were no firearms in D block and that those involved had retreated to another section of the prison. He made it clear that many innocent men would die, if they continued to barrage them with gunfire.

On May 3, at about 12 noon, the convicts phoned Warden Johnston to try to discuss a deal, but he would only accept their unconditional surrender. That night, a constant fusillade was fired at the cell block. The following morning, squads of armed guards rushed into the cell house firing repeatedly into the narrow corridor, after nearly forty-eight hours of battle, the gunfire finally ceased, and in the violent aftermath, Cretzer, Coy, and Hubbard were killed, their bullet- and shrapnel-riddled bodies were found in the corridor. The mastermind, Coy, was found dead wearing a guard uniform. One officer, William Miller had died from his injuries, and a second officer, Harold Stites, had been shot and killed during an attempt to regain control of the cell house.

On December 3, 1948, Thompson and Shockley were executed together in the Gas Chamber at San Quentin for their role in the murder of Officers Miller and Stites; inmate Clarence Carnes received an additional ninety-nine-year sentence, but would eventually gain his release in 1973. It would take months before the cellblocks returned to any normalcy and the scars on the cement and cell walls would remain strong reminders until the closure of the prison in 1963.

The Black Dahlia

(Los Angeles, 1947)

One of the most infamous unsolved murders of the twentieth century, the Black Dahlia case, has for over sixty years fascinated scores of professional and amateur sleuths. The grisly 1947 murder of aspiring starlet and nightclub regular Elizabeth Short, has over the decades transformed from Los Angeles' crime of the century into an almost mythical symbol of unfathomable Hollywood Babylon. This is the cautionary story of a pretty young girl who came to Hollywood to be a movie star but wound up in a weed-filled dirt lot, hacked in two.

During her life time, Elizabeth Short was probably not called the Black Dahlia, though some accounts claim she was. Short probably received her exotic nickname in death, and according to newspaper reports, shortly after the murder, Elizabeth Short received the nickname "Black Dahlia" at a Long Beach drugstore in the summer of 1946, as a word play on the then-current release of the 1946 Raymond Chandler crime film, *The Black Dahlia*.

She called herself Beth; friends and family knew her as Betty. She was born on July 29, 1924, and grew up during the depths of the Great Depression in the working class neighborhood of Medford, Massachusetts, outside of Boston. She found an occasional escape from the drudgery of the real world at the movie theater and was determined to become a star. In pursuit of her dream, she eventually wound up in Hollywood. Elizabeth Short embodied the feminine ideal of the 1940s, with her meaty legs, full hips and a small, up-turned nose. She was drama personified. She dyed her mousy brown hair raven black, painted her lips blood red and pinned white flowers in her hair. With her alabaster skin and startling light blue eyes, she looked like a porcelain doll. At one point during World War II, Short worked as a cashier at a local military base where she won the title "Camp Cutie of Camp Cooke."

In the last six months of her life, Short moved constantly between a dozen hotels, apartments, boarding houses, and private homes in Southern California. She was chronically short on cash. From November 13 to December 15, Short lived in a cramped two-bedroom apartment in Hollywood with eight other young women, cocktail waitresses, telephone operators, dime dancers, and other out-of-towners who hoped to break into showbiz. The women paid $1 a day for a bunk bed and a couple feet of closet space. But Short couldn't even afford this paltry sum, and snuck out a side door to avoid the manager when the rent was due.

Her roommates told the *LA Times* after her death that Short was out "with a different boyfriend every night" and didn't have a job. "She was always going out to prowl [Hollywood] boulevard," Linda Rohr, 22, told the paper.

The Black Dahlia, murder victim Elizabeth Short. *Courtesy of the Herald Examiner Collection/ Los Angeles Public Library.*

Short was elusive in life as she remains in death. She didn't have close friends, male or female, but preferred the company of strangers and a constant change of entourage. The last person to see her alive was a recent acquaintance, a 25-year-old married salesman named Robert Manley, nicknamed "Red" for his flaming auburn hair. According to press reports, Manley picked her up on a street corner in San Diego. He noticed her standing alone, a beautiful woman with no apparent destination, and pulled over to ask if she wanted a ride. Short played coy, turning her head and refusing to look at him. But Manley kept talking, reassuring her that he was harmless, that he just wanted to help her out, give her a lift home. At the time, Short was staying with a family who took pity on her after finding her at a twenty-four-hour movie theater, where she'd gone to spend the night. But they soon tired of her. She lazed around their small house during the day and spent her evenings out partying. In early January 1947, they asked her to leave. Manley came to pick her up.

The pair stayed in a local motel but Elizabeth slept in her clothes and the pair didn't have sex, he later told a reporter. The next day, January 9, 1947, he drove her to Los Angeles and helped her check her luggage at the bus station. She told him she was going to Berkeley to stay with her sister, whom she was meeting at the Biltmore Hotel downtown. Manley accompanied her into the hotel lobby, but took leave of her at 6:30 p.m. to return to his family in San Diego. The Biltmore was exactly the sort of place Short loved to hang out. It was as glamorous as she aspired to be, filled with wealthy travelers and luxuriously appointed. Built in the early 1920s, it was the largest hotel west of Chicago, with 1,000 rooms. Its lobby was its centerpiece, featuring hand-painted cathedral ceilings, crystal chandeliers, and marble floors. This elegant setting could offer no greater contrast to the dirt lot where her desecrated body was dumped one week later. She was seen in the lobby of the hotel making phone calls while waiting for her sister, who was suppose to meet her there. She was never seen alive again – except by her killer.

A number of people claimed to have spotted Short here or there, in the company of various people, during the six days that passed between her disappearance from the Biltmore and the discovery of her brutally mutilated corpse. In the early morning hours of January 15, 1947, Betty Bersinger was walking with her 3-year-old daughter, when they stumbled upon what Bersinger first thought to be a discarded department store mannequin in a vacant lot on the west side of South Norton Avenue, between Coliseum and 39th Streets, in the Leimert Park district of Los Angeles.

The Biltmore Hotel at Pershing Square in downtown Los Angeles (present day).

It turned out to be the body of Elizabeth Short, severed at the waist, naked, drained of blood, and posed with the legs spread and the corners of the mouth cut, so that they extended to each ear thus forming a frightful smile. The body had been washed and cleaned and she had been posed with her hands over her head and elbows bent at right angles. The police quickly determined that Short had been bound, tortured, and killed elsewhere, then dumped. The autopsy found that there were marks on her ankles and wrists made by rope, consistent with being tied either spread-eagle or hung upside down. There was evidence she had been forced to eat feces. Although the skull was not fractured, Short had bruising on the front and right side of her scalp with a small amount of bleeding in the subarachnoid space on the right side, consistent with blows to the head. The cause of death was determined to be from blood loss from the lacerations to the face combined with shock due to a concussion of the brain.

Although a popular portrayal amongst her acquaintances and many true crime authors was of Short as a call girl, a Los Angeles Grand Jury investigation proved there was no existing evidence that she was ever a prostitute and the district attorney's office attributes the claim to confusion with a prostitute of the same name. Another widely circulated rumor holds that Short was unable to have sexual intercourse because of a congenital defect that left her with "infantile genitalia." Found in the Los Angeles district attorney's files and in the Los Angeles Police Department's summary of the case, Short's autopsy describes her reproductive organs as anatomically normal although the report notes evidence of what it called "female trouble."

The autopsy also states that Short was not and had never been pregnant, contrary to what had been claimed prior to and following her death. Short was buried in Oakland's Mountain View Cemetery in a quiet ceremony attended by six family members. A handful of cops were also present, on the odd chance that the killer would appear to say one last scornful goodbye to his victim. On her modest pink marble headstone is simply engraved: Daughter, Elizabeth Short, July 29, 1924 - January 15, 1947.

The killer contacted the editor of the *Los Angeles Examiner* on January 23, 1947, expressing concern that news of the murder was tailing off in the newspapers, he offered to mail items belonging to Short to the editor. The following day a packet arrived at the Los Angeles newspaper containing Short's birth certificate, business cards, photographs, names written on pieces of paper and an address book with the name Mark Hansen embossed on the cover. The killer would later write more letters to the newspaper, calling himself "the Black Dahlia Avenger." On January 25, Short's handbag and one shoe were found in a garbage bin a short distance from Norton Avenue. William Randolph Hearst's papers, the *Los Angeles Herald-Express* and the *Los Angeles Herald-Examiner* sensationalized the case; the black tailored suit Short was last seen wearing became "a tight skirt and a sheer blouse" and Elizabeth Short became the "Black Dahlia," an "adventuress" who "prowled Hollywood Boulevard." As time passed, the media coverage became more outrageous with claims her lifestyle "made her victim material," when in fact those who knew her all reported that Short did not smoke, drink, or swear. Due to the notoriety of the case, police would be swamped with tips every time a newspaper mentioned the case.

The LAPD refrained from speculating on the identity of killer. The truth is that Elizabeth Short's killer is most likely dead, if not of disease, of old age, and will never be brought to justice. This fact hasn't stopped a large group of amateur sleuths from picking up the torch in an attempt to solve the case. Their conclusions range from plausible to downright ridiculous. Mary Pacios pins the blame, incredibly, on movie director Orson Welles, who once did a magic act where he "sawed" a woman in half.

In another book, *Daddy Was the Black Dahlia Killer*, a public relations specialist named Jan Knowlton blames her father for the murder. She writes that therapy helped her recover childhood memories of her father forcing her to watch him torture, murder, and hack up Short. Knowlton goes on to accuse her father of nine such killings, including that of a son he engendered with her. Her book was a flop, but Knowlton harassed anyone writing about the case who did not support her claims until she committed suicide in 2004 with a drug overdose.

Robert Manley was the last known person to see Short alive. He was initially booked as a suspect, but released after he passed a polygraph test. Beset by a long history of mental health problems, in 1954, his wife committed him to a psychiatric hospital after he told her he was hearing voices. That same year, doctors gave him a shot of sodium pentothal, aka the "truth serum," in another attempt to glean information about the Black Dahlia murder from him. He was absolved a second time. He died in 1986, thirty-nine years to the day, after he left Short at the Biltmore. The coroner attributed his death to an accidental fall.

Mark Hansen's name was embossed on the address book that was mailed to the Examiner; it's unclear how the item fell into Short's hands. He was the manager of the Florentine Gardens, a sleazy Hollywood nightclub featuring burlesque acts. Many of the young women working for Hansen lived at his home, which was located behind the club. Short was his guest for several months in 1946.

In 2003, a retired LAPD detective named Steve Hodel published another daddy did it book, but this one became a national bestseller. According to the *Black Dahlia Avenger: A Genius for Murder,* Hodel Jr. depicts his dad as a tyrant and misogynistic pervert who held orgies at the family home and was put on trial for raping his 14-year-old daughter (he was acquitted). After his father died in 1999, Steve Hodel acquired his father's private photo album, which contained two snapshots of a dark-haired woman. Hodel claims the woman was Short, but Elizabeth's family has refuted his claims.

In *Severed: The True Story of the Black Dahlia Murder*, crime writer John Gilmore fingers an alcoholic drifter named Jack Anderson Wilson. When Gilmore interviewed him in the early 1980s, Wilson purportedly divulged details about the murder that only the killer would have known, including knowledge a supposed vaginal defect which would have prevented Short from having sexual intercourse. A few days before his pending arrest, Wilson died in a hotel fire. The book's validity has been questioned by other Dahlia devotees who have failed to track down many of Gilmore's primary sources, leading them to question the sources' existence.

In 1997, a *Los Angeles Times* writer named Larry Harnisch suggested yet another suspect: Dr. Walter Alonzo Bayley, a surgeon whose house was located one block south of the lot where Short's body was found. Bayley's daughter was a friend of Short's sister, Virginia. Harnisch theorizes that Bayley suffered from a degenerative brain disease that made him kill Short. The police believed Short's killer was affiliated with a cutting profession, a surgeon or butcher. Bayley was sixty-seven at the time of the murder, and had no known record of violence or crime. Neither is it known whether he ever met Short.

Other crime authors have speculated on a link between the Short murder and the Cleveland Torso Murders, which took place in Cleveland between 1934 and 1938. As with a large number of killings that took place before and after the Short murder, the original LAPD investigators looked into the Cleveland murders in 1947 and later discounted any relationship between the two cases. However new evidence implicating a former Cleveland torso murder suspect, Jack Anderson Wilson, with Short's death was investigated by Detective John St. John in 1980, who claimed he was close to arresting Wilson for the death of Short, when Wilson died in a fire on February 4, 1982.

Numerous other crime authors have suggested a link between the Short murder and the 1946 murder and dismemberment of 6-year-old Suzanne Degnan in Chicago. Among the evidence cited is the fact that Elizabeth Short's body was found on Norton Avenue three blocks west of Degnan Boulevard, Degnan being the last name of the girl from Chicago, and there were striking similarities between the writing of the Degnan ransom note and that of "the Black Dahlia Avenger." Currently, convicted serial killer William Heirens is serving time for Degnan's murder. Initially arrested at age 17 for breaking into a residence close to that of Suzanne Degnan, Heirens claims he was tortured by police, forced to confess, and made a scapegoat in the Degnan murder.

None of these suspects have been endorsed by the LAPD. And because most of the key physical evidence has disappeared from the Black Dahlia file, including thirteen scornful letters the killer sent the police and media, it's unlikely the case will ever be solved.

At the time, the Black Dahlia murder investigation was the largest LAPD investigation, since the murder of Marion Parker in 1927. Because of the size of the investigation, the case also enlisted the help of hundreds of officers borrowed from other law enforcement agencies. Because of the complexity of the case, the original investigators treated every person who knew Short with suspicion until eliminated as a suspect. Around 200 people were considered suspects and thousands were interviewed by police. Owing to the nature of the crime, sensational and sometimes inaccurate press coverage focused intense public attention on the case. Most of the approximately fifty people who confessed to the murder were men.

Elizabeth Short has been portrayed many ways in the six decades since her body was dumped in two pieces on an empty lot in Los Angeles: manipulative playgirl, aspiring starlet, and troubled soul. Above all, time has immortalized Elizabeth Short as the pin-up girl of Los Angeles Noir. Fascination with her life and especially her gruesome, violent, unsolved murder continues to this day. The story of the unemployed 22-year-old waitress has inspired dozens of books, websites, a video game, and even an Australian swing band. The quest to pinpoint her killer has become a hobby for generations of armchair detectives. The Los Angeles Police Department has all but given up hope of ever closing the Dahlia case; the department has more urgent crimes to investigate, and the killer has likely been dead for years. Yet, it is precisely the unsolved status of Elizabeth Short's murder that gives it such an enduring allure. It needs to be emphasized that the case is so cold, the information so musty and bungled, that it's difficult to get a lucid picture of Elizabeth Short's brief life, much less her grisly death.

The Unsolved Slayings of Evelyn May Winter and Laura Trelstad: The Los Angeles County Murder Spree of 1947

(Los Angeles County, 1947)

On March 11, 1947, Los Angeles police were called to the scene of the sixth brutal murder involving a female victim in eight weeks. The first was "Black Dahlia," Elizabeth Short, on January 15th; a second murder victim, 45-year-old Jeanne French was found beaten to death on February 11th on a West Los Angeles hill top near Grandview Boulevard, a third victim; 40-year-old waitress Gladys Cantrell was found beaten and murdered near the Los Nietos railway station on March 2nd; a fourth victim, forty-six year old Mae Lorena Preston was found dead in the San Gabriel River near Norwalk, she had been strangled and her head was smashed in; a sixth and final murder victim, Laura Trelstad, was found beaten and strangled on May 12, 1947 near Signal Hill.

The latest, found at 1:45 a.m., in the Gashouse District where Ducommun Street crossed the Santa Fe railroad, was 49-year-old Evelyn Mae Winters. She had been clubbed to death; her clothes had been pulled nearly off. The victim's underwear and shoes were found a block away, at the corner of Commercial and Center Streets.

A musician and Vassar graduate, once described as a brilliant scholar, Evelyn had been married to Sydney Justin, head of Paramount Studios legal department, from 1936-1941. She too had worked at Paramount, as a music copywriter. In 1942, she had married a soldier named Horace Wyndham, but they divorced two years later. Lately she had fallen on hard times, including a series of arrests for intoxication and drunk driving. At the time she died, her blood alcohol level was .28, nearly three times the legal limit. Two days before her corpse was found, on March 9, 1947, Winters had spoken to her mother in the lobby of the Clarke Hotel. She had borrowed five dollars "for expenses" but refused to say where she was living, remarking that "It's too terrible a place. I don't want to tell you." Her mother reported that Winters had once resided at 1850 North Cherokee, a few doors from January victim Elizabeth Short.

Police detained George Wickliffe, the 28-year -old railroad section hand who discovered the body, after they found a woman's coin purse in his possession and noted lipstick smudges on his mouth. No stranger to jail, having been arrested for vagrancy in February of 1947, Wickliffe had a simple explanation for the lipstick: He admitted kissing Winters when he found her sprawled beside the railroad tracks, allegedly before he realized that she was dead. He was subsequently cleared of involvement in the crime, and police never identified another suspect.

On May 12, 1947, the body of Laura Trelstad, a 37-year-old mother of three, was found dead in a Signal Hill oil field, twelve blocks from her Los Angeles home. According to the autopsy report, she had been beaten, raped, and strangled with a strip of cotton cloth. There was no mutilation per se, but various reports described the beating as savage and ferocious enough to have fractured her skull.

Trelstad's husband, a truck driver, told police he had taken his wife to a party on Sunday, May 11, but she left to go dancing while he stayed behind to play cards. Detectives tracked down a sailor who was seen leaving a Long Beach café with the victim on Sunday night, but he was later cleared of suspicion in the case. Police believed him when he said he had escorted Trelstad to a bus stop and put her aboard a Huntington Park bus at 11:50 p.m. From there police declared, she kept a date with another girl, but no details were forthcoming. The crime was speculatively linked to the January 1947, Black Dahlia case, and with the exception of the Gladys Cantrell murder case, the Evelyn Winters, Jeanne French, Mae Lorena Preston, Laura Trelstad and Elizabeth Short slayings all remain open and unsolved.

The Newport Beach Yacht Murders

(Orange County, 1947)

Walter and Beulah Overell, were killed in March of 1947; their yacht exploded in Newport Harbor in Newport Beach. Their daughter and her boyfriend were arrested and charged with murder, and the resulting trial attracted nationwide attention, becoming what was described at the time as "the trial of the century." It certainly contained all the necessary elements – sex, wealth, lust, and greed.

Walter and Beulah Overell were wealthy socialites who lived in Flintridge, California. Walter Overell made his original fortune in the furniture business in the 1930s and early 1940s, and followed that with successful investments in real estate. The Overells had one child, a daughter named Beulah Louise. People who knew the family said that she, like many children of wealthy parents, was very spoiled. When she was 17, Beulah Louise, a student at the University of Southern California, decided that she wanted a boyfriend, and she picked a 20-year-old World War II veteran named George "Bud" Gollum. But the Overells did not share Beulah Louise's enthusiasm for her boyfriend. In fact, they told her that if she married him, they would refuse to acknowledge her. Nevertheless, Beulah Louise and Gollum planned to marry, and scheduled the ceremony for April 30, 1947.

On Saturday evening, March 15, 1947, the Overells, their daughter, and Gollum were together on the Overell's yacht, a forty-seven-foot cabin cruiser called the Mary E., which was moored in the harbor at Newport Beach. Beulah Louise and Gollum decided that they wanted to get a midnight snack, so they took a skiff to go and get some hamburgers at a late-night cafe. At just about the time they were ordering their food, the Mary E. was rocked by a powerful blast. By the time Beulah Louise and Gollum returned, the Coast Guard was at the scene. The bodies of Walter and Beulah Overell were found in the wreckage of the boat, after it was towed to shallow water. Although the initial theory was that the explosion had been caused by a gasoline leak, further investigation discovered that more than thirty sticks of dynamite had been placed in the boat's engine room, wired to an alarm clock detonator, and attached to the boat's battery. Another collection of dynamite was found in another area, but had not exploded. The first blast, investigators theorized, was supposed to have set off the second cache of dynamite, but a heavy wooden bulkhead confined the first blast to the engine room. Nevertheless, both Walter and Beulah Overell were dead. Walter had been impaled on a plank, while Beulah died of multiple skull fractures. The coroner, however, determined that the couple could have been dead for up to an hour before the explosion. And the wounds on Mrs. Overell's skull matched injuries which could have been caused by blows from a hammer-like object.

Four days later, Beulah Louise and Gollum were arrested and charged with murder. A check of Gollum's car turned up pieces of wire and adhesive tape similar to that which had been used to prepare the bomb on the Mary E.; bloody clothes were also discovered in his car. A sales receipt showed that the couple had purchased fifty sticks of dynamite the day before in Chatsworth, with Gollum signing a different name on the receipt, also found in his car. Gollum told police that Walter Overell had asked him to buy the dynamite to remove tree stumps in his yard. Police theorized that Walter and Beulah Overell were beaten to death, and then the bomb was detonated, blowing up the Mary E. The motive was the Overell's dislike of Bud Gollum, and Beulah Louise's expected inheritance.

While they were in jail, Beulah Louise and Gollum wrote love letters to each other, which were leaked to the press, and added to the sensationalism and the nationwide public interest in the trial. Gollum wrote, "Because I love and adore and worship and cherish you with all my heart, I'll kidnap you and carry you off somewhere where no one will ever be able to find us and I'll make passionate and violent love to you. If you ever marry another person, I will kill him." Beulah Louise wrote to Gollum, "Would you still marry me if I were broke, Oh Pops darling, please promise you will marry me. You're an uplifted human being. You're the most intelligent person I ever heard of. Einstein was a moron compared to you. ... Yes, sir, you're the object of my adoration and the creature of my determination."

When their trial started on May 26, 1947, Judge Kenneth Morrison of the Orange County Superior Court allowed radio microphones in the courtroom to broadcast the trial, but with one restriction, the order permitted only "hometown" radio stations, and there was only one at the time: KVOE in Santa Ana.

The trial of Beulah Overell and Bud Gollum at the Orange County Court House, (Overell and Gollum, seated 2nd and 3rd from the left). *Courtesy of the Herald Examiner Collection/ Los Angeles Public Library.*

The station contracted with the Mutual Broadcasting System to rebroadcast the trial all over the United States, and soon everyone in the country was listening to the testimony. In addition to coverage by the Orange County and Los Angeles newspapers, *Life* and *Time* magazines, New York newspapers, and wire services were there. The *Los Angeles Examiner* sent famed Hearst columnist Adela Rogers St. John to write her observations.

The trial lasted four and a half months, at that time the longest murder trial in American history. Defense attorney Otto Jacobs cut apart the prosecution's case, arguing that it was built entirely on circumstantial evidence. After two days of deliberations, the jury agreed. On October 5, 1947, Beulah Louise Overell and George "Bud" Gollum were found not guilty. The jury decided that Walter Overell was depressed over his deteriorating financial situation, and the explosion on the Mary E. was the result of "the accident of suicidal tampering with dynamite by Walter Overell."

After the trial, reporters asked Gollum if he and Beulah Louise were going to get married. "We'll see," he replied. But Beulah's answer was more direct: "No." Gollum, who was a pre-med student at the time of the trial, never went on to medical school. Instead, he worked for a carnival, did some traveling, and wound up serving time in prison after he was caught riding in a stolen car in Florida. Gollum later went back to school, eventually earning a doctorate degree in biophysics, teaching in Northern California, and disappearing into obscurity.

e Old Orange County Court House (present day).

A year after the trial, Beulah Louise discovered that the huge fortune she expected to inherit was nothing close to her original estimates. She got some money, married twice, moved to Las Vegas and started to drink heavily. On August 24, 1965, she was found dead in her bed, two empty vodka bottles near her head and a loaded, unfired .22 caliber rifle at her feet. The cause of death was determined to be acute alcoholism; she was 36 years old.

Walter and Beulah Overell gravesite at Forest Lawn Memorial Park, Glendale.

Bumped Off: The Killing of Mobster Bugsy Siegel

(Los Angeles, 1947)

A New York City native, Benjamin "Bugsy" Siegel was born Benjamin Siegelbaum on February 28, 1906 in Williamsburg, Brooklyn. As a young boy, he was an incorrigible delinquent who joined a gang on the lower east side of Manhattan. He was infamously known for his ferocious temper and impulsive violent behavior. As a teenager, Siegel befriended Meyer Lansky and they formed a small gang that committed petty crimes. Crime obviously paid for Siegel, a handsome man who wore only the best fashions. He was very charming and was comfortable cavorting with politicians and celebrities. He became the East Coast mob's ambassador to high society. Known as a hot head, he was always quick to resolve disagreements with physical violence. He had no problem with murder and rose quickly up the ranks of the criminal underworld.

During the early 1930s, Siegel and Lanksy aligned themselves with powerful mob bosses, Charles "Lucky" Luciano and Frank Costello. Siegel was sent to the West Coast in 1937 to develop the gambling rackets in Los Angeles. There he recruited gangster Mickey Cohn and together set up a book-making service. On November 22, 1939, Siegel along with other gang members, murdered Harry "Big Greenie" Greenberg. He had become a police informant and the mob ordered him killed. Siegel was arrested for the murder and it was during this proceeding that he gained his infamous nickname of "Bugsy." Local Los Angeles newspapers began to refer to Siegel as such, which was based on the slang "bugs" which meant "crazy." Siegel hated the nickname and no one dared to call him it to his face.

Artificial respectability was a goal for many mobsters, who longed to rub shoulders with movie stars and captains of industry. Siegel yearned for this as well but the respectability he dreamed of was way beyond the bounds of reality. A window of opportunity opened for Siegel and others when, in 1931, the state of Nevada legalized casino gambling. Siegel, along with fellow mobster Moe Sedway, were ordered by the East Coast mob to go to Las Vegas to expand operations. Siegel initially wanted nothing to do with the new venture and retreated to Hollywood. But pressure from Lansky forced him to go to Nevada anyway. This meant that Siegel would have to forsake his Beverly Hills playboy life style.

By the spring of 1946, Siegel, bankrolled by Lansky and the east coast outfit, was able to reinvent himself in Las Vegas with the construction of the Flamingo Hotel. He named the hotel on a whim, choosing the nickname of his mistress Virginia Hill for the venue. Hill, a fiery redhead had definitely been around the block when she met Siegel and had been paired with numerous other mobsters. Their relationship was marred by numerous arguments and violent outbursts that often distracted from Siegel's supervision of the construction of the Flamingo Hotel.

Siegel demanded the most luxurious hotel that money could buy and spared no expense in its building. Adding to budgetary woes were problems with contractors, and builders often went unpaid. As costs soared, checks began to bounce, and by October 1946, building costs had reached 4 million dollars. Mob bosses in the east ordered Siegel to cut costs and to remain on budget, but he ignored their pleas and proceeded with the hotel as he'd planned. Under order to have the hotel make some money, Siegel moved the opening from March 1, 1947 to December 26, 1946. Although the hotel was incomplete, he hoped to generate enough money to complete the project and to fend off the mob bosses. The opening of the Flamingo was a bust with only locals and no celebrities in attendance as promised. After two weeks in operation, the gaming tables were not making a profit and the mob shut the whole operation down. In early 1947, Siegel traveled to New York and met with Meyer Lansky in one last ditch effort to get the Flamingo open again. His pleading worked and was granted a temporary extension and second chance to make the Flamingo profitable. Siegel thought that he was back in the good graces of mob bosses, but he did not know they had grown weary of his antics and lack of follow through.

On the evening of June 20, 1947, with Virginia Hill absent on yet another vacation, Siegel lounged with friend Alan Smiley in the living room of Hill's Beverly Hills home at 810 Linden Drive. Siegel was reading the newspaper when an unknown assailant armed with a .30 caliber rifle fired several shots through a window striking him in the face and upper body. Within moments of Siegel's murder, a delegation of mobsters invaded the Flamingo Hotel in Las Vegas and took over control of all operations. No one questioned the move and play at the casino tables continued as normal.

Who killed Bugsy Siegel? The case was never officially solved, but it was most certainly a gangland hit. Even today, speculation concerning the mysterious identity of the triggerman continues. Some believe that mobster Jack Dragna, who was frequently humiliated by Siegel, fired the fatal shots. Others point to hit man Frankie Carbo, named by FBI informant Aldena Fratianno as the shooter. Another possible scenario has mobster Moe Dalitz, a former lover of Virginia Hill, as the killer. Some say that he was offended by Siegel's tendency to beat Hill. He had warned Siegel to stop the violent outbursts, but Bugsy paid no attention. When Hill showed Dalitz what Siegel had done after their last altercation, the contract for Siegel's murder went out. Fact or fiction, in 1949, the Dalitz-run syndicate moved its headquarters to Las Vegas, where Dalitz was soon dubbed as the gambling Mecca's "god father." As for the source of Siegel's death sentence, most agree that the hit was ordered by both Lansky and Luciano and that it was postponed, to give Bugsy plenty of time to pay off his debts before the murder.

Benjamin "Bugsy" Siegel was laid to rest at Beth Olam Cemetery (today part of Hollywood Forever Cemetery) in Hollywood, California. The cemetery is bordered by Paramount Studios. Ironically, Siegel always dreamed of becoming a movie star and he now rests for eternity just a few yards away from where movies were made. Only his immediate family was in attendance at his funeral and no one from the movie industry came to pay their respects. Even his close friend, actor George Raft, stayed away. As the man who helped found America's future playland was put in his crypt, only five people mourned his passing. His crypt is simply, yet mockingly inscribed "In Loving Memory from the Family."

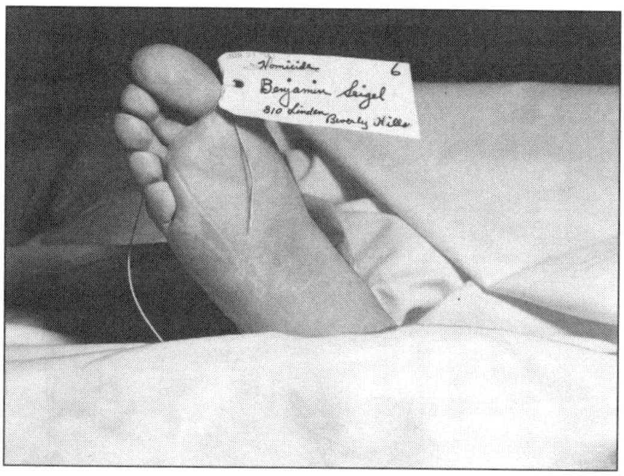

Identification toe tag of Benjamin "Bugsy" Siegel as he lay in the Los Angeles County Morgue. *Courtesy of the Herald Examiner Collection/ Los Angeles Public Library.*

Benjamin "Bugsy" Siegel's crypt in the Beth Olam section at Hollywood Forever Cemetery.

The Werewolf Murderer: Fred Stroble

(Los Angeles, 1949)

A werewolf, also known as a lycanthrope, is a mythological or folkloric human with the ability to shape shift into a wolf or an anthropomorphic wolf-like creature, either purposely, by being bitten by another werewolf, or after being placed under a curse. This transformation is often associated with the appearance of the full moon. Werewolves are often attributed superhuman strength and senses, far beyond those of both wolves and men.

Fred Stroble was dubbed the "Werewolf killer" by the Los Angeles press for his brutal 1949 murder of six-year-old Linda Glucoft. He had the uncanny anthropomorphic type ability to appear like an innocent grandfatherly type character on the outside, but could knowingly shape shift into a murderous pedophile.

On the afternoon of November 14, 1949, six-year-old Linda Joyce Glucoft walked from her home at 1968 South Crescent Heights Boulevard, to visit her best friend, Rochelle Hausman, who lived two blocks away, she was never seen alive again. Unknown to Linda was the fact that Rochelle, and her mother, Ruth Hausman had just left for a birthday party. Fred Stroble, 68, Mrs. Hausman's father was home alone at the family residence at 2003 South Crescent Heights Boulevard. At 6 pm., Linda's father Jules Glucoft, notified police that his daughter was missing. At 6:30 a.m. the next day, Linda's body was found behind an incinerator in the yard of the Hausman home. She had been brutally beaten, strangled, and sexually assaulted.

A city-wide manhunt was immediately pressed for the missing Stroble, known as "Grandpa," who was well liked by the neighborhood children and known for giving out chocolate bars. On November 16, 1949, two days after the murder, Stroble was captured. Linen service truck driver, William Miller, spotted him drinking beer at the bar of Leighton's Restaurant at 451 South Hill Street. Miller immediately notified police officer Arnold Carlson, who was directing traffic at a nearby intersection that he saw a man fitting the description of Stroble. Officer Carlson rushed inside the bar and took Stroble into custody without incident. He was taken to police headquarters and interviewed by homicide detectives. After hours of questioning, Stroble broke down and confessed to killing Linda Glucoft, stating "I had to kill her to stop her screaming."

Stroble in his confession admitted to police that over the past ten years, he had molested four or five other children, and that this wasn't the first time with the Glucoft girl. Stroble detailed to police what lead up to the murder:

> Around 3 p.m., the little girl rang the door bell asking for Rochelle, I invited her in and gave her a chocolate bar and led her to the back bedroom. She wanted to play outside but I told her we could play here for a little bit. This wasn't the first time. I had played with her once before. She refused. I threw her on the bed, began to fondle her and she began to scream. When she screamed too much I put my hands on her face. I held her throat. I tried to choke her. That didn't work so I got a necktie and used it to choke her. I wrapped her in a blanket. I got a ball-peen hammer from the kitchen and hit her with it on the side of the head through the blanket. Then I dragged her into the back yard and stabbed her in the heart and then in the back with an ice pick, while she lay beside the incinerator. She was resisting and trying to get away. I slammed her six times with the flat side of an ax that was standing there. I killed Linda because I didn't want her to suffer anymore and because I feared she would tell her parents.

Stroble went on to detail the hours after the murder telling police that he went to Venice, where he spent the night in a rooming house under an assumed name. There he went to a local bar, got drunk and contemplated suicide by jumping off of Santa Monica Pier. He returned to Los Angeles the next day, stopping at the Hill Street restaurant, where he planned to have a drink prior to turning himself into law enforcement authorities. That same day, little six-year-old Linda Joyce Glucoft was laid to rest at Home of Peace Cemetery; she was buried in her favorite blue plaid dress.

At his preliminary hearing on December 2, 1949, Stroble pleaded not guilty and not guilty by reason of insanity. At his trial in January 1950, defense attorneys tried to show that Stroble had no mental capacity to deliberate and premeditate the killing. They characterized him as an old man, senile, going through a male change of life. Attorneys went on to explain that he was a chronic alcoholic and that hardening of the arteries affected his brain. The jury of ten women and two men did not buy the assertions of the defense, and on January 19, 1950, found him guilty of first degree murder and sentenced him to death in the gas chamber. After two years of appeals, one of which was heard by the U.S. Supreme Court, and several stays of execution, Fred Stroble was put to death in the gas chamber of San Quentin prison on July 25, 1952; he made no final statement.

Conclusion

The horrific stories that have been retold in this book only touch the surface of crimes that were committed during this period (1849-1949). The small smattering of tales that I have decided to retell serves only as a reminder of mankind's inhumanity towards its fellow man. Our society is characterized by a culture of fear about crime, but it also a culture that is fascinated by it. We are seemingly both seduced and repulsed by crimes and criminals. Nor is this fascination with crimes and criminals simply the stuff of fiction. Acts defined as criminal may both seduce and repulse us because they involve, on occasions, both risk-taking and challenges to "normal" ways of doing things. But what makes the human mind seek and cling to facts about a gruesome murder, rape, or ritual killing with such resolve that they just cannot seem to let it go? It is interesting that such stories are talked about for so long, they end up becoming legend; it shows you that however old a true crime story is, it does not lose its allure.

It is normal for humans to want to know the facts behind a criminal act, and then immediately after that, question why it was committed? A crime story grows more and more fascinating as people continue to speculate as to why a crime was perpetrated. Like everything else, media attention tends to hype crime and criminals. It chases down every bit and morsel and shows you bloody crime scenes, car chases, and even bodies. Listen to or watch news broadcasts for a day, and you will most likely hear of three or four crimes. If the media were to highlight crime less, perhaps society would be less aware of it, and its fascination would somehow lessen. Whatever the justifications given for fascination with crime, we must admit that being human, we want to know what happened, we want the gory details, and we will go after them until we get the last bit of information that we possibly can.

The remaining decades of the 20th century and early 21st would witness even more horrific and legendary crime. Crimes such as the 1968 assassination of Robert F. Kennedy at the Ambassador Hotel, the unsolved Zodiac killings of the 1960s and 1970s, the Manson Family slayings of 1969, the Freeway Killers of the late 1970s and early 1980s, the mass shooting at Cal State Fullerton in 1976, serial killer Richard Ramirez "the Night Stalker" and his murderous rampage through southern California in the mid-1980s, the mass shooting at McDonalds in San Diego (1984), and the O.J. Simpson and Menendez brothers murder cases, just to name a few.

In the end, crime is a nasty business to be certain, but it is also a fascinating one. We all disapprove of crime, and find ourselves shocked and appalled by it, but a moment later we simply find that we can't get enough of it. Not all misdeeds are created equal. Some are more sensational than others, some more baffling, some more audacious. The fifty-two notorious crimes revisited in this book are all of these things and more. In the end crime is awful, but it can be, in retelling, awfully exciting. Millions have come to the golden shores of California in search of fame and fortune but scores have found misery and pain. From the Gold Rush of 1849 to the rise of Hollywood, this book has detailed much of that hurt and wretchedness. My objective was to bring to light, what I perceive to be some of the most notorious and long forgotten crime stories of the first 100 years of this state's history.

Bibliography

Anger, Kenneth. *Hollywood Babylon*. San Francisco: Straight Arrow Books, 1975.

Asbury, Herbert. *The Barbary Coast: An Informal History of the San Francisco Underworld*. New York: Garden City Publishing, 1933.

Bancroft, Hubert H. *History of California, 1860-1890*, Vol. VII. San Francisco: The History Company Publishers, 1890.

Barry, Michael Thomas. *Final Resting Places Orange County's Dead & Famous*. Atgeln, Pennsylvania: Schiffer Publishing, 2010.

Boessenecker, John. *The Life and Times of Tiburcio Vasquez*. Norman, Oklahoma: University of Oklahoma Press, 2010.

Burns, Walter Noble. *The Robin Hood of El Dorado*. New York: Coward-McCann, 1932.

Carr, Harry. *Los Angeles: City of Dreams*. New York: Grosset & Dunlap, 1935.

Caughey, John Walton. *California*. New York: Prentiss-Hall, 1940.

Chermak, Steven & Frankie Y. Bailey. *Crimes & Trials of the Century*. Santa Barbara, California: Greenwood Publishing, 2007.

Cleland, Robert Glass. *From Wilderness to Empire: A History of California, 1542-1900*. New York: Alfred A. Knopf, Inc., 1944.

Cleland, Robert Glass. *California in Our Time, 1900-1940*. New York: Alfred A. Knopf, Inc., 1947.

Doing, Leroy L. *The Village of Garden Grove*. Santa Ana, California: Pioneer Press, 1962.

Donnelley, Paul, *501: Most Notorious Crimes*. London: Bounty Books, 2009.

Duke, Thomas S. *Celebrated Criminal Cases of America*. San Francisco: James H. Barry, Company, 1910.

Ellis, Julie. *The Mammoth Book of Celebrity Murder*. New York: Berghahn Books, 2005.

Edmonds, Andy. *Hot Toddy: The True Story of Hollywood's Most Sensational Murder*. New York: William Morrow, 1989.

Enss, Chris. *Outlaw Tales of California*. Guilford, Connecticutt: Twodot Books, 2008.

Fanning, Pete. *Great Crimes of the West*. San Francisco: Pete Fanning, 1927.

Friis, Leo J. *Orange County Through Four Centuries*. Santa Ana, California: Pioneer Press, 1982.

Garden Grove Historical Society. *Garden Grove: Images of America*. San Francisco: Arcadia, 2005.

Gilmore, John. *Severed: The True Story of the Black Dahlia*. Los Angeles: Amok Books, 2006.

Gray, A.A. *History of California from 1592*. New York: D.C. Heath & Company, 1934.

Hallan-Gibson, Pamela; Don Tryon and Mary Ellen Tryon. *San Juan Capistrano*. Charlestown: Arcadia Publishing, 2005.

Higham, Charles. *Murder in Hollywood: Solving a Silent Screen Mystery*. Santa Barbara, California, Greenwood Press, 2007.

Hoeper, George. *Black Bart: Boulevardier Bandit*. Freson, California: Word Dancer Press, 1995.

Jacobs, David. *The Mafia's Greatest Hits*. New York, New York: Kensington Publishing, 2006.

Kirsch, Robert & William S. Murphy. *West of the West: Witness to the California Experience, 1542-1906*. New York: E. P. Dutton, 1967.

Kulczyk, David. *California Justice*. Sanger, California: Quill Driver Books, 2008.

Lawson, Kristan & Rufus Anneli. *California Babylon*. New York: Macmillan, 2000.

Leal, Luis. *Life & Adventures of the Celebrated Bandit Joaquin Murrieta: His Exploits in the State of California*. Houston, Texas: Publico Press, 1999.

MacLean, Angus, *Legends of the California Bandidos*. Arroyo Grande, California: Bear Flag Books, 1977.
Monroy, Douglas. *Thrown Among Strangers: The Making of Mexican Culture in Frontier*. Berkeley and Los Angeles: University of California, 1990.
Mullen, Kevin J. *Let Justice Be Done: Crime and Politics in Early San Francisco*. Las Vegas: University of Nevada Press, 1989.
Munn, Michael. *The Hollywood Murder Casebook*. New York, New York: St. Martin Press, 1987.
Newton, Michael. *The Encyclopedia of Unsolved Crimes*. New York: Checkmark Books, 2004.
Nolan, Fredrick. *The Wild West: History, Myth & the making of America*. London: Arcturus Publishing, 2003.
Pourade, Richard F. *The Glory Years: The Boom and Busts in the Land of the Sundown Sea*. San Diego: The Union Tribune Publishing, 1964.
Ramsey, Merle & Mabel. *This was Mission Country: The Reflections in Orange of Merle & Mabel Ramsey*. Laguna Beach, California: Mission Printing Company, 1973.
Reasoner, James. *Draw: The Greatest Gunfights of the American West*. New York: Berkley Books, 2003.
Secrest, William B. *California Desperadoes: Stories of early California Outlaws in their Own Words*. Clovis, California: Word Dancer Press, 2000.
Starr, Kevin. *Inventing the Dream: California Through the Progressive Era*. New York: Oxford University Press, 1985.
Sullivan, Robert, ed. *Life: The Most Notorious Crimes in American History*. New York, New York: Life Books, 2010.
Wilkes, Roger, ed. *The Giant Book of Unsolved Crimes*. London: Magpie Books, 1999.
Wolfe, Donald H. *The Black Dahlia Files: The Mob, the Mogul, and the Murder that Transfixed Los Angeles*. New York: Harper Collins, 2000.

Newspaper:

Alta Californian, various years and contributors.
Los Angeles Star, various years and contributors.
Los Angeles Examiner, various years and contributors.
Los Angeles Times, various years and contributors.
New York Times, various years and contributors.
Sacramento Record-Union, various years and contributors.
San Diego Tribune, various years and contributors.
San Diego Union, various years and contributors.
San Francisco Chronicle, various years and contributors.
San Francisco Examiner, various years and contributors.
Santa Ana Daily Register, various years and contributors.
The Southern California, various years and contributors.

Websites:

Wikipedia.org
Findagrave.com

Index